INQUIRING INTO THE TEACHING PROCESS:

TOWARDS SELF-EVALUATION AND PROFESSIONAL DEVELOPMENT

John Haysom

DATE DUE

Research in Education Series/12

OISE Press/The Ontario Institute for Studies in Education

The Ontario Institute for Studies in Education has three prime functions: to conduct programs of graduate study in education, to undertake research in education, and to assist in the implementation of the findings of educational studies. The Institute is a college chartered by an Act of the Ontario Legislature in 1965. It is affiliated with the University of Toronto for graduate studies purposes.

The publications program of the Institute has been established to make available information and materials arising from studies in education, to foster the spirit of critical inquiry, and to provide a forum for the exchange of ideas about education. The opinions expressed should be viewed as those of the contributors.

CANADIAN CATALOGUING IN PUBLICATION DATA

Haysom, John 1938-
    Inquiring into the teaching process

(Research in education series ;12)
Bibliography: p.
ISBN 0-7744-0293-8

1. Teachers — Self-rating of. 2. Teaching — Evaluation. I. Ontario Institute for Studies in Education. II. Title. III. Series.

LB2838.H39 1985   371.1'44   C85-098486-6

ISBN 0-7744-0293-8

Printed in Canada

2 3 4 5 AP 98 88 78 68

For Steven, Jenny, Matthew

Contents

Introduction

This book is not a review of the study of teaching, neither is it a textbook in the traditional sense. Rather, it is designed to be a stimulant to action and reflection for teachers who are concerned to make a study of their own teaching. The book naturally divides into two distinct but closely related parts.

The first part contains invitations to teachers to make a personal appraisal of their teaching. To reduce the complexity of this task, I have developed an analytic procedure which involves gathering information about four major aspects of the teaching process:

- the teacher's frame of reference: the ideas the teacher has about teaching;
- the teacher's actions: what the teacher actually does;
- the pupils' actions: what the teacher or observer is able to see the pupils doing;
- the pupils' covert experiences; what is going on inside the pupils' minds, in terms of the thinking and feeling they are experiencing.

The second part of the book — the last two chapters — contains invitations to teachers to implement and monitor changes. These invitations naturally follow self-appraisal.

Studying one's own teaching is not an easy matter.

No doubt many teachers will have difficulty in making explicit their thinking about their practice — their frames of reference. It is not a simple matter even to begin articulating one's "philosophy" of teaching.

I expect that many teachers believe that they know what is happening in their classrooms — after all, they are there every working day. What conceivably could they discern that is not already quite apparent? And yet I would be surprised if, after careful observation and analysis, they didn't notice things they hadn't noticed before and perceive interaction in ways they hadn't previously considered.

Many teachers will find the process of examining their thinking and their practice an uncomfortable one. Some teachers will be reluctant to tape record or video record their lessons, and some will be reluctant to show their recordings to others. Concern for their public image, even amongst other teachers who are examining their own practice, will make it difficult for teachers to acknowledge almost inevitable imperfection. However, I would nevertheless anticipate that, as they begin to understand the value of self-appraisal, these reluctances will begin to diminish. The satisfaction gained from feeling more professional will gain ascendancy.

Many teachers will find it difficult, at least initially, to share my view that the notion of good teaching cannot be readily defined. We have become accustomed to believing that there is a straightforward answer and that someone with more authority than us has it. Checklists of teaching qualities abound and it might seem heretical to regard these critically. There is an aura about "educational theory."

In this book educational theory is used in two ways. First, at the beginning of the book and at the beginning of most chapters, it is used to locate and support the assumptions and the arguments I am making. Many authors have contributed ideas which influence the stance I take in the book. To refer to these ideas acknowledges the origins of my thinking. Moreover, it provides an opportunity for interested readers to probe the assumptions a little more deeply. Second, in the latter part of most chapters, I have highlighted a number of articles which relate to classroom practice. These tend to be personal favorites. Because I do not wish to present them as gospel, the good news about what to do and why to do it, they tend to follow the inquiries that have been discussed earlier. In this way I hope teachers will be encouraged to value them according to whether they personally find them relevant or illuminating. At the end of each chapter I have identified a small number of "Suggested Readings." These have been selected to provide some depth, and I hope that study of them will trigger discussion and enhance understanding. Many of them are widely referred to in the literature and have thus played a formative role in the development of our thinking about teaching.

Each chapter introduces a cluster of educational ideas. These provide the setting for a range of inquiries into the teaching process. Following the introduction of an idea, an invitation to inquiry is incorporated in the text. It is important to stress that these are only *suggested* inquiries. It may appear that the tone in which they are suggested is somewhat terse, but I hope this attempt to reduce waffle does not inhibit teachers using them from asking questions like, Why am I doing this? and, Is this the best way of going about it? All these inquiries have been field-tested with groups of teachers. From time to time I have described some of their experiences in the text. I hope that this will encourage other teachers to undertake similar explorations. If so, they might find it interesting to compare their experiences; if not, I hope they will find it valuable to share their experiences vicariously.

The methodology of inquiry implicitly advocated in this book is qualitative in essence. I have tried not to be doctrinaire about this and have from time to time deliberately sought to prompt critical reflection on the methodology. Nevertheless, here I would argue for the use of qualitative methodology largely because I view classrooms as complex and infinitely variable in terms of their contexts and of the personalities within them. I do not see the main purpose of teachers' researching their own classrooms as providing generalizations for others, rather I see it as deepening their understanding and appreciation of their own particular situations.

To date, the draft of this book has been used in many settings. Beginning teachers, studying for their Bachelor of Education degrees, have used selected inquiries as the basis for observing other teachers and in the latter stages of their teaching practice. Teachers studying for their Master of Arts degrees have used the book to provide a foundation for research into pertinent aspects of their own teaching. Sections have been used to provide a focus for short in-service courses and workshops.

In my view, one of the most interesting and potentially valuable applications of the book would be by small groups of teachers in a school or department of that school. They might like to begin by dipping into some of the inquiries which appeal to them. It wouldn't seem to matter where they start; each inquiry is part of the larger whole. My guess is that teachers will find the inquiries outlined at the end of chapters 4, 5, and 6 of particular appeal. Once a beginning has been made, the inquiry can be put in context by reading the chapter in which it was introduced.

In conclusion, I should try to make clear and underline the position this book takes on the nature and process of professional growth. Certainly, I hope the book enables teachers to become better at their work — to become more professional. As I see it, growth may take place when teachers begin to question what they are doing; when they seek to relate their thinking to what is happening in their classrooms, and when they seek to relate their thinking to the thinking of others in the professional community. This is in contrast to the view shared by some change agents, trainers, and staff development specialists, who see their task in terms of "demonstrating specific techniques so that skill-mastery becomes possible." I do not see professional growth taking place when tips are passed from the trainer to the teacher.

Closely connected with the position the book takes on professional growth is the relationship between the staff development specialist and the teacher or this book and its reader. I regard education (and teacher education) as a moral enterprise insofar as it involves the teacher making value judgments and choices. On account of this I do not consider it appropriate for a person, a group of people, or a book to tell another person what to do. Simply put, I believe teachers themselves should take responsibility for their actions.

Finally, this book takes the optimistic view that many individuals *are* motivated to improve and grow. Thus, as I see it, an appropriate role for the staff development specialist is that of facilitator, and an appropriate role for this book that of resource. But I do not wish to imply that the facilitator should adopt a laissez-faire approach or that the book be used casually. For professional development to take place, I believe that individuals need encouragement and stimulation, that the traditional isolation of the teacher needs to be broken down, that constraints need to be removed. Without organizational support the efforts of committed individuals may flounder.

PART I:
Appraising the Teaching Process

1

Good Teaching: A Historical Perspective

A Trip Back in Time

There's no evading the questions, "What makes a good teacher?" and "What makes good teaching?" Teachers want answers in order to sharpen their practice. Administrators want answers, not only to help them make informed decisions about whom to employ, but also to illuminate such problems as the effects of class size on teaching quality. Teacher educators want answers: the courses they offer should have solid foundations.

In order to explore the dimensions of the problem of answering these questions, a group of fourteen teachers were cast in the role of an early twentieth-century research team, when research into what makes a good teacher and what makes good teaching was in its infancy. The team divided into four subgroups, A, B, C, and D, and each group proceeded to prepare an outline of a research design. You might like to pause at this point to consider the sort of design you would have suggested (see Inquiry 1.1 at the end of this chapter).

The challenge was not simply met. Group A — Gord, Dawn, Dave, and Laurie — began by exploring the possibility of identifying teacher characteristics which were generally recognized as being important.

Gord: . . . .Then possibly after you've found these good teachers you might ask students and parents why they thought they were good teachers and try to discover — do a system of trait selection. . . .

Dawn: You think that after you did your observations and so on and you found similar coinciding traits, that many people thought made a good teacher; you feel these would be acceptable traits?

Gord: Well, they'd certainly be a beginning point to look at. If you found them reoccurring consistently, I think they'd have to have some validity — if they were the things that people valued in a teacher.

Doubts about the "validity" of this were expressed and a little later Laurie wondered if these might be overcome by restricting the survey to those who were professionals.

Laurie: . . . .I would think an examination of supervisory reports where you're going to see good things noted and bad things noted. . . .

Gord: I think we might have to expand a little broader. Because if the supervisors set up a value system . . . their evaluations may be colored by the fact that they like control and quietness and neatness and the rest of it. But in another area, in another culture, they may allow a different type of sitting around a circle on the floor, and one on one. A looser kind of structure that may be very practical for certain other goals. I guess we have to look at that and compare the two.

Laurie: I think we also have to assume too that because a person has reached a supervisory role, he was a good teacher. That's why he's there.

Dawn: I can't go along with that.

Laurie: I said it was an assumption (laughter). . . .

Gord nevertheless continued to focus on the problem of making generalizations about the teaching process. Dave tried to resolve this by shifting attention to the product.

Gord: One of the things we have the greatest difficulty with is that we might have great trouble coming up with operational definitions and ways of actually measuring these things. Now, for instance, if we took consistency, consistency of behavior. Students like a sense of security, a certain evenness of personality, a teacher who didn't go through wild mood swings. Then we might find, gosh, when a teacher goes through mood swings it's stimulating, so. . . .

Laurie: Then we'd have to measure that. . . .

Gord: Well I suppose! . . . .But clinical observation is often the beginning that you start with before you get into rigorous design. . . .

Dave: I am not necessarily saying that you don't observe what is going on in the classroom. I think that is necessary. But also that you would have to evaluate what was learned in that classroom session to be able to tell whether the techniques used in that session resulted in good learning.

Gord: All right! Let's start defining good learning. Is good learning that you're able to reproduce it on an exam? Is good learning that you remember it next week or next year? Is good learning the fact that what you've learned is worth learning?. . .

This line of thinking seemed to offer some hope. The group pursued it vigorously.

Gord: . . . the fascinating thing you know. Alexander the Great called a man out of his army one day and took his sword and cut the man's head off and held it up. And he lectured on the anatomy of the head for 4½ hours. Everybody listened.

Laurie: Attention getter!! (laughter)

Dave: If you look at what he was trying to teach though?

Dawn:	He was a good teacher at that time.
Dave:	He was trying to teach the importance of good discipline.
Gord:	Or was he trying to teach the anatomy of the head?
Laurie:	I think there are as many things that constitute good teaching as there are teachers.

Again Gord tried to find a way out of this dilemma.

Gord:	But maybe we need to change the question a little. We have to say what makes effective teaching?
Dawn:	But what's the difference?. . .
Gord:	The only thing about the word good that I get a little hung up on is that we get back on that other problem of whether you value what was taught. And if you ask about effective teaching then you may be effective at doing something but the value of what you do may be called into question.
Dawn:	I think that's really good!
Dave:	How do we tell when the teacher has been effective?
Dawn:	Ah hah! (approvingly)
Gord:	Well. . . .
Laurie:	Well there are visible signs. . . .

The different groups produced a variety of designs. Group B settled for the idea of surveying experienced teachers' opinions about the qualities of good teachers, anticipating a consensus. Group C was concerned to relate teacher's qualities to student examination performance. With hindsight, it is interesting to examine the focus and scope of these designs in terms of the variables identified by Mitzel (1957):

Type 1 Variables — Prediction sources: personality characteristics of teachers, training.
Type 2 Variables — Contingency factors: pupil individual differences.
Type 3 Variables — Classroom behavior: teacher behavior, pupil behavior.
Type 4 Variables — Criteria: pupil growth (reading, social maturity, etc.).

Clearly group C was interested in correlating Type 1 variables — prediction sources — with Type 4 variables — criteria related to pupil growth. Group B, on the other hand, although evidently concerned with Type 1 variables, did not seek to establish the basis on which their experienced teachers intuitively form their own opinions. Had the research director the insights of Mitzel, he might have usefully commented on the contributions of each group so as to help the whole team to orchestrate its efforts.

Although it wasn't feasible to proceed with implementing the designs produced, the simulation continued by considering what might have transpired. The scene was set two years later. We supposed that the different groups were meeting to present the findings of their studies to date and to review the direction the team should take. The studies examined took the form of synopses of two actual pieces of research (see Boxes 1.1 and 1.2 on pages 6 and 7).

These two studies are clearly inconclusive. Why didn't they yield definitive answers? Was it because the research designs are weak? Was it because research methodology of the scientific type is inappropriate? Was it because certain assumptions about the nature of teaching were made and these do not hold? (Inquiry 1.2).

6

Box 1.1   Synopsis of a Research Study I

*"An Analysis of the Views of Supervisors on the Attributes of Successful Graduate Student Teachers"** *

The researcher asked the question, "Which attributes of student teachers do you think are most helpful to success in practice teaching?", when accompanying supervisors on visits to student teachers. In this way he collected a wide range of opinions from a number of supervisors. From these opinions he prepared a list of fifty attributes. He tried to ensure that there was little overlap between the attributes and that vague items like "health" and "intelligence" were left out.

   Here is a sample of the attributes:

Ability to interest . . . "can hold a group"; makes work meaningful;
Equable temperament . . . poised; not easily put out; stable;
Enthusiasm for subject . . . "can communicate a devotion";
Multiplicity of interests . . . brings outside interests to bear in teaching;
Grasps of principles and aims of subjects;
Ability to organize class . . . can supervise all activities; manage;
Interest in people . . . knows the pupils; seeks to understand and help them;
Good appearance . . . "well dressed and groomed"; likely to appeal to young.

   He then asked the eighteen cooperating supervisors to put the attributes in rank order of importance. Each supervisor's ranking was correlated with the other seventeen. The highest correlation found between supervisors was $r = 0.73$ and the lowest, $r = 0.16$. The coefficient or concordance, a measure of the communality of judgements for a number of rankers, was 0.38. The researcher concluded that "the degree of general agreement about the attributes which contribute to success in practice teaching was not high."

---

*This is a summary of a study reported by Robertson (1957).

Box 1.2   Synopsis of a Research Study II

*"A Pilot Investigation into the Effects of Writing on Learning"** *

Two researchers who considered writing to be an important learning activity wanted to study the question, "Do students learn better if they prepare their own notes rather than copying the teacher's?"

   They encountered a science teacher who used copying exclusively but who was very interested in helping them with their inquiry. He planned to teach the topic, properties of matter, over a three-week period to two of his grade 6 classes which were well matched.

   One class, the control, followed the established lesson routine: teacher reviewed previous lesson using quick-fire questions, teacher presented new material using transparencies or demonstration, students copied notes from chalkboard filling in some blanks.

   The other class, the experimental one, followed a different routine: small groups

Box 1.2 — continued

of students compared and revised notes from previous lesson, teacher presented new material using transparencies or demonstrations, students made their own notes.

Both classes were given the same two-part test, before and after the topic had been taught. The first part tested factual recall. The second part tested understanding. The results were as follows:

	Mean percentage gain in recall	Mean percentage gain in understanding
Control class	35	32
Experimental class	28	23

In addition the researchers made the following observations:
(i)   The notebooks of the control class were identical, whereas those of the experimental class varied in length and accuracy.
(ii) The control class seemed keen when copying notes.
(iii) The morale of the experimental class seemed lower and the teacher seemed less relaxed and confident with it.
(iv) The teacher said he expected the experimental class to be superior on the test of understanding.

*I am grateful to Bryant Fillion and David Mendelsohn of OISE for making this available to me.

Historical Review

The history of research into teacher and teaching effectiveness seems to have moved through a number of phases.

Early studies focussed on the qualities and attributes of the teacher with a view to identifying these from both pupil and "expert" opinion. (The first research study is of this type.) Later this type of research was refined with a view to correlating the teachers' attributes with the pupils' achievement, often measured in terms of examination performance.

Subsequently, the focus of the studies moved from the teacher to the teaching. Many attempts were made to compare one method with another, for example, lecture versus discussion, to see how well the pupils performed in tests. (The second research study is of this type.) The approach was in turn refined by changing the focus from methods either to features of the teacher's behavior, such as the way they praise pupils and the way they ask questions, or alternatively to features of the teacher's interaction with the pupils. For instance, scores of studies were made in the sixties which attempted to correlate the teacher's style, described in terms of Flanders' Interaction Analysis, with the pupils' performance in tests designed to measure a wide range of cognitive abilities and affective states.

In a nutshell then, the focus of research seems to have progressively moved from the teacher to the methods he or she uses and to characteristic features of his or her behavior and interaction on the one hand, and from opinion to pupils' examination scores, to pupils' performance in a wide variety of tests on the other. Donald Medley's review, "The Effectiveness of Teachers" (1978), provides an interesting elaboration of this history.

What has this research revealed? How successful were the efforts of the researchers? The disappointing answers to these questions are captured in these quotations from the literature:

> "The simple fact of the matter is that, after 40 years of research on teacher effectiveness during which a vast number of studies have been carried out, one can point to few outcomes that a superintendent of schools can safely employ in hiring a teacher or granting him tenure, that an agency can employ in certifying teachers, or that a teacher-education faculty can employ in planning or improving teacher-education programs."
>
> Committee on Criteria of Teacher Effectiveness of the American Educational Research Association (1953), p. 657

> "The Eternal Note of Sadness. It is possible that the patterns of effective teaching for different ends are so idiosyncratic that they will never be isolated; it is possible that studying teaching in natural settings is unproductive because the settings are not functional for the desired outcomes; it is possible that descriptive systems and research within the descriptive-correlational experimental loop will be unproductive;. . . . At the moment there has not been enough research to make any firm statement about any of these concerns."
>
> Rosenshine and Furst, in *Second Handbook of Research on Teaching,* American Educational Research Association (1973), p. 175

Diagnosis of Failure

Why has so much research effort into teaching effectiveness yielded so little? In this brief section we will examine some of the possible reasons:

- The complexity of teaching
- The lack of focus on the teaching process
- Paucity of description of the process

The Complexity of Teaching

I would not be surprised if you could write down one hundred factors which likely affect what your pupils learn in your classroom — the number of pupils in the class, the content being studied, the time of day, the grouping procedures you use (Inquiry, 1.3). The vast range of these factors has been neatly summarized by Dunkin and Biddle (1974), who show how what you are like as a teacher (pressage variables) and the situation in which you work (context variables) affect what happens in the classroom (process variables) and what the pupils learn (product variables). (See Figure 1.1.)

Now it is apparent that a huge number of studies, if not the majority, have tried to ascertain the importance of these variables. To do this, investigators have usually used a scientific methodology, which, in essence, is an attempt to control or

9

Figure 1.1 A Model for the Study of Classroom Teaching (Dunkin and Biddle, 1974)

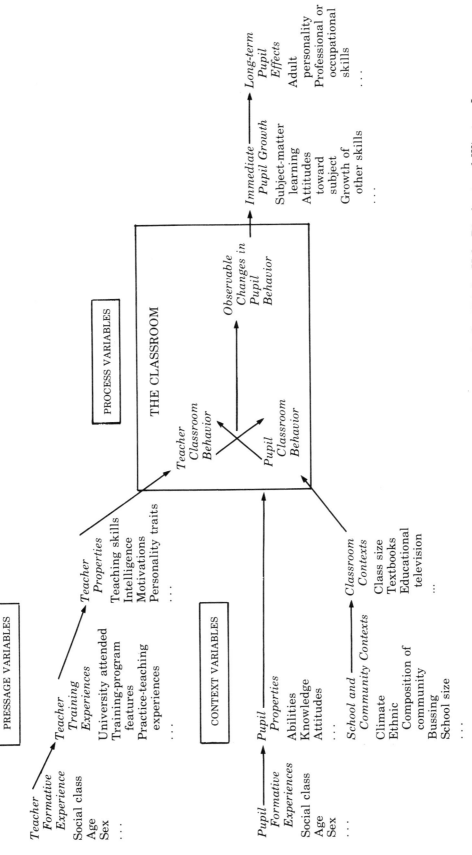

Source: From *The Study of Teaching* by Michael J. Dunkin and Bruce J. Biddle. Copyright © 1974 by Holt, Rinehart and Winston, Inc. Reprinted by Permission of CBS College Publishing.

eliminate from consideration all those variables except those whose interdependency is being examined. In this light, could it be that failure should be associated with the use of an inappropriate methodology?

Dunkin and Biddle didn't think so, but one can argue that teaching is such an idiosyncratic activity that to attempt to make generalizations to reveal universal truths is unlikely to be very productive.

Teaching does indeed appear to be idiosyncratic in at least three distinct ways. First, the teachers themselves will have different values, and, in particular, will place different weights on different educational objectives. For example, some will give more weight to developing their pupils' knowledge and understanding, others to developing their pupils' self-concepts. Second, neither two pupils nor two groups of pupils will be the same, and it seems insufficient to describe them merely in terms of their achievement or their socio-economic status. Third, there is a spontaneous uncontrollable element in every classroom. Teaching is a dynamic activity.

Doyle (1977) made similar points when he discussed three aspects of classroom complexity: multidimensionality, simultaneity, and unpredictability. Multidimensionality refers to the interacting network of purposes, events, and processes. Teachers face a multiplicity of tasks, which include such matters as "processing subject matter information, judging student abilities, managing classroom groups, coping with emotional responses to events and behaviors, and establishing procedures for routine and special assignments, distribution of resources and supplies, record keeping, and so on." Many such events occur simultaneously and their consequences are often unpredictable.

The Lack of Focus on the Teaching Process

Many of the earlier studies, especially those which sought to correlate teacher attributes with pupil performance, ignored the process. Gage (1963) described these studies as considering the classroom as a "black box" and was clearly dissatisfied with them because they failed to enhance significantly our understanding. A classic example of this type of study is *Pygmalion in the Classroom: Teachers' Expectations and Pupils' Intellectual Development* by Rosenthal and Jacobson (1968). They told a group of teachers that on the basis of an intelligence test some of their pupils would "bloom" during the year. Although in fact these pupils had been randomly selected, they did indeed bloom by comparison with others. Rosenthal and Jacobson concluded that the teachers' expectations had become self-fulfilling prophecies. However, the value of their study was limited because they did not give any indication as to the process by which this came about. In order to examine the way in which the teachers' expectations influenced the way in which the teachers interacted with pupils, a number of studies followed (Brophy and Good, 1974). These studies were characterized by increased focus on the process than ever before. Not only were the teacher's interactions with the class as a whole monitored, but also those with individual pupils (dyadic interaction). The results obtained from these studies, however, were rather contradictory. The process itself is evidently very complex (Inquiry 1.4).

Paucity of Description of the Process

If you were to tell somebody about a car, what would you tell them? Would you tell them about its color? its fuel consumption? how the designers had sought to compromise between aesthetic appeal and aerodynamic shape? There are so many things you might mention that it is difficult to know which to select and where to begin. If an analogy is drawn between this problem of describing a car and the problem of describing the teaching process, a number of important questions emerge:

- Have our descriptions merely been of the obvious?
- Have we been examining the trivial rather than the important?
- Have our descriptions been sufficiently comprehensive?
- Have all the important features been identified?
- Have we merely examined component features rather than their interdependence?
- How do we decide what an important feature is? And from whose viewpoint is this decision made?

I suspect that the failure to make substantial progress in answering the question as to what makes good teaching may be associated with our failure to be able to provide convincing responses to these questions, and moreover that before real progress can be made, effort needs to be directed towards providing richness and power when describing the teaching process. (In passing, I would prefer to measure this richness and power in terms of what is of practical value to teachers.)

It does appear that the beginnings of this effort have been made. In the last two decades, there has been a growth of interest in applying the qualitative methodologies used by *social* scientists to the study of classrooms, with a view to perceiving and understanding what is happening in them. The extracts (see Box 1.3) from a review by Hinely and Ponder (1979) outline the state of affairs.

Box 1.3 "Theory, Practice and Classrooms Research." Extracts from a paper by Hinely and Ponder (1979).

". . . . Generations of critics and theorists have lamented the minimal impact exerted by the various theories of education on the practices of schooling. . . . This notable lack of success in improving practice has typically spawned redoubled efforts to generate new theory, again intended to serve the function of improvement. But in the last several years an alternative function of theory has gained ascendancy. This function is that of description of practice with the intention of increasing understanding of the ways classrooms work. . . .

The primary question for researchers interested in improvement is: How can things be changed? For describers, at least three questions are of key importance: A descriptive question — What seems to be happening here? An analytic question — Why are these events occurring? And a question of understanding — What do these events mean in the context of the classroom? . . . . Improvers wish to maximize the efficiency and effectiveness of instruction primarily by modifying the behaviors of teachers. . . . Describers on the other hand tend to view the stability of teaching practices as a phenomena to be explained and understood. While improvement of practice may be their ultimate aim, they view the discrete pieces of teacher behaviour — questions, responding tactics, and so forth — as micro-phenomena embedded in a larger and more complex whole.

Box 1.3 — continued

The differences between improvers and describers in questions and assumptions have led to alterations in research procedures. While descriptive and inferential statistics borrowed from the field of psychology are still widely used, classroom researchers interested primarily in explanation have increasingly adopted the perspectives of sociology, ethnography, and linguistics, as well as the formerly little-used fields of ecological psychology and cognitive science, to add depth and meaning to collections of data. . . .

In sum, the growing body of literature in the field of classroom research signals significant departures from the directions established by previous studies of teaching and learning. Its search is for the causes of phenomena that occur in classroom settings rather than the cures for supposed ''ills'' of schooling. It assumes that the classroom environment plays a large role in shaping the behavior of its inhabitants. It suggests that teachers and students who inhabit classrooms actively construct their own meanings for events that occur there, and that they are thus to be valued as potential partners in the research enterprise.

The growing body of research directed toward classrooms describes an .increasingly complex portrait of the academic and behavioral systems existing there . . . . The work remaining to produce a reasonable understanding of the workings of classrooms will be time-consuming, intricate, and sometimes perplexing. Yet its products hold significant promise for the practices of schooling and the education of teachers.

Source: Extracts from R. Hinely and G. Ponder, "Theory, Practice, and Classroom Research," *Theory into Practice* 18 (1979): 135–37. Copyright 1979, College of Education, The Ohio State University.

Suggested Inquiries

This appendix contains outlines of a number of suggestions for inquiries which were introduced in the chapter. There is no reason why individual teachers shouldn't use them by themselves. I would hope they would find it a worthwhile experience. However, their separate experiences might well be enriched if shared with others. Hence, the following activities have been written as if addressed to a group of teachers.

Inquiry 1.1   Research Team Simulation

In groups of three or four, spend forty minutes or so formulating the outlines of research designs into the questions, what makes a good teacher or good teaching? You might prepare for a five-minute presentation using an overhead projector transparency if you wish. At the beginning of this chapter you will find a brief description of the experience of other teachers who undertook this activity. Their designs are categorized according to Mitzel's model. Where does yours fit?

Inquiry 1.2   Making Critiques of Research Studies

Examine the two synopses. How do you explain the findings being somewhat inconclusive?

Inquiry 1.3 Appreciating the Complexity of Teaching

In order to get a feel for the complexity of teaching, write down as many things as you can which might have affected how much you think your pupils learned from the last lesson you taught. Then classify these as pressage, context, or process variables using Dunkin and Biddle's model (p. 9). Some of the ideas in the model and some which your fellow teachers have included might cue you to add to your list.

Inquiry 1.4 Comparing Your Expectations and Your Actions

Brophy and Good (1974) suggested "Teachers need to become more aware of their classroom behavior in general and their interactions with lows (low achievers) in particular."

Select a class for study. Place the students in rank order of achievement so that later you can divide the class equally into high achievers and lower achievers. Tape-record the lesson. Afterwards, use the following checklist to tally your behavior with the "highs" and with the "lows."

Teacher behavior	Number of occurrences with high achievers	Number of occurrences with low achievers
Asking a question		
Praising, rather than just accepting an answer		
Criticizing, rather than simply rejecting an answer		
Rewarding, inappropriate answers		
Staying with pupil, e.g., asking a supplementary question, in a failure situation		
Waiting a second or more for an answer		

Try to identify other ways in which you behaved differently towards the higher and the lower achievers. This is important since the behaviors in the checklist may be of lesser consequence. How did your findings compare with those of other teachers?

This activity might have given you some indication of how your behavior varies with lows and highs. However, the challenge of moving towards a rationale for your action remains. Good and Dembo (1973) were moving in this direction when they asked a group of teachers which of the following methods of dealing with the lows would be appropriate:

• Call upon lows less often than other students, but call upon them when they are likely to know the answer.
• Call upon lows equally without concern for whether they know the answer.

- Call upon lows more often than other students, but call upon them when they are likely to know the answer.
- Call upon them equally, but call upon them often when they are likely to know the answer.

Suggested Reading

Dunkin, M. J., and Biddle, B. J. "Research Failure and Ideological Response," *The Study of Teaching,* Ch. 2. New York: Holt, Rinehart and Winston, 1974.

After reviewing some of the possible reasons why research on teaching effectiveness has yielded so little, Dunkin and Biddle reiterate their support for the use of the scientific methodology.

Hinely, R., and Ponder, G. "Theory, Practice and Classroom Research," *Theory into Practice* 18 (1979) 135–37.

This paper makes the case for using the qualitative methodologies of the social sciences. It provides a stimulating contrast to the previous article.

2

Appraising Teaching

Key Aspects of the Teaching Process

In the previous chapter, it should have become clear that making comments, criticisms, or judgments about teaching is not a matter of comparing a teacher with a list of traits or comparing teaching with a list of process characteristics which have been correlated with pupil achievement. But this does not necessarily mean that judgments are not possible to make, just that the business is more complex than making a number of comparisons with a series of criteria. Moreover, in critically examining the research into what makes good teaching, a variety of considerations have emerged which should be taken into account if any form of judgment is to be more than naive or simplistic (Inquiry 2.1).

- The criteria of good teaching are not simply established. Although a strong case can be made for these being closely associated with good learning, it is not clear what good learning amounts to. There is no consensus about the relative value to different ends and hence there is no consensus about good teaching. It would seem somewhat inappropriate to judge the effectiveness of a teacher, who has one set of ends in view, using another set of ends as criteria. To do this would be to compare apples and oranges. In addition, means as well as ends are important. For example, most of us would have reservations about using brainwashing techniques, however desirable the ends.

- Every teaching situation is different: a different teacher, a different group of pupils, a different context. These differences need to be taken into account when making judgments. Although there will be similarities between one situation and another, to apply criteria of effectiveness which do not recognize these differences is indefensible. If and when any criterion is ventured, I would suggest that it is important to ask, "Is it possible to visualize a 'good' teaching situation where this criterion does not hold?"

- Each teaching situation is complex. Many, many factors combine in unpredictable ways to produce the resulting sequence of events. Furthermore, even to describe what happens is not a simple matter. Our understanding of what is happening will be limited by our powers of perception. And the quality of our judgments will be limited by our understanding.

In this chapter, around which the first part of this book is built, we will take a fresh look at the problems of describing and appraising teaching. In order to describe teaching I will argue that it is necessary to consider fully four closely related aspects of the teaching process:
- the teacher's frame of reference
- the teacher's actions
- the pupils' actions
- the pupils' covert experiences.

In doing so a variety of implications for appraisal will emerge.*

The Teacher's Frame of Reference

This phase is designed to capture the notion of a network of ideas that influences the way a teacher acts when taking the role of a teacher. I have noticed that the phrase is used from time to time in the literature but it is seldom ascribed a technical meaning. Some authors have clearly felt the need for such a technical phrase, however. For example, Bishop and Whitfield (1972) introduced the idea of the teacher's "decision framework," and Sharp and Green (1975) develop in some detail the idea of a "teacher's perspective."

I would maintain that one cannot fully understand classroom interaction without knowing what the teacher has in mind. For example, an apparent lack of praise for pupils' responses becomes meaningful when this is associated with a concern of teachers to preserve their intellectual independence or with concern to help them develop realistic self-concepts. An important dimension of meaning is added to the teacher's actions if one knows the rationale underpinning them. This is not a new insight. It is recognized as being fundamental to any phenomenological study.

In the course of their lives, all teachers will have accumulated a considerable range of ideas about the teaching process. Some ideas will be brought to a level of consciousness and made explicit, some will remain intuitive. These ideas originate from the teachers' attempts to make sense of their own experience as children, as pupils at school and college, as student-teachers, as practising teachers, as parents, and so on. From a theoretical point of view, I see these ideas about classroom interaction falling into three general categories: ideas about aims, ideas about principles of procedure, and hypotheses about interaction.

Within the category of aims, I would include objectives as well. The category includes qualities which the teacher deems it worthwhile developing in pupils. Not all teachers will value the same aims equally. It is possible that two individuals teaching the same content to the same pupils in the same school would emphasize different aims. For instance, one science teacher might place an emphasis on the

---

* These ideas were first presented in a paper given at the meeting of the Association for the Study of Curriculum at Nottingham in 1983. See J. T. Haysom, "Towards Relating Curriculum Development and Teacher Education", in C. Day, D. Morton, and G. D. Yeoman, eds., *Prospect for Curriculum* (Association for the Study of Curriculum, 1985).

pupils' remembering the facts and another on pupils' being able to use scientific processes.

The category of principles of procedure is distinct from the category of aims (see Peters, 1963, and Stenhouse, 1975). I would include in this category the ideas teachers have as to *how* pupils should be treated: ideas relating to equality, indoctrination, autonomy, punishment, and so on. Again, these ideas will vary from teacher to teacher. Not all will share the same ethical positions. Not all will have questioned their positions to the same extent.

The third category, hypotheses about interaction, refers to ideas about how teachers and pupils are likely to respond to one another. I call these ideas hypotheses for two major reasons. First, I believe that to express them in terms of "if . . then . . ." propositions disciplines us to think more precisely. For example, I believe the challenge to express an idea, such as "pupils should be allowed to work in friendship groups," as a hypothesis, such as "if pupils work in friendship groups, then there is less deviant behavior," encourages a clarification and development of the idea. Second, to call the ideas hypotheses emphasizes their tentative nature and underlines the dangers of making universal generalizations.

In discussing possible ways of categorizing teachers' thinking, several important points have emerged. First, every teacher will be unique. Different teachers will value different aims, adhere to different ethical positions, and use different hypothesis about interaction. Moreover, in this context, it is important to recognize that there are no absolute values or clear-cut resolutions of ethical problems and that hypotheses about interaction may vary from situation to situation. Second, it is evident that teachers will have a vast array of ideas which influence their classroom behavior. The problem of identifying the more influential remains. Both these points have considerable implications in making appraisals.

Clark and Yinger (1978), in reviewing studies of teachers' thinking, were only able to identify a handful of studies. Since then this has been a rapidly developing area of inquiry. One interesting development is the shift of interest from theoretical categorizations towards the categories teachers actually use (see, for example, Elbaz, 1981).

The Teacher's Actions and the Pupils' Actions

The claim that it is necessary to describe the teacher's actions and the pupils' actions in order to describe the teaching process does not require justifying. However, even if it were possible to make a list, in sequence, of everything a teacher said or did and everything a pupil said or did, then some (myself included) would still argue that this was not sufficient, that this did not fully describe what had actually happened in a classroom. We would be concerned to make the case that these different actions should be viewed in relationship to one another and would be arguing for some form of classification of these actions. Moreover, some might also argue that not all these actions or classifications should be given equal weight. Some might be more significant than others.

A wide variety of ways exists for classifying the teacher's actions, for example, teaching methods, teaching approaches, and teaching styles. To use these, however, is to align oneself to the view that they are valuable and powerful descriptors. More recently, attention has been directed towards examining the raw data for patterns and significant features in them (see, for example, Doyle, 1978). In similar vein, Yinger's (1979) concept of routines could guide the way we look for structure and might lead us towards producing rich and powerful descriptions of classrooms in action.

With respect to appraisal, one should expect to find a close relationship between the teacher's frame of reference and the teacher's actions. But this is not necessarily the case; much will depend upon the teacher's awareness. Teachers who are aware of both will have probably wrestled with the problem of matching their actions to their thinking. However, teachers who are aware of their thinking but not of their actions could be trapped into idealizing their actions, and those who are aware of their actions but not thinking, trapped by rationalization.

Teachers will regard some pupil actions as desirable and some as undesirable. It is reasonable to expect that they should act in such a way as to increase the desirable and decrease the undesirable. The efforts they make to manage the situation will be closely related to their hypotheses about interaction. In passing, it is worth noting that teacher–pupil interaction is not a one-way street. There is evidence that pupils in turn try to manage their teachers (see, for example, Holt, 1969).

Most teachers value pupil participation and with good reason. They could argue with force that if all the pupils are actively engaged on tasks which they can justify as being worthwhile, then this warrants a perfect score. This argument underpins much of the current research on teacher effectiveness (see, for example, Berliner, 1978, and Bennett, 1979). However, one needs to be cautious. How does one recognize participation? How does one ascertain the quality of participation?

The Pupils' Covert Experiences

The phrase is meant to capture what is going on inside the pupils' minds, the thoughts and feelings taking place. It is not the same thing as a learning outcome; a pupil may be attempting to make sense of a paragraph in a book but may fail. A pupil may solve a problem but achieve this by guessing. Learning outcomes usually refer to pupils' actions in a test situation. Bloom (1953) made the distinction clearly in his study, which compared the lecture and discussion methods. He was not content to measure outcomes. Instead he invited the pupils to relive their experiences by listening to recordings and then interviewed them about the thought processes they had had. His findings were striking (see chapter 6).

The pupils' covert experiences have a central position in the learning process. Winne and Marx (1977) argue the case from a psychological point of view.

> "Specifically we see the mental life of both teachers and students in classrooms as critical items to be studied if we are to understand the process by which teaching influences students' learning. . . . The body of prior research must now take account of the mediating phenomena such as teacher decision making and student cognitive processes and structures to achieve a sufficiently accurate description of what happens in teaching and learning from teaching." (p.670)

Although one can never know for certain what is happening in pupils' minds, one can make inferences from their actions. The more these inferences corroborate one another, the more certain one can be. Teachers watch children's faces. They listen to what they say. They make inferences about their actions and adjust their responses accordingly. The degree to which teachers are conscious of the importance of this process and their capacity to use it could significantly determine the quality of their teaching.

In summary then, I have argued that in order to describe teaching it is necessary to describe the teacher's frame of reference (TFR), the teacher's actions (TA), the pupils' actions (PA), and the pupils' covert experiences (PCE). They are at the core of the teaching process (Figure 2.1).

Figure 2.1   The Core of the Teaching Process

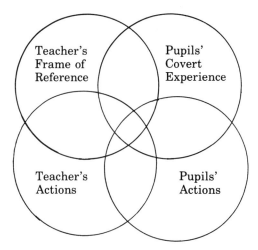

The extract from Muriel Sparke's *The Prime of Miss Jean Brodie* (Box 2.1) describes a short teaching sequence. You might find it interesting to identify the four aspects (TFR, TA, PA, PCE) discussed in this chapter. As you will see, there is more to the description than a simple record of the teacher's and pupils' actions. An observer's simple field notes about what happened would not provide the illuminating information about what the teacher and pupils are thinking (TFR and PCE).

Box 2.1   Extract from *The Prime of Miss Jean Brodie*

Miss Brodie was reciting poetry to the class at a quarter to four, to raise their minds before they went home. Miss Brodie's eyes were half-shut and her head was thrown back:

> In the stormy east wind straining,
> The pale yellow woods were waning,
> The broad stream in his banks complaining
> Heavily the low sky raining
> Over tower'd Camelot.

Sandy watched Miss Brodie through her little pale eyes, screwed them smaller and shut her lips tight. Rose Stanley was pulling threads from the girdle of her gym tunic.

Box 2.1 — continued

Jenny was enthralled by the poem, her lips were parted, she was never bored. Sandy was never bored, but she had to lead a double life of her own in order never to be bored.

> Down she came and found a boat
> Beneath a willow left afloat,
> And round about the prow she wrote
> The Lady of Shallot.

'By what means did your ladyship write these words?' Sandy enquired in her mind with her lips tight shut. 'There was a pot of white paint and a brush which happened to be standing upon the grassy verge,' replied the Lady of Shallot graciously. 'It was left there no doubt by some heedless member of the Unemployed.' 'Alas, and in all that rain!' said Sandy for want of something better to say, while Miss Brodie's voice soared up to the ceiling, and curled round the feet of the Senior girls upstairs.

The Lady of Shallot placed a white hand on Sandy's shoulder and gazed at her for a space. 'That one so young and beautiful should be so ill-fated in love!' she said in sad low tones.

'What can be the meaning of these words?' cried Sandy in alarm, with her little eyes screwed on Miss Brodie and her lips shut tight.

Miss Brodie said: 'Sandy, are you in pain?'

Sandy looked astonished.

'You girls,' said Miss Brodie, 'must learn to cultivate an expression of composure. It is one of the best assets of a woman, an expression of composure, come foul, come fair. Regard the Mona Lisa, over yonder!'

All heads turned to look at the reproduction which Miss Brodie had brought back from her travels and pinned on the wall. Mona Lisa in her prime smiled in steady composure even though she had just come from the dentist and her lower jaw was swollen.

'She is older than the rocks on which she sits. Would that I had been given charge of you girls when you were seven. I sometimes fear it's too late, now. If you had been mine when you were seven you would have been the **crème de la crème**. Sandy, come and read some stanzas and let us hear your vowel sounds.'

Appraising Teaching

In describing these four aspects of teaching, a variety of issues has been raised, sometimes implicitly, which pertains to the problem of appraisal. I summarize them here in the form of questions which, in my view, should be addressed when making appraisals.

- What is happening in the classroom, not only in terms of the teacher's and pupils' actions, but in terms of patterns of interaction and significant features of this interaction? How does one decide what is significant?
- Is the teacher aware of what is happening?
- To what extent is each pupil participating (in the covert sense)? What types of thinking and feeling are they likely experiencing? Are the teacher's inferences about the pupils' covert experiences reasonable?

- Has the teacher a well articulated rationale for action? What are its major features? Is the teacher able to justify this rationale?
- Is the teacher able to manage the interaction in accordance with this rationale?
- Is there a good match between the teacher's frame of reference, the teacher's actions, the pupils' actions, and the pupils' covert experiences? (Inquiry 2.2.)

No attempt has been made to make this a comprehensive list. Other questions come to mind, such as, "Is the teacher aware of alternative courses of action, which *prima facie* have advantages?" This question does not immediately follow from the previous discussion.

This list of questions bears a marked resemblance to those considered important by others. In laying the foundations for its course on practical classroom evaluation, the Open University (1980) sought to identify the questions teachers would need to pose in order to evaluate their work in classrooms. After more than six months working with teachers, the course team arrived at the following list:

- What did the pupils actually do?
- What were they learning?
- How worthwhile was it?
- What did I do?
- What did I learn?
- What do I intend to do now?

Although derived independently, the two lists contain many interesting similarities.

I do not believe it is possible to say exactly how one proceeds to gather data to answer these questions. However, the most productive starting point would seem to be with a close examination of the teacher–pupil interactions. Thereafter, one might well try to make sense of these, noting occurrences of particular interest, perceiving patterns which emerge, using conceptual descriptions of practice as they occur in the literature as a basis for analysis, and so on. Thenceforth, one might proceed to relate these findings to pupils' actions, the pupils' participation, and to inquire into the pupils' covert experiences. Whether one does this before or after probing the teacher's frame of reference, underpinning these classroom events, does not seem particularly consequential.

An observer or a helper can be of great assistance to a teacher who is gathering data and carrying out personal appraisal. A second viewpoint is provided. Recognizing that both the observer and teacher tend to perceive what is happening in the classroom in terms of their individual frames of reference offsets the danger of biased observation and interpretation.

Appraisal in Perspective

So far in this chapter I have taken a fresh look at the problem of appraising teaching. In a nutshell, I have argued that description is a necessary prerequisite to appraisal and that a full description should at least include the four aspects of the teaching process (TFR, TA, PA, PCE). Some may have found these arguments rather pedantic and heavy with references to the literature. However, it is timely to be careful. For too long, we have built our practices on shaky foundations. Although the conclusions to these arguments do not seem particularly extravagant,

22

they warrant scrutiny. In this last section I will place them within a critical perspective.

The writings about curriculum evaluation provide one such perspective. They contain a diversity of ideas, many of which pertain to judging teaching (see Stenhouse, 1975, for a useful review). Here I shall consider the contributions of Tyler (1949), Parlett and Hamilton (1972), and Eisner (1979). The procedures they advocated, which are radically different from one another, have received wide recognition within the education community.

Tyler's ideas (1949) dominated thinking about evaluation for twenty years. This is scarcely surprising; the argument, that the pupils' learning matters, is simple and compelling:

> ". . . the process of evaluation is essentially the process of determining to what extent the educational objectives are actually being realized by the program of curriculum and instruction. However, since educational objectives are essentially changes in human beings, that is, the objectives aimed at are to produce certain desirable changes in the behavior patterns of the student, then evaluation is the process for determining the degree to which these changes in behaviors are actually taking place." (pp. 105–106)

On this basis, some might argue that the procedures I have been advocating should be extended to include the pupils' learning (PL) and possibly the pupils' actions in a test situation (PAT). They would be arguing for the schematic diagram, TFR-TA-PA-PCE, to be extended to become TFR-TA-PA-PCE-PL-PAT.

Consideration of what the pupils' learn in a lesson and the pupils' actions in test situations could well enhance the quality of our appreciation of classroom events. They sometimes however tend to be peripheral rather than central: some learnings clearly take place over an extended period of time and not all lessons contain formal test situations.

Parlett and Hamilton (1972) launched a vigorous attack on the school of researchers which followed in Tyler's footsteps. They objected to evaluation being focussed on the measurement of anticipated outcomes and regarded it as divorced from reality because of the problem of controlling parameters. They scathingly described it as the "agricultural-botany" type of evaluation.

> "Students — rather like plant crops — are given pre-tests (the seedlings are weighed and measured) and then submitted to different experiences (treatment conditions). . . ." (p.7)

Instead of measuring the products of learning they proposed that evaluation should be concerned with describing and interpreting the process of learning, focussing on the "learning milieu" with the aim of "illuminating" it. They tellingly illustrated this idea by referring to the case at the Massachusetts Institute of Technology, where a switch was made from "distributed" to "concentrated" study (a change from students' taking several subjects concurrently to intensive full-time study of a single subject). The switch was accompanied by dramatic changes in the learning milieu: new pedagogic forms replaced lectures, interaction between students increased, normally silent students asked questions, the relationship between faculty and students changed. They did not ignore the pupils' learning and proceeded to add,

> "Connecting changes in the learning milieu with intellectual experiences of students is one of the chief concerns for illuminative evaluation." (p. 12)

The procedures discussed in this chapter for judging teaching find much sympathy with these ideas. Classrooms are recognized as complex. The concern to describe what is happening in terms of teacher actions (TA) and pupils' actions (PA) and to relate these to the pupils' covert experiences (PCE) is explicit.

However, Parlett and Hamilton went further. They also showed concern to locate classroom practice in a broader context.

> "To take an example: teaching and learning in a particular setting are profoundly influenced by the type of assessment procedures in use; by constraints of scheduling; by the size and diversity of classes; by the availability of teaching assistants, library, computing and copying facilities. These, in turn, are dependent of departmental priorities; on policies of faculty promotion; on institutional myths and traditions; and on local and national pressures." (p. 12–13)

There's no doubt that what happens inside classrooms is affected by what goes on outside. It is well recognized that constraints such as shortage of resources and adequate facilities also have dramatic repercussions. Cognizant of this, the co-ordinators of the Atlantic Science Curriculum Project carried out a detailed survey of all the junior high school teachers in Nova Scotia and New Brunswick *prior* to developing even one learning experience (McFadden, 1980). For them, curriculum development began with the type of situational analysis advocated by Reynolds and Skilbeck (1976). The design criteria they subsequently adopted emphasized "teachability." Recently, the Schools Council funded the Teacher–Pupil Interaction and Quality of Learning Project. This project was concerned to carry out research into "Understanding those factors which constrain the development of pupils' understanding in classrooms, and evaluating strategies designed to remove such constraints." Two books describing its findings are scheduled for publication.

Clearly the feasibility of the teacher acting in a particular way may sometimes take precedence over desirability. Teachers' aims and principles of procedure may be moderated by context. This may be expressed diagrammatically: Context-TFR-TA-PA-PCE. Appraisal should thus take context into account.

The problem is that most, if not all, teachers are to some extent unaware of the effects of context on their teaching. Sometimes they are oblivious of them. Sometimes they underestimate them. And sometimes the effects are exaggerated!

How can teachers become more aware of the most serious constraints? How can teachers develop an understanding of the way in which these constraints affect classroom interaction? It seems to me to be a matter of establishing links between the world of the classroom and the world outside. One might either begin with the classroom or alternatively, and possibly more productively, begin by identifying possible constraints. Once a constraint has been tentatively identified, evidence may then be collected with a view to developing hypotheses as to how teacher–pupil interaction is affected. Once this understanding is developed the teacher is then in a position to respond (Inquiry 2.3).

A concern to keep control was one such constraint identified by a teacher (Knight, 1984). She identified this by keeping a diary of noteworthy events over a six-week period. As you might expect many problems and difficulties were mentioned. Foremost amongst these were entries which related to control. For example,

> "September 8th. I feel as though I have been in a boxing ring all day! Half a dozen children spoil it for the rest. . . .
>
> September 12th. The children appear unused to sitting in groups, so I have isolated some of the more disruptive elements. . . ." (p. 7)

She followed this up by asking other teachers about the major constraints on their teaching (using the normal group techniques described in Inquiry 2.3). Top of the list was "time spent disciplining rather than teaching." Further inquiry reveal- ed how this was likely related to a range of school policies and practices, such as the amount of content to be covered and the purchase of workbooks. Having gain- ed this understanding, she implemented with some success a teaching strategy which encouraged self-discipline.

The third approach to curriculum evaluation that I should like to discuss was advanced by Eisner (1979). Eisner's orientation to evaluation found its origin in his involvement in art and art education. He called it "educational connoisseur- ship and educational criticism." This involved appreciating teaching in a way analogous to the way an art or literary critic proceeds in appreciating a piece of art or literature. The critic's task was that of "rendering the essentially ineffable qualities constituting works of art into a language that would help others to perceive the work more deeply." The critic acted as a "mid-wife to perception."

Gail McCutcheon, who worked with Eisner developing these procedures, has published a number of examples of educational criticism. She did not hesitate to make explicit the procedures she used (see McCutcheon, 1978). Criticism involv- ed three stages — description, interpretation, and appraisal — and culminated with the attempt to answer two questions: Was it well done? Was it worth doing?

What she had to say about interpretation is particularly relevant here. She viewed interpretation as encompassing three perspectives and it is these that I want to juxtapose with the ideas I have been developing in this chapter.

- She was concerned about establishing the social meanings of events. Behavior has to be related to the thinking underpinning it. She argued for the interpreta- tion of PA in terms of PCE and of TA in terms of TFR.
- Through the second interpretative perspective, she was concerned to relate events to external factors, particularly general theoretical principles. She envisioned a dialectic occurring between specific events and theory. In my view such a dialec- tic is a source of professional growth for the teacher. For growth to occur, the teacher needs to perceive the rationale underlying classroom actions, that is, to make explicit his or her frame of reference, and to see this in the context of theoretical discussions of teaching, which are to be found in the literature.
- The third perspective involved relating events, one to another, in the forma- tion of patterns. The important point that McCutcheon made here is that the individual teacher actions, TA, and the pupils' actions, PA, should not be seen as discrete. They need to be related to each other so as to build a picture of the fabric which constitutes the visible life of the classroom (Inquiry 2.4).

The positions of Tyler, Parlett and Hamilton, and Eisner on curriculum evalua- tion are radically different. It seems to me that they have different views about the nature of the study of teaching: Tyler (see also, Dunkin and Biddle, 1974) approaches it scientifically; Parlett and Hamilton (see also, Smith and Geoffrey, 1968) anthropologically, and Eisner aesthetically. And there are other views in addition. For example, Stenhouse (1978) considers the study of education to be akin to the study of contemporary history. If one were able to resolve the problem of the epistemological nature of the study of teaching, one would be able to say with some certainty how one should proceed to test the truth of different judgments. However, this matter has yet to be resolved.

To conclude this chapter I should like to make clear my reasons for writing it. Not only do I consider the systematic gathering of information about the teacher's frame of reference, the teacher's actions, the pupils' actions, and the pupils' covert experiences to be necessary to the description and appraisal of teaching, but I hypothesize that it is an important precursor to professional development. I hypothesize that growth may occur when teachers seek to understand and resolve the almost inevitable mismatch between their thinking (TFR) and classroom events (TA, PA, PCE). In tune with McCutcheon, I also anticipate that growth will sometimes occur when teachers critically review their thinking (TFR) in the light of the thinking of others.

Suggested Inquiries

Inquiry 2.1 Making Appraisals of a Lesson

In order to probe the dimensions of the problem of making appraisals, you might watch a film or video recording of a lesson with some fellow teachers. Afterwards, write a brief evaluative report on the lesson, up to say 500 words. Compare your evaluation with someone else's and list the major differences. Does this throw any light on the dimensions of the problem? Put another way, the end product of this activity might be a list of the difficulties your group encountered in making appraisals.

Inquiry 2.2 Improving Your Judgment

Examine the evaluative report you prepared in the previous activity in terms of the the four components described in this chapter.

Teacher's frame of reference: Did you speculate about what is in the teacher's mind? Does your judgment depend on knowing?

Teacher's actions/pupils' actions: Which teacher action and pupil action or patterns of interaction caught your eye?

Pupils' covert experiences: Did you make inferences about the pupils' actions? Did you speculate about what is happening in the pupils' mind?

Prepare a brief comment on how your evaluative report might be improved (if possible!). Note: The description of teaching (Figure 2.1) was presented with a view to making more comprehensible the problem of making judgments. Its value might be assessed, at least partially, in terms of whether you found it helpful. Did it enable you to get a grip on some of the difficulties you encountered in the previous activity? If you rewrote your evaluative report, how would it differ?

Inquiry 2.3 Identifying Constraints on Your Teaching

The purpose of this inquiry is to begin to *identify the major contextual restraints on your teaching — the factors that inhibit your teaching as you would really like to teach.*

If you are working with other teachers as a group, you might like to use the Nominal Group Technique (Collinson and Dunlop, 1978, and Elliott, 1982). NGT is basically a structured form of brainstorming which allows each member of the group to contribute opinions on an equal footing and for the group as a whole to move towards consensus.

- Write the task (above) on the blackboard. The group may decide to change the wording so as to make the meaning clearer.
- Silent nominations (approximately ten minutes). Individuals list the major constraints and rank order them.
- Round-robin listing of items (approximately twenty-five minutes). In turn each member contributes an item until their individual lists are exhausted. These are written on the board by the co-ordinator. Items should be written down without comment or change.
- Clarification (approximately fifteen minutes). Each member is given the opportunity of seeking clarification. Providing it is acceptable to the nominees, items may be clarified by rewording and overlapping ones combined.
- Evaluation (approximately five minutes). Each member selects the five factors he or she believes to be particularly consequential. Five points are allocated to the most constraining, four to the next, and so on.
- Compilation (approximately ten minutes). The co-ordinator tallies the number of points allocated to each item.

This inquiry raises a number of questions for discussion. Elliott (1982) considered the following to be especially important:

(a) Whether the areas of consensus are based on shared prejudice or sound evidence.

(b) Why do some individuals view certain factors as constraints while others don't? Is it because some teachers adopt strategies which prevent the factor in question from operating as a constraint? Is it because certain individuals are more aware

These questions prompt further inquiry. What evidence needs to be collected? What methods and techniques can be used to collect it?

Inquiry 2.4 Putting the Problem of Judgment in Perspective

Read McCutcheon's (1978) paper, "Of Solar Systems, Responsibilities and Basics: An educational criticism of Mr. Clement's fourth grade." Identify the similarities and differences between her approach to educational criticism and the approach outlined in this chapter.

Suggested Reading

Open University *Curriculum in Action: An Approach to Evaluation.* Milton Keynes: Open University Press, 1980.

These materials are very much in harmony with the spirit of this book and provide a most valuable supplement. The first unit (pp. 7–26) provides an easy to read introduction.

Parlett, M., and Hamilton, D. "Evaluation as Illumination: A New Approach to the Study of Innovatory Programmes." Reprinted in *Beyond the Numbers Game,* edited by D. Hamilton, et al. London: Macmillan, 1977.

This article contributed to opening up the flood gates to a "new wave" of ideas about evaluation. It moves far beyond the simple notion of appraising teaching merely according to how well the pupils learned.

McCutcheon, G. "Of Solar Systems, Responsibilities and Basics: An Educational Criticism of Mr. Clement's Fourth Grade." *Qualitative Evaluation: Concepts and Cases in Curriculum Controversy,* edited by G. Willis. Berkeley: McCutchan, 1978.

It is useful to have a good example of what a piece of educational criticism looks like. The introductory pages are particularly useful because they spell out the process the author used.

3

The Teacher's Frame of Reference

In Justification

Can one really understand classroom interaction without knowing what the teacher has in mind? I suspect the answer is a vigorous "No!" For example, a social studies teacher recently told me that she was very concerned to involve more students in classroom discussion. I later observed one of her lessons. Her struggle was apparent. "How many of you have visited Ireland?" Half the class put up their hands. "Tell me about it. You're the experts. I've never been there." She played down her authority position. Earlier when discussing the value of punishment, she remarked, "I was caned when I was at school." She emphasized her humanness. In her mind perhaps she had the idea that this would help to overcome her pupils' reticence. Unless she had earlier told me what was worrying her, I might not have attached any significance to these events. It is even less likely that I would have made these inferences.

Teaching is a human act. To separate the act from its intention is to render it less meaningful. Moreover, I would suspect that from an analytical point of view you could make a case that an act cannot be classified as teching unless reference is made to what is in the agent's mind. Suppose, for instance, a teacher selects a film to show to pupils, with the intention of merely occupying them whilst attending to personal matters. One would surely be right to say that, in this case, showing the film did not count as teaching. If this line of argument can be rigorously upheld, then it would mean that teaching must be conceived in terms of the agent's intentions and that these intentions therefore constitute necessary elements of our concept of teaching.

In summary then I have suggested two reasons why the teacher's thinking is important in the study of teaching: first, that the meaning of the teacher's actions is enriched when we associate them with his/her thinking; second, that the concept of teaching logically should be defined by making reference to what is in the teacher's mind.

Having claimed so much for the importance of being concerned with the teacher's thinking, it is perhaps surprising that it is such a neglected area of study. But there is no hiding the fact. In their comprehensive review of the research, Clark and Yinger (1979) cite less than forty studies and find space to cover them in some detail in one chapter. However, they conclude their review on a note of great optimism:

> "Researchers have made a promising start toward understanding why teachers behave as they do. This understanding should grow and develop as more of this kind of research is done. But the most exciting possibility is that the research may bring research on instruction and the behaviour of teachers together with that on curriculum and materials. All of these concerns come together in the minds of teachers as they make plans, judgments, and decisions that guide their behaviour. Indeed, the first practical theory of instruction may evolve from research on the thinking of teachers." (p. 259)

The Concept in Personal Terms

In order to capture the idea of what is in the teacher's mind, I have selected the phrase "the teacher's frame of reference." The phrase is not original (Runkel, 1958). The idea is also evident in the writings of others; Bishop and Whitfield (1972) talk about the teacher's "decision framework"; Dunkin and Biddle (1974) incorporate aspects of it when identifying "pressage variables"; Sharp and Green (1975) discuss it fairly extensively under the heading of the "teacher's perspectives." Yet, possibly because interest in it is only at the germination stage, the concept remains undefined.

In a broad sense everyone has a frame of reference which guides actions. But here, we are concerned with the teacher's frame of reference in a narrow sense. We are concerned with the professional aspects of life. The teacher's frame of reference is the framework of ideas, ways of thinking and feeling which are used in perceiving and interpreting what is happening in the classroom (and school) and in guiding actions. Whenever the teacher makes plans for action or responds thoughtfully to a situation, it is likely that unconscious reference will be made to this framework, checking that action or response is in harmony with it. If you were to ask the teacher why he or she did something or acted in a particular way, you might find that the answer made explicit some of the considerations taken into account — these considerations would be part of his or her frame of reference.

Specifically, what sort of things might we expect to be included in a teacher's frame of reference? During childhood a person's parents might have stressed the importance of being polite and this might account for its being valued in the present classroom. (Many of us tend to respond more warmly to the request prefaced by "Would you mind if I . . . ." rather than the more abrupt "I want to . . . .".). Whilst at school the same person might have done well in a subject where the teacher insisted on pupils' keeping neat notes. As a consequence this practice might be encouraged in the classroom and the pupils' assignments marked with this in mind. These two illustrations remind us that the teacher's frame of reference will include values acquired in childhood and which now in turn color his or her classroom behavior. It is evident, however, that we should not just be considering the teacher's experience as a child but the total experiences of the world and the values distilled from these. A teacher might have done very poorly whilst at university, might have been apprenticed to a plumber, might have found it hard to make ends meet, might have found solace in music, might be the parent to a wayward child. We have all enjoyed powerful experiences such as these and what we have learned from them will be incorporated into our frames of reference as a person. When the values we have acquired in this way affect our classroom behavior, then they become part of our frames of reference as a teacher.

When teacher education institutions talk about changing the outlook or extending the perceptions of their clientele, they might well be talking about changing and extending the frames of reference of their students. Students in one institution might be presented with a digest of the work of B. F. Skinner, its psychological foundations and its implications for classroom action. In another institution they might study, in an equally exhaustive way, the contrasting work of Carl Rogers. The extent to which these studies are realized in the classroom will bear witness to the effects that the institutions have on the teacher's frame of reference. In passing, it has often been lamented that such changes in a teacher's frame of reference are short-lived.

> "Almost every relevant investigation, whatever the instrument used, has found that the changes in expressed attitudes during training are followed by changes in the opposite direction during the first year of teaching." (Morrison and MacIntyre, p. 70, 1973)

Apart from life experience and professional education, it may be that the most important contribution to teachers' ideas, ways of thinking and feeling, lies in their own teaching experience. By trial and error they will have learned something about how to maintain classroom control or something about books which pupils seem to like, or something about mistakes which pupils commonly make. Impressed by a colleague's arguments, they may vary their own procedures. Enthusiastic about an in-service presentation, they may try out some specific suggestions with their own classes.

In summary then, I have suggested that the teacher's frame of reference incorporates ideas about teaching and that the teacher will have derived these from experience as a pupil and in life more generally, experience in teacher education and experience as a teacher.

The Components in Educational Terms

What exactly might we expect to find in the teacher's frame of reference? We can say with some certainty that the components will be a range of ideas about teaching. As far as I can see these ideas tend to fall into three major categories:
- ideas about worthwhile aims of education, desirable qualities which it is intended the pupils should develop;
- ideas embodying principles of procedure which should be followed, ethical considerations prescribing action;
- ideas about managing the classroom with a view to optimizing the achievement of worthwhile aims and/or following desirable principles of procedure. I have called them hypotheses about interaction.

Aims of Education

Many teachers conceive of their job in terms of helping their children to develop various skills, abilities, and attitudes. For example, a science teacher might include skills in manipulating scientific equipment, the ability to make inferences from data, and an attitude of curiosity. When teachers are asked why they set a particular task or did what they did, they often answer in such terms, that is, in terms of their aims, their view of an educated man or woman, their idea of the contribution they might make to their pupils' physical, intellectual, emotional, and spiritual growth. Many teachers thus conceive their role as an instrumental one.

Whether or not teachers should consider their role as an instrumental one is a matter of unresolved debate. Some philosophers such as Hirst proceed towards an analysis of teaching as an instrumental act. In his paper, "What is Teaching?" (1974), he characterized it as necessarily being an attempt to bring about learning (albeit not always a successful one) and argued that for this to be the case the act must have instrumental meaning for the teacher, that is, the teacher must have aims in terms of end states of learning. (In order to appreciate the thrust of his argument you might try testing these two old adages: The teacher isn't teaching unless the pupils are learning. When the pupils are learning, the teacher must be teaching.) However, a number of philosophers have called Hirst's analysis into question. Peters (1963) raised the issue with his paper, "Must an Educator have an Aim?" As you might expect his answer was "No!" In making his case he declared that very general aims, such as wisdom, could not be made concrete. He challenged the teacher's authority (it is the task which should exert the discipline rather than the teacher), asserted the pupils autonomy ("educere" means to lead out), and emphasized the morality of communication. Instead of having aims, Peters argued that teachers should follow principles of procedure and these, of course, would lead to a range of end states which could not be pre-specified. His argument was developed by Stenhouse (1975), who presented a process model of teaching. In a nutshell Stenhouse makes a case for education being an "initiation into knowledge," that is, principles of procedure should be derived from the nature of knowledge.

Principles of Procedure

I would like to broaden the notion of principles of procedure beyond that which is seen in opposition to the teacher having aims. Teachers have views about equality, about what it means in the context of teaching, and the procedures which are contingent upon the meaning they associate with it. Teachers have views about flexibility, about what it means, the extent to which it is desirable and hence the principles of procedure which should be adopted in this light. Teachers have views about violence and this will influence the way in which they discipline their pupils.

Hypotheses about Interaction

Every teacher has a range of ideas about how best to initiate and sustain the tasks which the pupils are undertaking and how to control pupils' behavior. Of consequence is the way tasks are introduced, the way pupils' questions are responded to, the way seats are arranged, the way assignments are marked, the way deviant behavior is dealt with. As well as being influenced by ideas about worthwhile aims or principles of procedure, the teacher's practice will also be influenced by hypotheses about how teachers and pupils interact. I call these ideas about interaction "hypotheses" for three reasons. First, I believe that to express them in terms of "if . . . then" propositions prompts us to think more precisely. For example, I believe the challenge to express an idea, such as "pupils should be allowed to work in friendship groups," as a hypothesis, such as "if pupils work in friendship groups then there is less deviant behavior," encourages the teacher to clarify and develop the idea. Second, to call the ideas hypotheses emphasizes their tentative nature and indeed underlines the possibility that they may not be universal generalizations. And finally, the word hypothesis contains within it an invitation to test.

In summary then, I have outlined three categories of components which teachers include within their frames of reference: their aims of education, their principles of procedure, and their hypotheses about interaction. However, I would not wish to imply that these components each exist in isolation. It is evident that they are interrelated in complex ways. The word "framework" contains notions of order, interrelationship, dependence of one part upon another, and that upon which the visible is secured. I hope the phrase "the teacher's frame of reference" captures these notions and thus invites us to consider the components as comprising more than a higgledy-piggledy collection of education ideas (Inquiry 3.1).

Making Explicit the Teacher's Frame of Reference

The most obvious way of revealing the teacher's frame of reference would seem to be to ask; but this superficial approach doesn't appear altogether satisfactory — problems emerge in practice. A small group of teachers were asked to discuss their reactions to the task of listing items in their frames of reference. They showed concern about the listing being comprehensive and being situation or context specific. Box 3.1 records some of their comments.

This evidence suggests that this approach may neither be very revealing nor indeed valid. In brief, we are faced with a serious methodological problem: that of truly getting an understanding of the thinking a teacher actually uses to guide his/her practice. An indirect rather than a direct approach may be more useful. This is not a new idea, teachers themselves use it extensively. Instead of asking a child directly whether he or she understands, they often put the child in a (test) situation which is designed to reveal his/her understanding indirectly. Methodologically, of course, this focusses our consideration on such problems as reliability and validity. In the next four sections we will examine some indirect procedures for revealing the teacher's frame of reference:

- discussing a recent innovation;
- evaluating teaching in action;
- comparing plans and actions;
- stimulating recall of decisions.

They are all imperfect, some more so than others.

Box 3.1 Teachers Discuss the Problem of Listing Items in Their Frames of Reference

Paul: I don't think anybody would ever achieve the full list. I don't think anybody ever sits down and says what is the total list. You would come up with certain concepts that you saw as being important as a classroom teacher . . . .
I don't think people go around with that sort of information in a box . . . .
I think there's a danger in saying that I've got 15 things that are important . . . .
I think the situation greatly affects your interpretation of what's happening . . . .

Don: The thing is so diverse, you see, that it helps to make it context specific. In other words, if you come and look at a lesson and present someone with a transcript of a lesson and ask them what they thought that lesson was about, then I think they are going to be able to say, "Right, well the aims behind my operation were . . . ." and trot them out nicely for you. Now, if you saw another lesson, maybe a whole different set of aims would be trotted out . . . . And the difficulty is, in sitting remotely (here), of articulating the things. I am not sure it's intuitive, but we are a sort of complex expression of all sorts of ideals and perspectives that we have, which come I suppose from notions of our humanity.

John: And you haven't got a list that you consult every day . . . .

Paul: I mentioned things that I felt were important but I wouldn't want that to be taken as the definitive article . . . because the danger is the one thing that didn't come up, that could be the very thing that is highly critical to what happens in the situation you see . . .

John: I would argue, you need something there to evoke these tacit assumptions.

Paul: I agree with what you're saying, but I think it's going to be a lot more than one stimulus. Because every time you meet a different stimulus you may well come up with a different set of . . . I mean, some will recur and recur and recur, but each time a new one would perhaps emerge which has always been there . . . .

Discussing a Recent Innovation

When a teacher introduces a change, the contrast between old and new highlights certain features of both practices. Moreover, in reflecting on the desirability of change, a teacher will have likely considered reasons for and against. With this in mind a group of teachers invited Gordon, who had some ten years experience, to tell them about an innovation he had recently adopted. He made his presentation as if to fifteen fellow math teachers on an in-service day. His topic was "the use of geoboards in helping children to understand fractions." Geoboards can be made by placing nails at 1 cm intervals in a 15 cm square of wood so as to form a grid. They are a commercially available formal device and Gordon saw them as part of the movement towards the use of concrete materials which had been a "bandwagon" in Nova Scotia for a number of years.

Gordon gave out worksheets, geoboards, and rubber bands. He used these to simulate some of the things he would do with his students, pausing from time to time to pass comment;

"Students could visualize operations which previously they were required to accept without question."

"Students love to participate in a hands-on event. I enjoy having the students activity involved."

"The use of practical examples in mathematics is very important to understanding a concept, rather than blindly accepting it."

After his presentation, the group delighted in taking the role of a critical audience. Although I sensed that some of their questions were asked to tease, Gordon seemed to take them very seriously; blushing, responding vigorously, arguing tenaciously. It was a pity that we did not tape the session, but later Gordon agreed to write down his responses to some of the questions that were asked. (Box 3.2)

At this point we might pause to reflect upon the strengths and weaknesses of the methodology involved in a teacher discussing a recent innovation as a means of revealing his frame of reference. To what extent is the procedure valuable? What are its limitations? Do Gordon's comments and answers to the questions reveal anything about his frame of reference: his aims, his principles of procedure, his hypotheses about interaction? How might the methodology be improved? (Inquiry 3.2)

In the next three sections we will examine some alternative procedures. The same sort of questions might also be applied to these.

Box 3.2   A Teacher Answers Questions about an Innovation

Q.1 Aren't geoboards just a gimmick? Why not use matches, paper squares?

A.1 Any teaching aid which can make the concept being taught more meaningful can and should be used. However, as Z. P. Dienes states in *Building up Mathematics,* "such devices may prove necessary for an efficient teaching and learning situation, but they are unlikely to prove sufficient."

Q.2 Aren't geoboards just crutches for feeble minds? Aren't the more able kept back?

A.2 I will again refer to a comment by Dienes. "A child may be quite conversant with all the technicalities of linear equations without having much idea what sort of thing a linear equation is. In other words, a child may well be under the impression that he understands mathematics when in fact he does not." It is my belief that most students do not have a solid grasp of the basic concepts of mathematics. Aids like the geoboard can reinforce basic concepts quickly as a prelude to working on more involved problems. The variable is the ability of the teacher to make the aid a meaningful experience.

Q.3   Don't the students just copy one another?

A.3 When the geoboard is used, a relaxed and informal atmosphere is necessary. If students desire to work in groups, they may. Some students may just copy a student whom they know will be right most of the time. However, it is the teacher's job to de-emphasize the correct–incorrect approach to teaching with the geoboard. Students are given specific tasks to work on but tangents are allowed to develop. The teacher must constantly remind himself that the goal of this exercise is not to evaluate but to create a learning situation where true understanding occurs.

Box 3.2 — continued

Q.4 When I teach my children fractions, they do it by making drawings. This works well!

A.4 Whatever is effective for a teacher should be used by that teacher. If you have created a willingness to understand in your students, then use the aids which you feel confident with.

Q.5 Don't the students become over-dependent on you when, step by step, you tell them what to do?

A.5 Students do become dependent upon a teacher if the teacher lays everything out for them in a step-by-step fashion. The more dependent the students are on the teacher, the easier it is for the teacher to control the class and inject his theories. True understanding and freedom of thought is suppressed by this type of teacher. True understanding and freedom of thought should be a desired goal in all classrooms. To achieve this goal the teacher must be totally aware of and in control of his classroom practices.

Q.6 Why not work with real life problems: Johnny promises a piece of cake . . . how much left?

A.6 Real life problems are important and should be a part of the total program. Again, it is the ability of the teacher that determines whether or not these real life problems are used in a meaningful way.

Q.7 How do you know children are more interested?

A.7 By observing the increased activity of students. As they become involved with manipulatives it becomes obvious that the interest level has increased. This is an assumption on my part, but I feel it is a sound assumption to make.

Evaluating Teaching in Action

I was a member of a group of teachers who took part in a study designed to reveal our own individual theories of teaching.* In practice the exercise lasted about ten hours, but I have abbreviated it here, at the expense of methodological rigor, so as to highlight its main components. These were:

- viewing a film of a teacher in action with a view to identifying patterns of behavior and surprising events;
- individually writing a one- to two-page evaluative report of the lesson;
- exchanging our reports with a partner and interviewing each other on tape, with a view to helping each other identify his or her major concepts, beliefs, and values about teaching;
- extracting from the report and the taped interview a list of concepts, beliefs, and values, and presenting these in written form.

The film was an edited version of a regular geography lesson, focussing on hydro-electric power and Ghana. The pupils, who were of mixed ability, came into the classroom, got themselves organized, and chatted. The teacher brought them to order, asked a few introductory questions, and set them to work. After some time, he organized a teacher-led discussion with the whole class. This was followed by a dictation. He concluded the lesson with another discussion and set an assignment for homework. I give this brief background since our evaluative comments were clearly related to what we saw: the way the pupils came into the classroom,

*This was conducted by John Elliott at the Cambridge Institute of Education in England in 1981.

the way the teacher asked questions and organized their activities, the way the pupils responded, and so on. Our comments are inevitably restricted by the stimulus: had there been serious problems of control, had the pupils been different, then our comments may well have been different too. In the context of helping each one of us to identify our theories of teaching it would seem, at first sight, that the closer the film resembled our own teaching situation the more likely it would have evoked comments which were closely related to our own theories of teaching. However, it was evident from the comments made that it was the difference between what each of us would have done, or at least liked to have done, that stimulated a reaction. The vast majority of the reactions were indeed negative.

After the film we each spent half an hour writing our evaluative accounts. An example (mine) is given in Box 3.3.

Box 3.3   Evaluative Account of a Geography Lesson

In a hurry!!
"Are you all with me?"
"I want you to draw a sketch there — it doesn't have to be that detailed."
"At 11:00 we go into the next stage."
"Why do you think Ghana would get involved?" Perhaps a student answered but he then proceeded to answer his own question.
"Imagine a 3rd world country . . . ."

"You have 7 mins."

The teacher created the impression that he was consumed with the importance of covering the material and tasks he had planned to cover. Perhaps this reduced the value of the tasks. For example, the question, "Why do you think Ghana would get involved?", could scarcely have prompted the students to think speculatively. (It's feasible of course that this invitation to answer a question was only a pseudo-invitation: that he didn't expect or want a response but was only setting the scene in a rhetorical way.)

I would like to be able to see the lesson introduction again with this in mind. If time is at a premium, then clearly the introduction to a task is important: setting the scene emotionally, intellectually, and organizationally. Failure in any of these respects will likely reduce efficiency. Perhaps the organizational and "informational" injections, which were common place, could have been reduced had attention been given to introducing the tasks. Do these interrupt the students' train of thought? Do they attend selectively? Do they ignore them?

Against this backcloth of being in a hurry, how does one proceed to justify time-consuming dictation. Is it the rock in a raging torrent? Is it the really important — every word matters — part of the lesson?

For me this lesson raised many issues. Where does the pressure come from? Does the teacher cope with the pressure effectively? What do the students learn from the pressure and how do they cope with it? What coping strategies do they adopt? More haste, less speed?

Box 3.3 — continued

In a positive mood, most of the pupils seemed to be involved in the lesson most of the time. Only David was reprimanded for not paying attention. There was little window-gazing, etc. There was a busy buzz, albeit that conversation could have been about ''What do we have to do?'' or the football match. How did he manage to get such an ability spread so well occupied?

Although I only saw three of these accounts, I was struck by both the similarities and differences between them. For example, all three alluded to the way in which the teacher did not allow the students time to answer the questions he asked. However, this was criticized for a variety of reasons: it was an affront to inquiry, it was symptomatic of the teacher's time-consciousness, the pupils were denied the opportunity of thinking. I think the point emerging here is that although the pattern of the teacher not allowing the students time was evident to all three, the reasoning underpinning their negative reaction was sometimes different. It was this reasoning that the next part of the exercise was designed to pinpoint.

In pairs we exchanged our evaluative comments, read them, and prepared to interview the other. The interview was designed to probe the thinking latent in the comments, that is, it challenged the author to reveal the ideas which were implicit in them. Each interview was taped recorded and on average lasted about twenty minutes.

After the interviews each of us proceeded to analyse both our account and our interview response with a view to compiling a list of concepts, beliefs, and values which we held important in teaching. We were not free to pluck these from thin air; on the contrary, we were asked to ground them in the evidence, referring to something that we had either written or said. An example of this analysis is given in Box 3.4. (The quotations in brackets refer to something which was actually said.)

As it stands, it should be possible to repeat this exercise in 2½ hours (Inquiry 3.3).

Box 3.4   An Analysis of the Evaluative Account and Interview

Concepts

  (i) Time consciousness/purposefulness
(''The teacher created the impression that he was consumed with the importance of covering the material and tasks he had planned to cover'')

  (ii) Pupils hidden/unintended learning
(''Is it (dictation) the really important — every word matters — part of the lesson'' and ''What do students learn from the pressure and how do they cope with it?'')

  (iii) Pupil participation
(''. . . most of the pupils seemed to be involved in the lesson'')

Beliefs (Hypotheses about interaction)

  (i) If the teacher doesn't wait or if he doesn't provide sufficient time, then the students won't engage in the type of thinking he wants to encourage. (''For example, the ques-

Box 3.4 — continued

tion, 'Why do you think Ghana would get involved . . .?' could scarcely have prompted the students to think speculatively'')

(ii) If the teacher rushes, the students will develop strategies for coping with it. (''What do the students learn from the pressure and how do they cope with it?'')

(iii) The quality of student participation (and attention span) in a task is increased if the teacher sets the scene emotionally, intellectually, and organizationally. (''If time is at a premium, then clearly the introduction to a task is important.'')

(iv) Teacher interruptions inhibit students thinking. (''Do these interrupt the students' train of thought?'')

* (v) If the teacher lines children up outside, etc., more time is spent off-task than if he allows them to filter in at the beginning of the lesson. (''In fact it may be more time consuming . . . if you bring them all in together.'')

* (vi) Children learn as much from duplicated sheets as they do from dictation. (''I certainly wouldn't have set the dictation. Instead I would have given them a little Banda handout.'')

* (vii) Children learn through talking with each other. (''When kids talk to each other about subject matter which is the concern of the lesson, they begin to formulate ideas and solve problems . . . .'')

* (viii) When teachers plan in detail they become less responsive. (''I underestimate how long it will take for an activity.''
''I want a lesson to flow rather well and neatly as I preordained.'')

Values

(i) Teaching should be a purposeful activity.
(''Perhaps this (rushing) reduced the value of the tasks'')
* (ii) Forming concepts and developing problem-solving skills are important objectives.
(''They begin to formulate ideas and solve problems (through talking)'')
* (iii) Given the institutionalization of exams, teachers should help students to pass them.
(''Given that they are there, I personally feel that I have to prepare those kids for them.'')
* (iv) Knowledge of facts is not the supreme objective.
(''I think he may concentrate more than he (the teacher) believes on the facts.'')

*asterisked items emerged in interview.

Comparing Plans and Actions

What exactly is the nature of the relationship between the teacher's frame of reference and his or her actions. It is not as simple as one might at first suspect. Thought does not simply translate into action. In order to explore the relationship I think it is useful to use the proposition that often thought is translated into plans for action before the plans are translated into action (see Figure 3.1).

Figure 3.1 The Teacher's Frame of Reference, Plans, and Actions

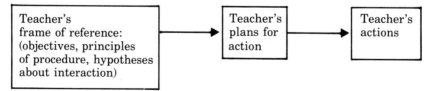

Let us consider each of the relationships shown in Figure 3.1 separately. First, the connection between the teacher frame of reference and the teacher's plans for action. Based on our previous experience, it is reasonable to expect logical consistency between the two. For example:

(i) Suppose a teacher values good handwriting as an educational objective, then it would be reasonable to expect to see opportunities or tasks planned in which the pupils are writing. If the children do not exercise their handwriting skills, then it is unlikely that they will develop them.

(ii) If a teacher upholds the principle of procedure that individual differences should be accounted for, it would seem reasonable to ask how his or her plans do in fact provide opportunities for individuals to behave in different ways.

(iii) Hypotheses about interaction may also influence a teacher's planning. For instance, if a teacher had found in the past that written instructions reduced the time spent in explaining tasks, then preparing an overhead projector transparency or a "hand-out" would be consistent with valuing this finding.

These examples have stressed that it is reasonable to expect logical consistency between teachers' plans and items in their frames of reference. However, one has to be careful not to oversimplify. For example, planning involves a host of considerations and some of these may well be in conflict. A teacher may recognize that written instructions reduce explanation time, but because of concern to develop pupils' listening skills may choose to give the instructions orally.

Nevertheless, if the teachers' thinking does indeed shape the teachers' plans, then it should be possible to learn something about it by exploring these plans. Indeed, I hope this discussion has prompted the idea that certain features of teachers' frames of reference may be uncovered by procedures which invite teachers to make explicit some of the considerations which they bear in mind when planning. Clarke and Yinger (1979) have reviewed a number of such procedures, ranging from simulation exercises to teachers' talking aloud whilst planning. One of the most attractive and straightforward, in my view, is interviewing teachers about their plans (Inquiry 3.4).

Let us now consider the connection between plans for action and the action actually observed. Stake (1967) used the idea of "congruence" to describe the match between the two. He held the view than an important part of program evaluation involved the comparison of the two for congruence. At first sight one might be inclined to jump to the conclusion that congruence is a good thing, but this misses the point. During a lecture/monologue, there may be substantial congruence — especially if the teacher reads his or her notes! But when there is interaction between the teacher and the pupils there will almost inevitably be less. Lack of congruence indeed may not be a bad thing. Moreover, it is possible to justify lack of congruence as a good thing. How could it be bad if the teacher declares that flexibility of response to the pupils is important. Before we accept this as a reason why we should always welcome lack of congruence, it would of course be important for the teacher to say what is meant by flexibility. And exactly what principles of procedure are involved in being flexible. A form of anarchy would prevail unless there was some relationship between the theories/rules in the teacher's mind and their actions! (In passing, you might ask yourself to define your stance on flexibility.)

So far we have merely considered two extreme possibilities: perfect congruence associated with one-way traffic from teacher to pupils, and complete congruence associated with anarchic flexibility. Let us now examine the middle ground. As a teacher moves away from one-way traffic, as plans are modified according to the responses of the pupils, one would begin to see incongruence appearing. This, in my mind, reveals a most important, if not crucial, area of study. How do pupils respond to teachers' actions, and how do teachers' modify their plans accordingly?

There is a vast substantially uncharted territory which involves describing and perceiving patterns of pupil responses and patterns of teacher modification. Moreover, examination of the way in which these patterns are related and the host of factors which influence them would be wonderfully illuminating. This, in my view, is at the very heart of the teaching process and will be looked at again in chapter 4. By way of summary I have outlined these ideas in the diagram below (Figure 3.2) and have inserted the teacher's frame of reference into the flow chart.

Figure 3.2   Modifications of Teacher's Plans

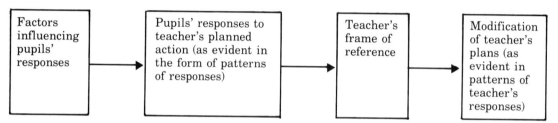

Although the teacher may be only intuitively aware of some of the patterns of modification used, these patterns will nevertheless have something to say about the teacher's frame of reference, if one assumes that response is indeed influenced by thinking, that is, is reflective rather than reactive. I would speculate that part of the process of the teacher gaining experience involves the casual, rather than deliberate, perception of pupils' patterns of response and the subconscious formulation of procedures — structured teacher response patterns — dealing with these. It is not inconceivable that the process of structuring responses could eventually become formalized to the extent that these could be built into lesson plans. Yinger (1978), for instance, suggested that teachers when planning thought in terms of routines as a means of simplifying their planning. Was he equating routines with patterns of interaction in the way they have been discussed above?

This discussion raises the possibility that it might be possible to reveal elements of the teacher's frame of reference by asking him or her to pinpoint and explain departures from plans (Inquiry 3.5).

Stimulating Recall of Decisions

In the previous section we examined the relationship between the teacher's thought and the teacher's action when some planning was possible. However, in the give-and-take of classroom interaction there is scant time for any planning. Moreover, when the teacher's action is reactive as opposed to being reflective, it would seem that there may not be even time for thought! In this section we will consider the teacher as a decision-maker, in situations where there is a close relationship between reflective thought and subsequent actions.

Many people have been interested in the idea of the teacher as a decision maker. Theoreticians have tried to map out what happens in the teacher's mind when faced with a critical incident and an "on-the-spot" choice between alternative ways of proceeding. In other words, they have speculated about how teachers think when confronted with such incidents as the following (Bishop and Whitfield, 1972):

> "You discover a pupil who thinks that (-5) (-3)=−15 is a true statement"

> "In a group of three girls working on a project, one girl is dominating and not letting the others help at all"

> "Having insisted that all pupils in your class read a section in the text book for homework, you find a pupil who has not done so"

> "You have based your lesson on a film, but when you try to project it the sound system fails" (pp.12-15)

Bishop and Whitfield's model of the decision process is shown in Figure 3.3.

Figure 3.3   A Framework for Decisions

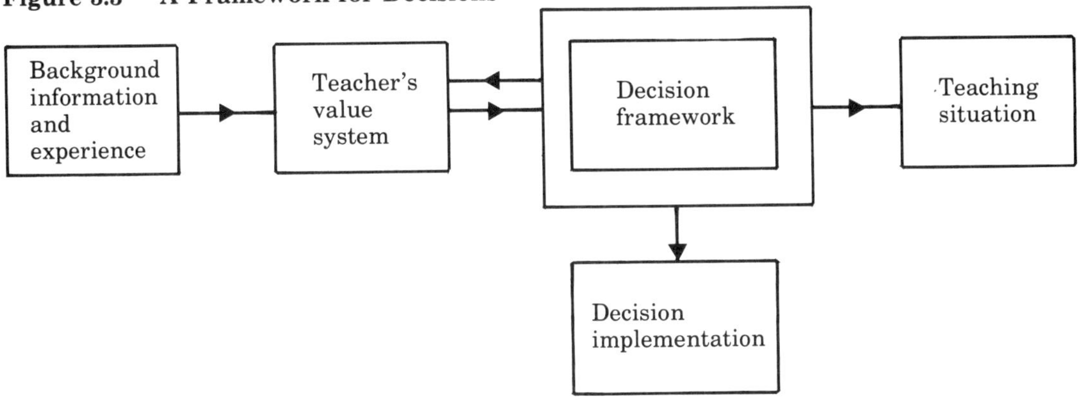

Source: A. J. Bishop and R. C. Whitfield, *Situations in Teaching* (Maidenhead: McGraw-Hill, 1972), p. 6. Reproduced by permission of the authors.

They say, "Experience and information related to life generally and to education specifically develop in the teacher a personal value system which forms the basis of his decision framework." Their model is similar in many ways to that of Bross (1953), which contains two interacting systems — a value system and a prediction system. Bross sees this prediction system as a tree in which alternative teacher actions are mapped out with predictions of the probability of certain consequences following these actions. Smith and Geoffrey (1968) used this idea of a prediction system when they tried to understand Geoffrey's response as a teacher to his finding Evelyn's two sisters absent. Smith, who was the observer, describes the episode:

> "Quizzes Evelyn regarding her sisters, both of whom are absent. She is embarrassed (looks uncomfortable) and he lets her off the hook gently, warmly, and with a smile. (LMS-Mr. Geoffrey does not probe hard when there is resistance.)"

They interpret this as follows:

"This illustrates very well a recurring pattern in the teacher's behaviour. In glowing terms one might call it 'respecting the privacy of the individual pupil.' Or in more analytical fashion one might argue the principle, if you probe too far or too deeply you put the child in a position of conflict: 'Should I tell or not tell?' If forced into this position, the child loses either way — the teacher is unhappy if she doesn't answer, or her friends (siblings in this instance) are unhappy if she admits that they stayed home because they were tired, uninterested, or for whatever inexcusable reason. The second significant inference we would make is that Geoffrey's considerate attitude alerts everyone, the audience and the child being quizzed, and ultimately the absent children, that while privacy is respected, absenteeism is not desirable." (p. 118)

They use the prediction tree to represent it (Figure 3.4).

Figure 3.4 Prediction Tree (after Smith and Geoffrey)

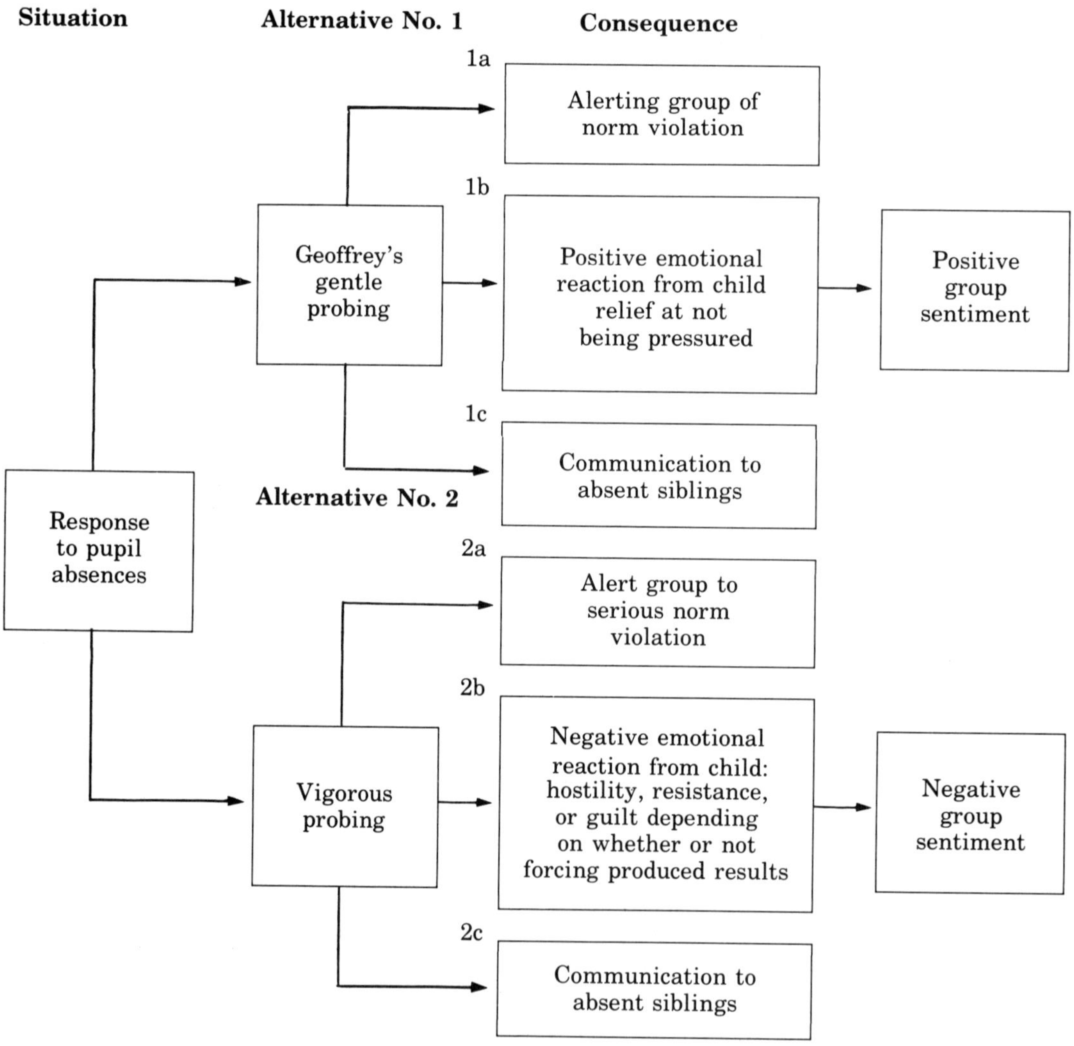

Source: L. M. Smith and W. Geoffrey, *The Complexities of an Urban Classroom* (New York: Holt, Rinehart and Winston, 1968). Reproduced by permission of the authors.

Even though these models of decision making are at present speculative (but open perhaps to empirical verification), they are of interest because they do at least attempt to relate the teacher's thought and action. Bishop and Whitfield's decision framework seems closely related to the teacher's frame of reference. Bross's value system bears resemblance to those items in the frame of reference where the teacher values certain objectives or certain principles of procedure (for example, respect for the privacy of the individual pupil) and Bross's prediction system is similar to the teacher's hypotheses about interaction. Hence, a further means of throwing light on the teacher's frame of reference would be to examine a lesson in terms of critical incidents and the decisions the teacher makes in response to them. The problem here, of course, is that this can scarcely be done during the lesson, at the time the decision is made. In order to help teachers recapture the moment of decision and to think about it, the technique of stimulated recall is often used. Here a video-recording is made during the lesson and this is played back afterwards. The recording is stopped at "interesting" moments (in practice this is often found to be when the teacher senses the lesson is going poorly) and the teacher is invited to talk about them: What was happening there? Why were you concerned? What thoughts ran through your head? A tape-recording of this interview is often made so as to render it open to follow-up analysis. If making a video-recording is not feasible, an alternative procedure would be to ask an observer to make field notes, giving a blow-by-blow account of the lesson. The observer should avoid making interpretations or inferences (Inquiry 3.6).

Suggested Inquiries

Inquiry 3.1 What Constitutes Your Frame of Reference?

This inquiry is described in a paper by Hunt (1980), which he introduced this way:

"This paper describes how to identify your implicit theories of teaching and learning."

The first step in this process is as follows:

"At the top of the first sheet write 'About my teaching,' and then imagine you are writing to another teacher, someone with whom you feel comfortable, and you want to communicate about your teaching so that this teacher will understand how you teach and what is most important in your teaching. Next, write what came to your mind . . . ." (p. 287)

I would suggest that you spend just fifteen minutes doing this. Afterwards try analysing your script so as to specify items in your frame of reference: aims, principles of procedure, and hypotheses about interaction. How comprehensive is your list? Does it reflect the "real you"? Keep your analysis for future reference.

I wonder whether or not you found the three categories (aims, principles, hypotheses) constraining. It could be, since they are derived from theory rather than from practice. If you wish to extend this exercise, you might re-examine the items with a view to seeing if other clusters naturally emerge.

44

Inquiry 3.2 Problems of Revealing the Teacher's Frame of Reference

Examine Gordon's comments and answers to the questions on pages 34 and 35. Identify items in his frame of reference. List the reservations you have about the value of this procedure. Suggest improvements.

Having done this, you might invite a colleague to talk about one of his or her recent innovations, building into the procedure any improvements you previously suggested.

Inquiry 3.3 Evaluating Teaching in Action

Reviewing the account of "Evaluating Teaching in Action" with a view to adapting it to your own purposes.

If you wish to add rigor, you might screen the interview responses with a view to eliminating those which were answers "at random," "romancing," or "suggested convictions" (see Piaget, 1929). If you wish to extend the exercise, you might pool the analyses of different individuals.

Inquiry 3.4 Your Frame of Reference in Planning

The point of this exercise is to help you discover what principles you use in planning. More precisely, it is designed to help you pinpoint items within your frame of reference which are revealed when you plan. The idea of suggesting that you should talk aloud whilst planning was rejected because of the difficulty of doing two things at once. Instead I'd suggest that you first simply draw up your plans for a lesson that you will shortly teach. Then alongside, add some explanatory notes so as to reveal your rationale. Give both the plans and notes to a colleague who will interview you in order to help reveal items in your frame of reference. Analyse your notes and your responses in the interview and list the aims you value, the principles of procedure you adhere to, and the hypotheses about interaction you consider important.

The interviewer may need to do more than merely invite you to apply the process of deduction. As well as asking why you planned something, he or she may well need to exercise imagination, asking, for example, what you expect to happen when the pupils embark on task X or why you chose task X rather than task Y. It might indeed enhance the exercise if the interviewer prepared a plan as if teaching the same topic to a similar group of pupils. The interviewer would then contain an element of discussion.

Inquiry 3.5 Plans in Action

Prepare a plan as in Inquiry 3.4 with explanatory notes. Tape record the lesson in action. List the significant departures you made from your plans. Identify, if possible, the responses of pupils which led to these departures. If possible, give your plan and list of departures to a colleague and invite him or her to tape record an interview with you which seeks to reveal your reasons for departure. Analyse the interview with a view to making explicit items in your frame of reference.

You might follow this activity by pursuing these research questions: Were there any patterns, recurring features, amongst the responses of pupils which led to departures from your plan? Were there any patterns amongst the departures?

Inquiry 3.6 Reasons for Decisions

Arrange for a colleague to make a video-recording or to write field notes in one of your lessons.

If a video-recording were made, review it after the lesson, stopping it at points which were of significance for you. At each of these points (you might choose about five), invite your colleague to tape record your thinking about the situation (why you thought it significant, why you responded as you did, and so on) with a view to his or her helping you to reveal your frame of reference. For interest, you might ask your colleague if he or she would have stopped the recording at the same points. Your opportunity to interview!

If your colleague has made field notes instead, first cast your mind back over the lesson with a view to identifying significant moments. Jot them down. Then ask your colleague to read you the field notes which surrounds one of these moments. Proceed to discuss each in turn as before.

After you have completed the interviews, analyse the tape-recordings of them with a view to making explicit the items in your frame of reference. Support each item by providing evidence in the form of a quotation from the interview.

Suggested Reading

Clark, C. M., and Yinger R. J. "Teachers' Thinking." In *Research on Teaching: Concepts, Findings, Implications,* edited by P. Peterson and H. J. Walberg. Berkeley: McCutchan, 1979.

The authors provide a comprehensive review of the research that has examined teachers' thinking in planning and decision making.

4

The Teacher's Actions and Interactions

Cleaning the blackboard, marking an exercise book, asking a question, reprimanding a disruptive child, distributing materials, listening to a child reading, pausing to capture attention — the teacher performs thousands of actions a day. When the extent and diversity of teacher action is so bewildering, how does one proceed to make sense of it all? Why indeed bother?

The answer to the first question really depends upon the answer to the second. The way you do something depends on why you want to do it. I suggested that educational criticism involves ascertaining what is happening in the classroom and in turn this involves more than giving an ''objective'' description of classroom events; it involves perception and interpretation of them from both the teacher's and the pupils' points of view. To have meaning, separate events need to be seen in relation to one another and in context. Unless one knows what is happening, one cannot proceed to say whether this is in harmony with the teacher's intentions, whether there is a match between teacher–pupil interaction and the teacher's frame of reference, whether the teacher's actions are consistent with his or her rationale for action.

The problem then, of making sense of the array of teacher's actions, becomes one of perceiving, interpreting, interrelating to one another, and of relating them to the context in which they occur. In order to make this manageable, I have in the first place classified/perceived the actions as falling into three major categories: methodological, organization, and managerial.

By methodological actions I mean those which are primarily concerned with the pupils' learning. By organizational actions I mean those which are mainly concerned with getting learning going. At a simple level this involves administrative matters such as handing out materials or making them available for pupils to collect. At a complex level it involves the way in which the classroom is organized for mixed ability teaching or team-teaching or self-paced instruction. By managerial actions, I mean those which are essentially concerned with gaining and maintaining pupil co-operation or controlling deviant behavior. The separation of actions into these three types is of course somewhat artificial. Conceivably one action could be classified in more than one way. Moreover, there is a strong interrelationship between them — one action affects another.

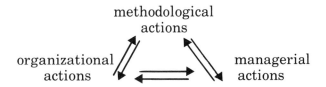

It soon becomes evident that it doesn't make sense to consider teacher action as separate from pupil action. Methodological actions are related to what the pupils do, organizational actions are related to the freedom the pupils have, and managerial actions are seen in the context of pupils' work involvement and deviancy. Although the focus of this chapter is on teacher action, it concludes by examining teacher– pupil interaction as an entity.

Methodological Actions

Teachers are familiar with talking about the methods they use: discussion, showing films, seatwork, lectures, and so on. However, possibly because these descriptions do not possess either richness or power, the concept of method tends to have been displaced by other ways of describing teacher and pupil actions. In this section three alternative ways of viewing methods will be considered:

- methods in terms of their characteristics or dimensions
- methods as learning tasks
- methods as routines

Methods in Terms of Their Characteristics

Instead of talking about methods, teachers often prefer to talk about approaches: a formal approach, pupil-centred approach, unstructured approach, traditional approach, and so on. Looking at this another way, they may be grouping certain methods together, often intuitively, according to characteristics which they have in common.

Teachers can learn a lot about the way they view their methods — and about their theories of teaching — by categorizing them. The following example shows how a beginning teacher, who was studying for her B.Ed., explored the characteristics of her methodology using Kelly's Repertory Grid Technique.

But first, a few words about the origins of this technique. George Kelly (1955) proposed that people make sense of their world by comparing things. They learn to recognize (conceptualize) an orange by its juicyness, its "pippyness," its sweetness, and so on. By comparison, a banana is less juicy, less pippy, but more sweet. These dimensions, from less juicy to more juicy, and so on, are called constructs. Constructs are bipolar concepts. Kelly proposed that people learn by the process of "construing." A simple way of finding out how people construe things is to take items (elements) in groups of three. By asking which is the odd one out, and why it is so, you can identify one pole of the construct. By asking how the other two are similar, you can identify the other pole. The two poles should be opposite of course — a useful check. This procedure forms the basis of the Repertory Grid Technique.

In the example (see Table 4.1) the teacher tried to identify how she construed methods. She wanted to find out her own personal view of the methods she used. She proceeded as follows:

- She listed the methods she used in the columns at the top of the grid.
- She selected the first three methods in her list and put circles in the boxes below to identify them. She asked herself, Which is the odd one out? Why? "Projects" were odd because they were "prepared by the student." She marked the "project" box with a cross. She then asked how "lecture" and "audio-visual" were similar. They were " prepared by the teacher." She ticked the corresponding boxes. Using the construct, "prepared by the student/prepared by the teacher," she then categorized her other methods, giving them ticks or crosses as she deemed it appropriate.
- She then selected another three methods and used the same process to elicit another construct. (And so on, selecting different sets of methods in threes.)

There are a number of pitfalls to be avoided when following this technique: duplication of constructs should be avoided; constructs should be bipolar; the way in which the constructs are expressed should be meaningful. (The teacher might have improved her analysis by using these criteria.)

Every individual teacher will have a unique way of perceiving the features that characterize the methods they each use. Many are surprised at how personally revealing it is to elicit their constructs in this way. Moreover, they are implicitly invited to say something about the significance of the constructs that emerge.

Once this basic analysis has been made, it is possible to derive other interesting information from it. A closer look at the grid reveals that construct B, "less interesting for student/more interesting for student," shares the identical pattern of ticks and crosses with construct C, "student–teacher interaction/student–student interaction." This means that these two constructs were somehow related in the teacher's mind. One can proceed to find out which constructs were related by counting the number of ticks and crosses they have in common. Construct B has 9 in common with C (the maximum). It has 8 in common with I, which represents very substantial overlap. With F it has zero in common, but if the construct poles are reversed, perfect agreement is obtained. (The polarity of the constructs in the grid is arbitrary since it merely depends on which triad of methods were selected.) The second chart shows how the teacher systematically recorded the extent to which her constructs were related. It records the number of ticks and crosses each construct has in common with others.

Her analysis indicated the following very close relationships: B to C, B to H, C to H, B to F, C to F, F to H. She expressed these in a diagram in words. The diagram represents pictorially how she construes her teaching.

"I feel that students will be more interested in their studies if they are allowed more student–student interaction, through a less rigid structure, in which the students are able to pursue subjects of their choice. It appears that the more the teacher controls the lesson, the less the opportunity the students will have to explore the aspects of the subject which interests them most."

Table 4.1   Applying the Repertory Grid Technique to Teaching Methods

Construct Pole (difference ×)		Lecture	Audio-Visual	Projects	Field trips/Labs	Questioning	Reading Periods	Group Discussions	Review	Games	Construct Pole (Similarity ✓)
Prepared by the student	A	✓Ⓞ	✓Ⓞ	✗Ⓞ	✓	✓	✗	✗	✓	✗	Prepared by the teacher
Less interesting (for student)	B	✗	✗	✓	✓Ⓞ	✗Ⓞ	✓Ⓞ	✓	✗	✓	More interesting
Student–teacher interaction	C	✗	✗	✓	✓	✗	✓	✓Ⓞ	✗Ⓞ	✓Ⓞ	Student–student interaction
Outside work (research) necessary	D	✓	✓Ⓞ	✗Ⓞ	✓Ⓞ	✓	✓	✓	✓	✓	Outside work unnecessary
Independent study	E	✗	✗	✓	✓	✓Ⓞ	✗Ⓞ	✓Ⓞ	✓	✓	Group study
Less structure (rigidity)	F	✓Ⓞ	✓	✗	✗	✓	✗	✗	✓Ⓞ	✗Ⓞ	More structure
No application of theory	G	✗	✓	✓Ⓞ	✓Ⓞ	✗Ⓞ	✗	✓	✗	✓	Application theory
Teacher controls direction	H	✗	✗	✓	✓	✗	✓Ⓞ	✓Ⓞ	✗Ⓞ	✓	Students pursue own interests
No teaching aids required	I	✗Ⓞ	✓Ⓞ	✓	✓	✗	✓	✓	✗	✓Ⓞ	Teaching aids required

Constructs	A	B	C	D	E	F	G	H	I
A	9	1	1	6	4	8	3	1	3
B		9	9	4	6	0	7	9	8
C			9	4	6	0	7	9	8
D				9	5	5	4	4	5
E					9	3	6	4	5
F						9	2	0	1
G							9	7	8
H								9	8
I									9

She also noticed that construct I, "teaching aids required," was closely related to all of the constructs in the diagram and speculated how this came about.

Once a teacher's thinking about methods has been made explicit an important and challenging question is prompted. Is there a match between it and the teacher's action in the classroom itself? The teacher is invited to look at his or her classroom and to collect data which throws light on important constructs (Inquiry 4.1).

The idea of viewing methods in terms of their characteristics has interesting historical roots. In the sixties and seventies this line of thinking appealed strongly to those who were investigating the interrelationship between process of teaching and products of it. As was pointed out in chapter 1, researchers' efforts to correlate method with product had drawn a blank and they perhaps saw new hope in describing teacher activities this way. The sixties indeed witnessed a flurry of work in the design of observation instruments which categorized teacher and pupil actions along a variety of dimensions. One of the most well known of these is Flanders Interaction Analysis. Flanders characterized teachers' actions according to the dimensions of indirectness and warmth. His categories are shown in Table 4.2 (Inquiry 4.2).

Table 4.2   Categories Provided in FIAC

Teacher talk	Indirect influence	1.	Accepts feeling: accepts and clarifies the feeling tone of the students in a non-threatening manner. Feelings may be positive or negative. Predicting and recalling feelings are included.
		2.	Praises or encourages: praises or encourages student action or behavior. Jokes that release tension, not at the expense of another individual, nodding head or saying "uh huh?" or "go on" are included.
		3.	Accepts or uses ideas of student: clarifying, building, or developing ideas or suggestions by a student. As teacher brings more of his own ideas into play, shift to category five.
		4.	Asks questions: asking a question about content or procedure with the intent that a student answer.
	Direct influence	5.	Lectures: giving facts or opinions about content or procedure; expressing his own idea; asking rhetorical questions.
		6.	Gives directions: directions, commands, or gives orders with which a student is expected to comply.
		7.	Criticizes or justifies authority: statements, intended to change student behavior from non-acceptable to acceptable pattern; bawling someone out; stating why the teacher is doing what he is doing, extreme self-reference.
Student talk		8.	Student talk-response: talk by students in response to teacher. Teacher initiates the contact or solicits student statement.
		9.	Student talk-initiation: talk by students, which they initiate. If "calling on" student is only to indicate who may talk next, observer must decide whether student wanted to talk. If he did, use this category.
		10.	Silence or confusion: pauses, short periods of silence, and periods of confusion in which communication cannot be understood by the observer.

Source: E. J. Amidon and N. A. Flanders, *The Role of the Teacher in the Classroom* (Minneapolis, Minn.: Association for Productive Teaching, 1963), p. 14. Reprinted by permission of N. A. Flanders.

By 1970 a large number of observation instruments reflecting a variety of dimensions of teaching had been devised. An anthology aptly titled *Mirrors for Behavior,* compiled by Simon and Boyer (1970) contained seventy–nine. And more emerge every year (see, for example, Borich and Madden, *Evaluating Classroom Instruction: A Sourcebook of Instruments,* 1977).

One of the problems coupled with the selection of such instruments is the tendency for them to reflect a theoretical rather than a practical point of view, that is, they don't reflect the teacher's way of seeing things. Elliott (1976/77) showed how this problem could be attacked in the Ford Teaching Project. The teachers participating in this project had declared their concern to adopt the inquiry approach. But what did inquiry mean? What dimensions characterized it? To answer these questions Elliott might have proceeded in a number of ways. He might have closeted himself and proceeded with a conceptual analysis of the idea. He might have gone to the library with the intention of reviewing and distilling the essence of the idea from the literature. Both of these procedures would have reflected a theoretical orientation. As it happened he and his colleague decided to ask teachers for their interpretation. They had noticed that much confusion existed amongst the frequently recurring terms that the teachers used to describe their practice other than "discovery" or "inquiry": formal/informal, structured/unstructured, framework, teacher-directed, self-directed (child), guided, open-ended, dependent/independent (child), subject-centred/child-centred. They proceeded as follows:

> "We invited teachers to discuss the meanings of these words at team and regional meetings and report back. We also went into schools and discussed them with teachers. We discovered that although teachers might be using different terms they were often doing so to label the same things. A surprising degree of consensus appeared to exist about which dimensions of meaning are significant in appraisals of teaching situations." (p. 6)

(If you wish to experience the type of process which Elliott and his co-workers went through, you should try Inquiry 4.3 before reading on.)

Three main dimensions emerged:

- Formal–informal: the degree of intellectual dependence on or independence from the teacher's authority position.
- Structured–unstructured: the degree to which the teachers were concerned with getting students to achieve preconceived knowledge outcomes, the degree of emphasis on the product as opposed to the process.
- Directed–guided–open ended: the degree to which teachers prescribe in advance how a learning activity is to be performed, the degree of control the teacher tries to exert over the learning activities of the student.

In clarifying these meanings the teachers had in our terms clarified their frame of reference about the types of classroom action they deemed desirable.

Methods as Learning Tasks

Doyle (1979) is one of a group of researchers who sees *the task* as "the fundamental organizer of classroom behavior." This is a provocative phrase and full of implication. We are invited to examine what goes on in classrooms from a different perspective, to see teacher actions and pupil actions from the vantage point of the task to which they are related. The very process of doing this offers a distinct and possibly new way of perceiving the kaleidoscope of classroom activity. Certainly to see things this way is to see them in terms different from method.

Observers and analysts adopting this stance frequently think of themselves studying classrooms from an ecological point of view. The metaphor, ecology, is a powerful one. When biologists talk of ecology they mean "the branch of biology that deals with the relation of living organisms to their environment and to each other." A feature of this definition is the duality of the relationships. Within the classroom there are the relationships between teacher and pupils and in addition there are the relationships between events within the classroom and the world outside.

In suggesting that the task is a fundamental organizer of classroom behavior, Doyle is suggesting that the task not only mediates the relationship between teacher and pupils, but also mediates life in classrooms and life outside, that is, by describing classroom events in terms of tasks he is hypothesizing that we will open new windows to understanding the effects of contextual features such as the examination system, ministry of education guidelines, parental expectations, school rules, and the availability of resources.

The selection of the word "task" is an interesting one. It has a "job-to-be-done" ring about it. It implies that schooling has purpose. This ring of purpose is less evident in concepts such as method or learning experience, which are often used to describe teacher and pupil activity. Moreover, because the word inclines one to be specific, and to talk about actual tasks, it also prompts one to ask specific questions: Who originated the task? How did the teacher introduce the task? To what extent was the task structured? What difficulties did the pupils encounter in doing the task? Why does the task exist?

But what exactly is meant by "task"? The way in which a task is specified is clearly going to be consequential. Should a lecture be redescribed as a "listening and taking notes" task or as a "remembering and understanding" task? Doyle suggests that both the product and the process should be specified.

> "A task is defined by two elements: (1) a goal and (2) a set of operations necessary to achieve the goal. In a window washing task, for example, the goal is to produce clean windows. To achieve this goal it is necessary to assemble appropriate materials — a ladder, brush, soap, water, etc. — and perform certain operations with these materials. The goal (clean windows) organises and gives direction to actions, including both the selection of items in the environment and the operations performed with these items." (p. 3)

According to this definition, would the following example count as a task?:

> "In small groups, prepare a poster showing life in the frozen north. You may cut out anything suitable from the magazine and pamphlets provided." (p. 3)

It seems difficult to decide. Does the poster count as the goal? Should the teacher's implicit goals (such as developing pupils' co-operation and awareness of the Eskimo's way of life) be made explicit? To raise such an issue may appear to be quibbling. But in the first place, it could be consequential if teacher and pupils see a task differently, valuing it according to the extent it is in harmony with their purposes. And secondly, it could be consequential to the analyst who is using the idea of a task to formulate an understanding of classrooms (Inquiry 4.4).

What sort of understandings have been developed by using the idea of a task as an analytic tool? Doyle's (1983) review provides a rich source of reference. Of particular interest to teachers is his second section which examines how the features of the tasks affect the ways pupils respond. For example, tasks may be classified according to the risk and ambiguity associated with them. A high risk task is one in which it is likely that the pupil will be unable to meet the demands made. An ambiguous task is one in which there is either ambiguity in how to proceed or ambiguity in terms of how the product is to be judged. Many aspects of classroom behavior may be interpreted in terms of the pupils adopting strategies to reduce both risk and ambiguity.

Methods as Routines

Yinger (1979) in a fascinating ethnographic study of a sixth-grade teacher was intrigued by how little attention she gave to detail when planning. It was as if once the essential ingredients of an activity had been decided upon, the rest followed naturally, almost automatically. To explain this he proposed that she reduced the complexity of planning and instructing by intuitively applying routines.

> "Instructional routines are methods and procedures established by the teacher to carry out specific instructional moves. These routines are in effect strategies or styles of teaching that have been developed over time and occur in regular configurations and sequences.... Decisions about instructional moves were rarely mentioned by the teacher in this study, usually only when an activity was not going well. When planning for a new activity, most of her attention was directed towards the instructional task itself rather than how it would be taught. When new activities were implemented, few new or unusual instructional moves were apparent." (p. 166)

I am attracted by Yinger's insights because I find they describe my experience and throw new light on my observations of others. Like Yinger, I suspect that many of the difficulties of adjustment experienced by beginning teachers may be associated with the time it takes them to develop routines. Moreover, I suspect that the reason why some innovations fail to be adopted is either because they are lacking in routines or because they are out of line with existing routines or because they are out of harmony with routines teachers deem desirable.

The real test of any relatively new insights like this depends on whether or not they evoke a sympathetic response from teachers and whether or not they find it illuminating to view their practice in these terms.
Do elementary teachers use routines for "show and tell"?

> Your turn, Andrea . . . ."
> "Where exactly did you find it? . . ."
> "Would anyone like to ask Andrea a question? . . ."
> "Now you, Billy . . . ."

Are textbooks used in routine ways?
Do teachers have routines for monitoring individual seat-work and group activities?

Do teachers have routines for starting lessons?
Can your lessons be conceived of in terms of routines?
What routines do you commonly use?
What instructional moves constitute one of your common routines? (Inquiry 4.5)

The concept of routines has other attractive features. By comparison with the concept of method it is rich in power of description — there may be vast differences in the way two teachers handle the same method. It reduces the complexity without undue distortion. And further, the concept is firmly grounded in the teacher's practice. Indeed it owes its origin from a perception of what a teacher did rather than from a theoretical analysis of the nature of education.

Organizational Actions

Some authors have been content merely to classsify the teacher's actions as either methodological or managerial but this seems to fall short of giving due emphasis to the classroom as a social system. Teachers can and do control the way they structure the classroom. They make decisions about how tasks are arranged and organized within it. In this section, two organizational aspects of the teacher's actions are considered:

- the way in which the class is divided into groups
- the way in which the teacher provides for the individual

Organization and Group Structure

Adams and Biddle (1970) in an extensive field survey of thirty–two mathematics and social studies teachers separated the tasks (the group function as they called it) from the group structure (number of groups, size of the groups, composition of the groups, communication roles played by group members). One of their most interesting findings was to reveal the range of significant variables. Complex relationships evidently existed between the subject matter, the grade level of the students, the age of the teacher, who is communicating to whom, the time spent discussing the subject matter as opposed to other things, and so on. This being the case, it scarcely makes sense to talk in terms of general rules for organizing groups. Rather, it would seem most appropriate for teachers individually to develop their perceptive and analytic capacities, with a view to answering two questions about their own teaching: What is happening? Why is it happening?

A group of ten teachers undertook the following exercise, previous to studying their own classrooms:

- They were divided into two groups of equal size. One group was given the task, "What makes a good small group discussion?"
  The other group was given the same task together with considerable elaboration "What makes a good small group discussion? You have considerable experience to draw upon: your observations of student discussion in your own classroom, your knowledge and experience as a teacher, and, not least, your participation in discussions (including this one!). Try to draw up a list of approximately ten features, the presence of which characterizes a good discussion. (When you can, formulate your criteria in terms of observable pupil actions.)"

- The discussions were scheduled to last twenty minutes. Each was video-recorded.
- In order to begin answering the question, "What happened?", each group viewed the video-recording of the other and listed significant differences between them. The lists were compared. A large number of differences emerged: one group spent longer orienting themselves to the task; one group contained a larger number of active participants; one group produced more ideas; one group was more critical of the ideas produced, and so on. The groups found the classification developed by Benne and Sheats (see Knowles and Knowles, 1972, for a useful summary), which is contained in Table 4.3, enhanced their perceptions.
- The focus then shifted to answering the question, "Why did it happen?" The teacher began speculating how these features were related to one another. Many, indeed, seemed to be interdependent. There was also speculation about how the task affected the discussion and how working relationships, previously developed between group members, affected the way the group functioned.
- Finally, reference was made to the literature. (A number of texts, for example, Gage and Berliner's *Educational Psychology,* 1979, provide useful reviews.) The teachers recognized within its findings which further illuminated their perceptions and analysis, albeit they also identified some which didn't seem to fit! (Inquiry 4.6).

Table 4.3 Classification of Group Behavior (after Benne and Sheats)

Group Building Functions:

(a) Encouraging: being warm to others, praising their ideas.
(b) Mediating: harmonizing, conciliating, making compromises.
(c) Gate keeping: drawing contributions from others.
(d) Standard setting: expressing standards, rules of conduct.
(e) Following: accepting others' ideas, listening.
(f) Relieving tension: draining off negative feelings, jesting.

Task Functions:

(a) Initiating: suggesting new ideas or activities.
(b) Information seeking: asking for relevant facts.
(c) Information giving: providing relevant facts or experience.
(d) Opinion giving: starting a pertinent belief or opinion.
(e) Clarifying: probing for meaning and understanding.
(f) Elaborating: building on a previous comment, giving examples.
(g) Co-ordinating: pulling ideas and suggestions together.
(h) Orienting: reviewing direction group is taking.
(i) Testing: checking if group is ready to make a decision.
(j) Summarizing: reviewing the content of past discussion.

Non-Functional Behavior:

(a) Blocking: interfering with group's progress, arguing too much.
(b) Showing aggression: criticizing, blaming, attacking, deflating others.
(c) Seeking recognition: drawing attention to oneself.
(d) Special pleading: claiming support for one's own concerns.
(e) Withdrawing: acting passively, indifferently.
(f) Dominating: asserting authority.

Organization and Individualization

Frequently reflected in arguments about the worth of mixed ability teaching, vertical grouping, and "informal" teaching is the concern teachers have for the individual pupil. Individualization for many teachers is an ultimate but seemingly elusive goal. The notion itself is hazy (What does it mean to individualize?) and the contingent demands on action hazier still (How can one individualize?). Instead of trying to unravel the problem theoretically by attempting to answer these questions, I have chosen here to examine the attempts made by teachers who were trying to provide for the individual and to look for distinctive features of their practice. In doing so I have come to the tentative conclusion that it is meaningful to discuss individualization in terms of the way the teacher structures the class and organizes the tasks so as to provide the pupils with certain degrees of freedom of action, and I have been able to perceive three such degrees of freedom of action:

- freedom of interpretation and response
- freedom to progress at one's own pace
- freedom of choice and initiative

Freedom of Interpretation and Response: This lies not so much in the way the tasks are organized but in the way the tasks are presented. A mixed ability class of twelve to thirteen year olds had been discussing what life was like on the remote island of Foula. For homework, their task was to write about "For and against living on Foula." Box 4.2 shows two of their responses (not edited for spelling, etc.).

Box 4.2 Pupils' Homework

To Be or Not to Be . . . On Foula? (by Jane)

This is an argument between a successful student and his conscience whether to stay on Foula after his school or to go to live on the mainland. Which would you decide? Answer after reading this argument:

   "If I stay on this island I shall become very bored and turn into a cabbage. If I go on the mainland there will be more chance of me meeting a wife."

   "If you go on the mainland you will breathe in all the fumes from cars, cigs etc. You will have a healthier life here. Foula isn't polluted at all."

   "But if I stay on here what chance have I got of getting a fulfilling job or going university and getting a degree?"

   "But on Foula you have a fulfilling job, what could be more fulfilling than growing your own food and bringing up lambs. It would also keep you at peak physical fitness,"

   "On the mainland I can earn better money and raise my standard of living. I can live in comfort on a decent wage."

   "On Foula you rely on yourself more. Your instinct of survival are sharpened. You grow all your own food and survive alone."

   "On the mainland the weather is better, it is warmer and less windy. You suffer less from chilblains etc."

   "On Foula you are tougher. You get your lungs clean and you do not get used to easy living."

   "You have a higher standard of living it is more comfortable on the mainland. Food

Box 4.2 — continued

is easier to come by and more of it. All the community facilitys are nearby. If anyone is ill a doctor can be called immiediately.''

''On Foula you are close to your family. The food is not varried but it is wholesome and natural. No additives or preservatives in our food!''

''But suppose I move to the mainland my kids are going to have all the opportunities available to them. If they were ill a doctor would be close on hand all of the time. They would be able to go to school close by and come home in the evenings to us.''

''On Foula your children could go school on the mainland. This would mean that they would become very independent of you and able to cope with life alone.'' WHAT WOULD YOU DO?

Points for and against living on Foula (by Sarah)

I would not like to live on Foula because it is so isolated and lonely. There is only one shop so you could not have a varied diet or selection of clothes. There are not many people on the island so it would be suprising if there were any my own age to talk to and go round with. I also doubt if there would be much money around. There is also nowhere to go out to on the island, nothing to do in the evenings unless I felt that I wanted to cut peat or shear sheep in the dark! I personally don't think that Foula has much going for it unless of course you count the fact that no-one would be blown up and you wouldn't find any bombs in department stores.

I do not know exactly how the teacher ran the discussion and introduced the task, but it is clear he provided considerable latitude as to how the pupils might interpret and respond to it. Somehow he contrived to encourage Jane to express herself in a vivid dialogue with her conscience. He told me afterwards that he had thrown out the idea of presenting the piece in the form of a discussion between two friends, but Jane has taken off — look at the title! The two girls are evidently of different ability — Jane was ranked first and Sarah tenth. Yet the task caters for this difference. It is open rather than closed. A wide range of responses is acceptable.

Freedom to Progress at One's Own Pace: A Teacher in Nova Scotia decided to change the way he organized his mixed ability grade 8 geography class. In the past the class would spend about two weeks studying a chapter of Crickmer and Hildebrand's *The United States.* Each chapter covered one major region. The teacher thought well of the book. It contained stimulating pictures and diagrams as well as provocative questions interspersed within the text. Typically he would discuss a short section of a chapter with the class, direct attention to a picture, diagram, or question, set a task based upon it, discuss the pupils' responses, and then move on to the next section. At the end of two weeks, a period of review would be followed by a test.

His new organizational format was very different. Although he continued to use the textbook and the tasks set remained substantially the same, by contrast, each student moved at his or her own pace. He now spent a period introducing the chapter and then distributed a sheet of assignments each of which directed the pupils to read a section of the text with a task to follow. Pupils who applied themselves during class time would find themselves with little homework to do.

The difference between the old and the new would have struck any visitor very forcibly. In the past you would have likely seen the teacher at the front of the class. Now you would most likely find him working with individual pupils. Herbert (1967) classified lesson formats according to whether the teacher alone was working on the subject matter, or whether the teacher and pupils worked together on the subject matter, or whether the pupils worked on the subject matter by themselves. He would have classified the old and the new very differently. The desks were no longer in rows, they were arranged in a "U." Some pupils worked by themselves, some helped each other, and some were evidently engaged in other matters! The classroom both before and after the change was orderly, but the quality of order rather different.

In terms of the tasks set both the old and the new organizational structure might be represented the same way:

However, the new structure makes provision for different pupils carrying out different tasks at the same moment in time. Lockstep progression has been reduced. A degree of freedom has been introduced.

This type of organizational innovation isn't unique. It is rumored that one of the reasons why the Schools Mathematics Project introduced their packs of workcards (1973) was to assist teachers who wished to operate in this way. When the Schools Mathematics Project's materials were available only in book form, some teachers cut out the exercises, mounted them on cards, and organized their classrooms so that their pupils could work on these at their own pace. This might indeed have been a stimulus to the production of the workcards.

A variation of this pattern of task organization — a circus of activities — was employed by the Nuffield Combined Science Project (1970). When covering certain topics such as "Estimating and Measuring," they were concerned to provide pupils with a variety of experience.

The pupils are divided into groups and given the opportunity of working on a range of tasks. The order in which they tackle the tasks is not important.

Figure 4.1 indicates the variety of tasks included in the circus. The project recommended that the pupils should be allocated sixteen periods for this piece of work. Notice that scope is provided for faster workers to pursue additional tasks or activities. Notice also that the quantity of apparatus required is much less than would be needed otherwise. The circus of activities is used only occassionally by the Project and may be of particular interest to teachers who explore the possibility of pupils doing different things at the same time.

There has been a boom in the production of curriculum materials designed to allow pupils to work at their own pace and, in conclusion, it would be remiss not to recognize the plethora of commercially available products such as those published by S.R.A.

Freedom of Choice and Initiative: Carl Rogers (1969) presented the case of Miss Shiels who dramatically altered the organizational structure of her classroom. Her

Figure 4.1 Circus of Activities: Estimating and Measuring

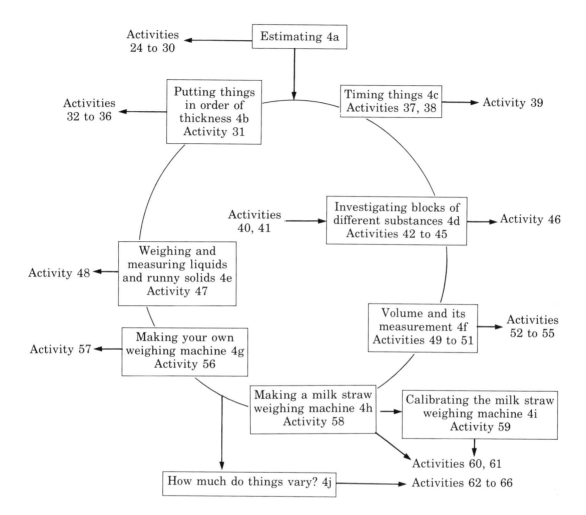

Source: Nuffield Combined Science, *Teacher's Guide 1* (London: Longman, 1970). Copyright © Nuffield — Chelsea Curriculum Trust.

diary is a fascinating chronicle of the change and is well worth studying in full. Here are a few extracts:

"A week ago I decided to initiate a new program in my sixth grade classroom, based on student-centered teaching — an unstructured or non-directive approach. I began by telling the class that we were going to try an 'experiment'. I explained that for one day I would let them do anything they wanted to do — they did not have to do anything if they did not want to. Many started with art projects; some drew or painted most of the day. Others read or did work in math and other subjects . . . .
The next morning I implemented the idea of a 'work contract'. I gave them ditto sheets listing all our subjects with suggestions under each . . . . Each child was to write his or her contract for the day — choosing the areas in which he would work and planning specifical-

ly what he would do. Upon completion of any exercise, drill, review, etc. he was to check and correct his own work using the teacher's manual. An interesting project has developed. I noticed that some of the boys were drawing and designing automobiles . . . .
Other ideas began to appear in other areas; the seed of initiative and creativity had germinated and began to grow. Many children are doing some interesting research in related (and unrelated) areas of interest. Some have completed the year's required work in a few areas, such as spelling." (pp. 12–15)

Source: C. R. Rogers, *Freedom to Learn* (Columbus, Ohio: Merrill, 1969). Reprinted by permission of the author.

Some of the tasks were open ended (automobile designing) and some were not (drill). The pupils were working on different tasks. In addition, the pupils were free to make choices amongst the tasks suggested by the teacher and free to show initiative in developing their own tasks. Miss Shiels provided for an enormous amount of different types of freedom.

Less dramatic perhaps is the case of Miss Simmons (see Cronbach, 1977). Miss Simmons was a high-school English teacher who also provided for some freedom of choice and initiative. She began her course by explaining that the study of English involved skill in the use of language, writing, and talking, and an appreciation of the many forms of communication. "Let's begin by listing the forms of communication we know of since we will select one of them as a topic for study for the next several weeks." On the second day she asked them to suggest some questions which were important to ask about the media. This brought the limited response she had anticipated, so she then divided the class into six groups, each charged with finding important questions about the medium of their choice, by talking amongst each other and searching the periodicals for recent controversies. Early in the second week the groups shared the questions they had identified and with Miss Simmons' guidance these were consolidated. Miss Simmons then used the class's interest in debating issues of taste and censorship in motion pictures as a basis for suggesting that the next four weeks should be devoted to preparing standards for judging a movie. She further suggested that they might begin by watching some movies and writing and exchanging their reviews.

One gains the impression throughout that Miss Simmons is in control of task selection, but it is also true that she does provide for some freedom of choice and initiative.

A further example of a teaching providing for this type of freedom is nicely documented in the film *Into Tomorrow*. Mr. Rose takes a group of primary-school children on a walk around the local environment. He uses their interests, the oil films in puddles, the different fruits in the greengrocer's shop, the lichens on walls, as a basis for topic work in these areas. (See Graham, 1974, for a review of the film.)

In summary then, I have identified three degrees of freedom which pupils might be provided with in the classroom: freedom to interpret and respond, freedom to progress at their own pace, and freedom to choose and initiate. These degrees of freedom are associated with the way in which the teacher organizes the tasks within the classroom. Whether the tasks are open, whether pupils work on different tasks at the same time, and whether pupils can select and develop their own tasks.

The temptation is to assume that the freer the form of organization the better. But is this the case? The question can be examined both ideally and practically.

Ideally one should ask:
- Other things being equal, are open tasks to be preferred to closed tasks?
- Other things being equal, is pupils' proceeding at their own pace to be preferred to pupils' working at the same pace?
- Other things being equal, is pupil choice of task to be preferred to teacher choice?

Even if the answers tend to be positive, judgment cannot ultimately be made without reference to what happens when some degree of freedom is introduced. For example, Miss Shiels in her diary at one point said, "The greatest problem I've encountered is discipline." Miss Simmons initially found her pupils puzzled and bewildered. A number of studies have indicated that unless pupils are closely supervised when they work by themselves, their involvement in work is lower. And Neville Bennett (1976) in his controversial study *Teaching Styles and Pupil Progress* indicated that more might be learned in the more formal classroom. The form of organization will, without doubt, have far ranging effects on teacher–pupil interaction.

Nevertheless, there is a challenge here for teachers to identify where they stand, to examine their versatility, their capacity to implement a variety of organizational structures, to experiment with them, and to monitor the changes in interaction which take place.

Managerial Actions

Classroom management is the theme of this section. It is evidently important — without a productive learning atmosphere there can be little or no learning. It is evidently complex — it depends upon the teacher, the pupils, the school, the tasks, the organizational pattern, the history of teacher–pupil relationships, and so on. Not surprisingly most teachers find it consequential and most beginning teachers daunting. And yet what may be surprising is that most teachers seem to cope rather well, if one is to judge from a number of published surveys. For example, H. M. Inspectors in *Aspects of Secondary Education in England* (1979) reported that "Observation of the 384 schools suggested that the very great majority were orderly and hardworking"; and their survey, *Primary Education in England* (1978) said, "There are a number of aspects of primary education that allow optimism for the future. The personal relations are good and the children behave well." How is it that such a state of affairs has come to be? My hypothesis is that these teachers have learned from their experience – they have observed, reflected, planned, and acted — and that their present practice has progressively evolved from moving through this cycle time and time again. What they have learned in this way has been incorporated into their frames of reference about management (Inquiry 4.8).

If teachers do develop their management practices through a tacit process of observing, reflecting, planning, and acting, then it is reasonable to hypothesize that their practices will be further developed by deliberately fostering the process. Action research involves doing just this with a view to improving our understanding and our control over our practice. A simple starting point for this type of research would be for you to take a close look at the status quo, to observe what is happening in the classroom. For example, Robertson (1981) invited a group of teachers with whom he was working to participate in the following inquiry (shown in Table 4.4).

Table 4.4 Research into Management Practices

UNDERSTANDING "DIFFICULT" BEHAVIOUR

The purpose of this exercise is to gain answers to three questions:

1. What do teachers regard as 'unwanted' pupil behaviours?
2. How do teachers *react* to unwanted pupil behaviours?
3. In what ways might we conceptualise unwanted pupil behaviours and teachers' reactions to them?

In the course of your teaching, or in any other interactions with pupils, you are asked to note your answers to the questions provided below, each time you notice or are involved in 'unwanted' pupil behaviour. Do this as soon after each 'event' as possible.

Could you please record *each event* on a separate sheet (i.e. your answers to Questions 1 to 4 below), and on an additional sheet your answers to Questions A to E.

Questions about each 'event'

1. What was the action, or lack of action, which drew your attention to the pupil(s)?
2. Did you react or change your behaviour in any way in response to the pupil's behaviour? Try to remember exactly what you said and/or did or felt.
3. What was the outcome of the action you took or chose not to take?
4. Can you suggest *why* the pupil(s) should have acted as he/she/they did at that time? Try to avoid vague generalisations, e.g. 'deprived child,' but rather suggest why the pupil chose to do what he did, rather than some other more appropriate behaviour such as doing what you wanted him to do.

Without conferring with other members of staff, can you in any way *categorise* the following?

A. The unwanted pupil behaviours you have listed in your answers to 1.
B. Your reactions listed in your answers to 2.
C. The reasons for unwanted behaviour you have suggested in your answers to 4.
D. Can you draw any conclusions about your own management of unwanted behaviour?
E. Please comment, if you wish, on the exercise you have engaged in.

Thank you for your cooperation.

Source: J. Robertson, *Effective Classroom Control* (London: Hodder and Stoughton, 1981). Reprinted by permission of Hodder and Stoughton.

The next stage of the action-research cycle involves reflection: looking at your data, examining it for characteristic features, speculating about the significance of these features. It may be that the data brings to light something that you hadn't noticed before and this starts you wondering. It may be that you are able to spot patterns in your action and this prompts you to ask questions which otherwise would have remained latent. Reflection doesn't come easily. Because it is rather like having a discussion with yourself, you might find it useful to consult others. For instance, you might ask other teachers to examine your data for characteristic features or you might compare and contrast your data with theirs. Alternatively, you might see the authors of relevant books and papers as distanced partners in stimulating discussion (Inquiry 4.9).

I have begun this discussion by considering how you might begin to examine your own practice. It seems particularly evident here that teachers possess such a vast wealth of tacit knowledge that it makes better sense to begin by making this explicit, rather than with the arbitrary selection of a theoretical starting point. And yet I do not wish to deny the value of theory. When inquiring into your own practice — here your management actions — you have a choice: either to start by looking at your practice and at the appropriate time seeking ideas from the literature which extend your perceptions, help you to reconceptualize events or call into question the hypotheses you have made, or otherwise to begin with an idea from the literature and seek to establish to what extent it describes your practice. To ignore the literature is to discard the opportunity of engaging in formative dialogue. In what ways then can theory be relevant in this context? In the paragraphs that follow, a few distinct examples will be briefly discussed.

A fairly extensive inquiry into class management was carried out by Teacher Education Project (funded by the Department of Education and Science, U.K.). Part of this focussed on first encounters with classes and has been discussed by Wragg and Wood (1980). The study is of interest on two counts: the research methods used and the preliminary findings outlined. The research methods ranged broadly, both qualitatively and quantatively, and some may be useful to teachers wishing to examine their own practice. For example, they described interviews focussing on details of first lesson procedures, in which teachers were asked to imagine they were about to enter a classroom for the first time; the gathering of substantially unstructured responses to deviant behavior illustrated in photographs; semi-structured observation schedules designed to record verbatim the teachers' first words and salient actions during the first fifteen minutes; structured observation of task involvement and deviance using the Nottingham Class Management Schedule; the application of critical events technique to the establishing of rules and relationships, in which the observer recorded what led up to an event, what both teacher and the pupil did, and what the outcome was. Their early investigations led them to this conclusion:

> "It became quite clear both from classroom observation and interviews that much of importance occurs in the very first encounters between teachers and pupils. Rules are established either explicitly or implicitly, events take place which may never occur again during the year, teachers role play, pupils experiment, and by late September for experienced teachers or by the end of the first two or three weeks of teaching practice for novices, patterns of behaviour have been established which may persist for a long period and be difficult if not impossible to renegotiate." (p. 1)

It also became evident that the practice of experienced teachers and novices differed substantially in these respects. For instance, experienced teachers pointed out that the rules had to be constantly restated and reinforced, whereas student teachers talked about introducing rules as the need arose. This is particularly relevant in the light of the hypothesis made earlier that teachers develop their management practices through the tacit application of the process of observing, reflecting, planning, and acting, and suggests that through this process they have formulated (tacitly) the generalization that if you are deliberate and attentive about formulating rules at the outset, then the task of establishing control will be facilitated. This is worth making explicit since it provides an invitation to examine your practice with this in mind. Moreover, the literature can throw further light on the process of establishing control. For example, Haysom and Sutton (1974) discuss it in terms of "negotiation." Against a backcloth of codes of behavior derived from the home, the school rules, and the expectations of other teachers, they perceived the pupils' actions in terms of their embarking on a strategy of testing the limits which involves them in making "bids" for freedom of speech and action and monitoring the responses of teachers. Wragg and Wood's study incidentally lends some support to this idea. They cited the case of a student teacher, "who within one lesson saw her second year science class dismantle the careful procedures established during the previous term by the head of science." In the context of making the action research cycle explicit, this concept of "negotiation" can provide a useful input during reflection; it is an invitation to examine your own observations to see if there is evidence of this taking place.

A rather different type of research into the nature of classroom management was pioneered by Smith and Geoffrey (1968). They used ethnographic procedures, which essentially involved making extensive observations in the form of field notes and interpreting these. They threw considerable light on the way in which one teacher went about establishing control and maintaining it.

The process of establishing control began with the teacher "grooving" the children, giving orders, and maintaining compliance. In this way the children began to establish their belief systems, "this is the way it's done." The teacher helped to develop these beliefs by clarifying the way he expected his pupils to behave and adding an "I mean it" quality. Finally, he softened his tone with humor, with a view to gaining his pupils' willing acceptance. He tried to build an emotional commitment to their belief systems with a view to shaping the classroom norms, "this is the way it should be done."

The process of maintaining control is evidently complex. Smith and Geoffrey perceived it as involving a variety of processes. They highlighted "banter," "skirmishing," and "getting off the hook."

Banter referred to the patterns of light-hearted exchange between teacher and pupil (comment — retort — counter) which seemed to have implications for the positive sentiment felt by the pupils.

Skirmishing was a category describing minor conflicts. For example, Edwin had lost his pen cap. The teacher asked "Edwin did you find it?" "No." "Who has it? Sam?" An interchange took place between Sam, Oliver, and the teacher. "I just want it. No questions asked . . . . I hope no one is playing tricks in here."

Getting off the hook grouped together actions which the teacher took to avoid growing conflict. After the "skirmish" described above, the observer noted: "(Teacher) leaves situation by picking up Sam's spelling, looking at it carefully, quietly putting it down, and walking off."

They proceeded to relate these in diagrammatic form which indicates tentative relationships between them (Figure 4.2).

Their findings prompt reflection. Do I engage in "banter," "skirmishing," and "getting of the hook"? Are these appropriate ways of describing my management actions? Do I perceive a similar relationship between them?

Yet another way of bringing the literature into conjunction with the teacher's management actions is to examine the nature of teaching from a philosophical perspective. For example, R. S. Peters (1966) in his analysis of punishment and

Figure 4.2

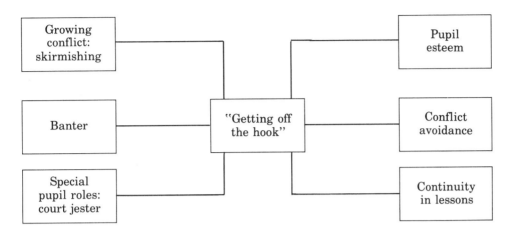

Source: L. M. Smith and W. Geoffrey, *The Complexities of an Urban Classroom* (New York: Holt, Rinehart and Winston, 1968). Reprinted by permission of the authors.

discipline raises a number of dilemmas for teachers. He proceeds from a clarification of the meaning of punishment towards an examination of the question, "What punishment should be given for a particular breach of a rule?" — the action question! In discussing this question he refers to the concepts of deterrence and reform. Implicitly, teachers are invited to examine their actions in terms of the way in which they mitigate the conflict between the deterrent and reformative aspects of punishment, and are drawn into considering the value they place on impartiality in administering rules, the motive of the culprit, the importance of enabling education to proceed and their responsibility for developing autonomy in the individual. By using the concepts of deterrence and reform as a basis of giving meaning to action, a dialogue with theory is provoked.

The most widely quoted and most influential of all studies of classroom management are probably those of Kounin and his co-workers. Kounin's book, *Discipline and Group Management in Classrooms* (1970), is a fascinating chronicle of the ebb and flow of two major research projects, rich in methodological considerations and findings.

His interest in management was sparked by a chance encounter in one of the classes he taught. One day he reprimanded a student who was reading a newspaper and was intrigued by the "ripple effect" on the other students. "Side glances to others ceased, whispers stopped, eyes went from windows or the instructor to notebooks on desks." This stimulated him and his co-workers to try to substantiate his finding by contriving a classically controlled experiment in which the effects of reprimanding a "stooge" in different ways were carefully monitored. Although they obtained positive results, they were left uneasy and chose to follow this experiment with an exploration of natural situations in beginning kindergartens. There, observers carefully recorded events surrounding "desist incidents": the deviant behavior, the interaction between teacher and pupil, and the effects on the pupil closest to the deviant. The results indicated that the clarity of the desist (whether the deviant and the deviant behavior were identified) and the firmness with which it was given made a difference. What the audience child was doing beforehand and how long he or she had been in attendance at school were also significant. Armed with increasing expectations of success, they then proceeded to observe the behavior of children at summer camp, to carry out structured interviews at high school, and to implement another meticulously designed experiment with high school pupils. However, the findings from these studies conflicted with one another. There was conflict between the field studies and the experimental studies, and conflict between those carried out in different settings. After five years of research they found themselves with as many questions as answers and concluded,

> "One must study real teachers in actual classrooms in order to learn about managerial techniques and any other aspects of teacher pupil relationships. . . . The classroom has its own ecology. It has a geographical location, physical setting, props, activities, time allotments, personnel, events, expectations, and purposes that make it different in many respects from other settings."

This conclusion prompted them to search for a more suitable methodology. First, they explored the possibility of making field notes, but because of the difficulty experienced in obtaining comprehensive and objective data, rejected this idea in favor of making video recordings. The first set of recordings indicated that the way in which a teacher handled a desist incident was important. And yet it was nevertheless evident to them that not all the teachers were equally successful in promoting work involvement and controlled deviance. To what could this be attributed?

They proceeded to make a second set of recordings in forty-nine different primary school classrooms, grades 1 and 2, and from a close examination and re-examination of these, perceived a number of aspects of the teacher's management actions which might be consequential.

With-itness:	Has the teacher eyes in the back of his/her head? Does he/she spot the deviant or mistakenly select the wrong target? Does he/she spot the more serious, rather than the more trivial, deviancy? Does he/she nip deviancy in the bud?
Overlappingness:	Can the teacher teach and maintain control at the same time?
Smoothness:	Does the lesson flow smoothly? Is there an absence of interfering behavior? Or does the teacher interrupt the students whilst they are busy, pay attention to irrelevant details, or terminate or leave an activity hanging in mid-air only to return to it later? Is the lesson free from slow downs?
Momentum:	Does the teacher overdwell on student deviancy, etc.?
Group alerting:	Does the teacher create suspense? Does the teacher present novel material?
Accountability:	Are the students held responsible?

Valence and challenge arousal:	Does the teacher make attempts to get the pupils more enthusiastically involved or curious?
Variety:	Are the activities truly varied, in items of content, covert experience provided, teacher presentation pattern, props, group arrangement, responsibility placed on the child, the child's activity and location?

They then went on to sharpen these qualitative concepts with a view to quantifying them. When they did so, they found that with-itness, smoothness, momentum, group alerting, and variety correlated very strongly with work involvement or with deviancy; and that it made a difference according to whether the pupils were working by themselves (seatwork) or as a class with the teacher.

What are the consequences of Kounin's work for teachers? Which methods recommend themselves to teachers who wish to study their own classrooms? How might teachers learn more about the ecology of their classrooms and the situational factors which indirectly affect their actions? How might teachers proceed to examine whether or not his findings hold for them?

Teacher–Pupil Interaction

In previous sections we have focussed on the teachers' actions from three vantage points (the methodological, the organizational, and the managerial). It will have emerged time and again that these actions and initiatives of teachers evoke responses from pupils. The pupils see (or fail to see) the teacher taking an initiative, they interpret it in one or indeed many ways, they consciously or unconsciously decide how to respond and respond they do (albeit not necessarily as intended!). A more complete picture of the classroom is provided when teacher action and pupil reaction are seen together as interaction.

A simple but revealing illustration of the way in which teacher action and pupil action interrelate is provided in Mary Budd Rowe's work on "wait-time." Rowe had become aware of the way many teachers were seemingly content to accept short responses from their pupils when they were answering questions. She was also aware that people in general frequently pause for thought when they are talking. What would happen, she speculated, if teachers introduced "wait-time" after a question and after a pupil responds?

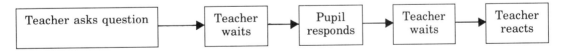

Her findings were dramatic. Not only did the length of pupils' responses increase but failure to respond decreased. The pupils seemed to grow in confidence — fewer responses were inflected, the number of unsolicited but appropriate responses increased, and the contributions by "slow" children increased as well. The incidence of speculative thinking grew and more pupil–pupil communication took place. And, moreover, the changed patterns of response seemed to affect the teacher, teacher-centred show-and-tell decreased.

Every lesson will contain hundreds of interactions. Not only T-P interactions but P-T interactions and P-P interactions and T-all interactions and P-all. Although every interaction will be unique, it would be surprising if some were not similar to others; for example, a teacher who gets no response to a question might often rephrase it. If you look carefully, you might see this happening time and again. This process of looking for patterns of interaction is often used as a starting point for analysing the teaching process. See if you can find any in this transcript of a conversation between a teacher and two pupils recorded by Rowe:

First child:	Ice is melting.
Teacher:	The ice is melting. What do we mean by melting?
Both children:	Getting smaller.
Teacher:	Getting smaller, very good.
Second child:	Shrinking.
Teacher:	Shrinking.
Second child:	The ice is reducing.
Teacher:	The ice is reducing, that's a good word, reducing.
First child:	And water is dropping and the ice . . . . (inaudible)
Second child:	Oh, I know what happens. Well, when the ice is dripping it causes water vapor.
Teacher:	Water vapor, that's very good. Water vapor. What else? . . . (p.287)

Even in such a short extract, you might have found more than one pattern emerging. Rowe perceived in this extract an example of a pattern which she called "mimicry." Had we been able to follow the teacher a little longer we might not only have seen this pattern reappearing but others emerging as well. Moreover, we might have been able to relate these to each other (to see patterns in the patterns). Rowe thought she could, and interpreted "mimicry" as part of the strategy used by the teacher to maintain control.

In summary then I have suggested that teachers might proceed to analyse the interaction going on in their classrooms by first perceiving simple patterns and then trying to relate them one to another so as to put them into a perspective. This process is called pattern analysis. (For a fuller description and another example see chapter 8, Inquiry 4.10.)

Interaction is not a one-way street. Although it may appear that interactions more naturally, more obviously, and more frequently emanate from the teacher, they also emanate from the pupils. John Holt's book *How Children Fail* (1969) was a landmark in this respect. It is full of anecdotal illustrations of strategies used by the pupils on the teacher. Here is a charming example:

"I remember the day not long ago when Ruth opened my eyes. We had been doing math, and I was pleased with myself because, instead of telling her answers and showing her how to do problems, I was 'making her think' by asking her questions. It was slow work. Question after question met only silence. She said nothing, did nothing, just sat and looked at me through those glasses and waited. Each time

I had to think of a question easier and more pointed than the last, until I finally found one so easy that she would feel safe in answering it. So we inched our way along until suddenly, looking at her as I waited for an answer to a question, I saw with a start that she was not at all puzzled by what I had asked her. In fact, she was not even thinking about it. She was coolly appraising me, weighing my patience, waiting for the next, sure-to-be-easier question. I thought, 'I've been had!'"(p.38)

I suspect that one of the reasons for Holt's appeal lay in teachers' being able to identify with him, realizing perhaps for the first time that their pupils use similar strategies to those he describes. And such knowledge is, of course, invaluable in reconceptualizing what is happening in the classroom — it is rather like a chess opponent telling you about his intentions after he makes a move. Unless we are alert to the notion that pupils exercise initiatives in interaction, and there may well be widespread patterns, then the teacher's responsiveness, and hence control, will be less than optimal.

Very little is known about interactions which emerge from the pupils. One of the first quantitative studies of "bidirectionality" of interaction was carried out by Martha Fiedler (1975). Her work is particularly interesting for the "Hit-Steer Observational System" she developed. This system enables an observer to assess the extent of the influence of the teacher on the pupils and vice-versa. Attempts to influence are described as "hits," a positive response as a "steer," a negative response as a "no steer," and an ambiguous response as a "conditional steer." She makes these categories clear in a simple short example.

"'Open your math book to page 51' and the students did. A teacher hit followed by a pupil steer would be scored. If the students said 'No, we won't. We want geography now instead' a pupil no steer and a pupil hit would be scored. Then if the teacher modified his behaviour to accommodate the students' suggestions, a teacher steer would be scored. Finally, if the teacher were to say 'O.K., then do the problems on page 54 tonight' and the student response could not be observed, a pupil conditional steer would be observed." (p. 737)

Although I have reservations about the value of premature quantification and wonder about the capacity of the instrument to detect the more subtle ways in which teacher and pupil actions influence one another, the use of this instrument may sensitize us to the view of interaction being more than a one-way street. Fiedler provides us with a starting point which focusses our observational efforts on a neglected area, and if these are then directed towards identifying different patterns of influence — different types of "hits" and "steers" — then we could be much the wiser (Inquiry 4.11).

Suggested Inquiries

Inquiry 4.1 *Characteristics of Your Methods*
Using Kelly's Repertory Grid Technique, identify the constructs you use when

you think about your teaching methodology. Neal and Tyrrell (1979) provide further details as to how this can be done if the procedure described earlier in this chapter is not clear.

Select two or three of your most important constructs and present an argument which explains why you value them so highly. Here you are making some of your educational philosophy explicit.

Draw a diagram to show how your constructs are related and then express your diagram in words. Here you are making some of the theories you have about teaching explicit.

Collect information/data which reveals the extent to which your teaching features one of the constructs you thought important. Compare your thinking with your action. (This is likely to be an uncomfortable task since most of us fall short of our ideals!!)

Inquiry 4.2   Using Flanders Interaction Analysis

If you value "indirectness," or if you are worried about teachers talking too much, you might find this inquiry provocative.

Tape record one of your lessons. Afterwards, analyse it using Flanders categories, identifying what was happening every 15 seconds for 25 minutes — 100 observations in total. Record your findings in bar chart form, filling out a grid such as that below:

45%										
40%										
35%										
30%										
25%										
20%										
15%										
10%										
5%										
0%										
Category	1	2	3	4	5	6	7	8	9	10

Write a paragraph commenting on your findings. What are your reflections on the value of this observation instrument?

(*When used for research purposes the instrument is used every three seconds. This is very demanding and unnecessary in this context. Moreover, because some of the categories are rather vague, at least five statements of ground rules have been devised to help investigators decide upon the appropriate category.)

Inquiry 4.3 Dimensions of Meaning

Write down the following items on slips of paper: formal/informal, structured/unstructured, framework, teacher-directed, self-directed (child), guided, open-ended, dependent/independent (child), subject-centred/child centred. Sort them into groups and then describe what each group has in common. Did similar dimensions to those perceived by Elliott emerge? Using either your dimensions or Elliott's, give examples of teacher or pupil actions that you would associate with either end of a dimension. Alternatively, you might like to examine a video recording of yourself with a view to locating yourself along each dimension.

Inquiry 4.4 Lesson Analysis with Tasks in Mind

Select a sequence of lessons. Identify the tasks that you set, defining them in terms of goals and procedures:

- How would you categorize the tasks? (Sort them into groups.)
- Doyle (1983) perceived four categories: memory tasks, which require pupils to recognize or reproduce what has previously been introduced; procedural tasks, which require students to follow a routine to find an answer; comprehension tasks, which require students to generalize knowledge or skill; and opinion tasks. Do your tasks fall into these categories?

Inquiry 4.5 An Inquiry into Your Routines

There are many unanswered questions about the concept of routines. Do they exist? If so, how can they best be described? How can the concept be profitably utilized? In this activity you and your colleagues are invited to explore such questions. Here are some suggestions which you should feel free to accept, modify, reject, or add to:

- Review a video-recording of yourself. Can you identify any routines? Do you share any of these routines with other teachers?
- Do you have a routine for introducing your lessons? Tape record the first five to ten minutes of every lesson for a day. Transcribe these introductions. Do you always use the same routine? Do other teachers use similar or different routines?
- Select a resource which you frequently use, for example, a textbook or a filmstrip. Tape record how you handle the resource on at least three different occasions.
- List a few factors which you think might affect the routines you use, for example, the ability of the students or the size of the class. Collect some evidence which throws light on this.

Inquiry 4.6 Monitoring Group Behavior

When you next organize group work in your classroom, tape record the interaction of one group. List features of the interaction you perceive. How are they related to one another ? How do you account for the way the group functioned?

If you think it might be useful, use Benne and Sheats classification. How do you explain the balance between different types of behavior?

Inquiry 4.7 Individualization: Where Do You Stand?

Identify actions that you have taken in providing pupils with freedom to interpret and respond, with freedom for them to progress at their own pace, with freedom
to choose and initiate. Better still, analyse a tape-recorded lesson with these ideas
in mind. Share you findings with your colleagues.

   If one of your colleagues has proceeded to individualize to a significant extent,
it would be very worthwhile making a video-recording of him or her in action.
This could be the beginning of a most pertinent research study of individualization and the way in which the provision of freedom by the teacher affects pupils'
actions.

Inquiry 4.8 Your Frame of Reference in Management

This inquiry is open to choice. On the one hand, you might be brief. You might
cast your mind back, recording some of the formative experiences you have had.
Or alternatively, you might clarify your present thinking by noting significant
items in your frame of reference, as if, for example, providing a list of pointers
to a beginning teacher.

   On the other hand, you might wish to probe more deeply. For example, you and
your colleagues might collaborate to survey your thinking and its origins.

Inquiry 4.9 Observing and Reflecting on Your Managerial Actions

This inquiry is designed to be a starting point in carrying out some action research
into your management practice. Three possibilities come to mind:
(1) Following Inquiry 4.8, some aspect of your practice may have emerged as being worth deliberately observing. Design a small-scale data- gathering schedule
and analyse the data you collect.
(ii) Modify Robertson's inquiry to suit your purposes.
(iii) Read the selection of examples of relevant literature and collect data which
relates to any one which you find pertinent. Analyse your data accordingly.

Inquiry 4.10 Analysing Interaction Patterns

This inquiry can be divided into three main phases: (a) collection and selection
of data, (b) perception of patterns, (c) interpretation.
(a) Make a tape recording of one of your lessons. Play it back and make a note
of any patterns you see. Afterwards transcribe a portion of it — say ten minutes.
My hunch is that although the transcription process is tedious, you will be surprised at how useful it is in revealing patterns you hadn't noticed earlier.
(b) Perception: Carefully examine the transcript and make a note of all the patterns you see. Give each a name (conceptualize it).
(c) Interpretation: This is a matter of looking for patterns in the patterns; of seeing relationships between them. Either write the patterns you have found on cards

and try grouping them, or select one pattern that interests you and provide an interpretation as to why it exists. This may prompt you to examine the other patterns with this interpretation in mind, or could feasibly prompt you to re-examine the transcript in a search for other patterns which support your interpretation.

It is natural to look for the patterns of the type TA→PA; however, you might find evidence for PA→TA interactions if you look carefully. Review your transcript with this in mind.

Inquiry 4.11   Seeing Interaction as a Two-Way Process

Obtain a video recording or a film of a class in action. View it with a group of colleagues. Collect as many instances as you can of the pupils trying to influence the behavior of the teacher. Transcribe them when possible and categorize them as either P. Hit – T. steer, P. hit – T. conditional steer, or P. hit – T. no steer. Now review your findings. Are there any patterns evident?

After examining the quality of the interaction in this way, you might find it provocative to quantify it. Use two simple grids, such as those below, to record the response to each teacher and pupil "hit," that is, for each instance, place a tick in the appropriate box.

	Pupil steer	Pupil conditional steer	Pupil no steer
T. HIT			

	Teacher steer	Teacher conditional steer	Teacher no steer
P. HIT			

Suggested Reading

Neal, M., and Tyrrell, F. "Sharing Meanings: An Introduction to the Repertory Grid Technique, *"Industrial and Commercial Training* 11 (1979): 327-33.

This short article not only provides a most readable introduction to the Repertory Grid Technique, it rehearses, step by step, how the technique can be applied to eliciting constructs about teaching methods.

Doyle W. "Academic Work," *Review of Educational Research* 53 (1983): pp. 159–73 and 178–87.

In these selections from his review, Doyle shows how our understanding of pupils in classrooms can be deepened by analysing classroom actions in terms of academic tasks.

Yinger, R. "Routines in Teacher Planning." *Theory into Practice,* Vol. 18, No. 3 (1979).

This describes an ethnographic study of a teacher as she planned her lessons. The findings are most insightful.

Smith, L. M., and Geoffrey, W. *The Complexities of an Urban Classroom: An Analysis Toward a General Theory of Teaching,* pp. 67–72 and pp. 96–121. New York: Holt, Rinehart and Winston, 1968.

This pioneering ethnographic study provides an interesting example of the way in which analysis and supporting data may be interwoven. In the selected pages Smith and Geoffrey analyse the processes of establishing and maintaining control.

Kounin, J. *Discipline and Group Management in Classrooms.* New York: Holt, Rinehart and Winston, 1970.

Rowe, M. B. "Wait time — Is Anybody Listening?" *Teaching Science as Continuous Inquiry.* Second edition, Ch. 9. New York: McGraw Hill, 1978.

Many teachers regard this chapter as having had more influence on their teaching than anything else they have read.

Rogers, Carl. *Freedom to Learn,* Ch. 1. Columbus, Ohio: Merrill, 1969.

In diary form a teacher describes the unfolding events as she provided her pupils with freedom to choose their activities.

5

The Pupils' Actions

In this chapter we shall be looking at the pupils' actions, the visible link between what the teacher does and what the pupils experience and learn:

Teacher's actions — Pupils' Actions — Pupils' covert experiences

Daily the pupils find themselves acting in a multitude of ways: hanging up their coats, answering their names at registration, reading books, writing notes, listening to the teacher, responding to questions, obeying directions, talking to friends, lining up for lunch, and so on. In passing, it would indeed make a fascinating study to shadow one or two pupils for a whole day, recording all they say (using radio-microphones perhaps), taking copies of all they write, making notes about their non-verbal communication, and interviewing them from time to time to get their view on what had been happening. Moreover, such a study could present us with a new way of looking at events in school through the eyes of the pupils.

Here, however, we will just make a beginning, taking a close look at what the pupils are doing when the teacher intends that they should be learning. In the first section we will examine how categorizing pupils' actions can help us to make sense of them. The second section is based on the idea of categorizing pupil actions according to whether they are on task or off task. In it we will examine important matters relating to the quantity and quality of pupil participation.

Making Sense of the Pupils' Actions

In the journal extract shown in Box 5.1 (Engel, 1975) the teacher's attention is caught by the behavior of Danny and John. Very quickly she recognizes their actions as those of "being stuck." She sensitively weighs the advantages and disadvantages of intervening and, as it worked out, made the right decision. A beautiful piece of teaching – very professional!!

It is worth making explicit the process this teacher spontaneously used. It may be one which we too can use in order to make sense of pupils' actions.

- The teacher *observed* what the pupils did.
- The teacher *perceived categories* of pupil actions. She put certain actions together in a group. (In our everyday lives we intuitively use this process to make sense of the situations and events we encounter.)
- The teacher *made inferences* about the thoughts and feelings the pupils were experiencing.
- The teacher *related her inferences* to the characteristics of the pupils and the task. She put them into the context of what she knew about the demands the task made, and the capacity of her pupils to overcome their frustration.
- The teacher *made a decision.*

Box 5.1   Page from a Teacher's Journal (Bobbie Snow)

Danny and John were making a spaceship. They cut off the end of a plastic bottle and painted it. They planned to put a balloon in the open end, attach the ship to a wire and let the balloon go, sailing the ship across the room. But they got stuck on how to attach the ship to the wire. So they painted the ship again. They stayed after school touching up some cracks in the now very paint-covered ship. The next day's work period they painted little windows on it and people's faces in the windows. They put up the wire across the room and stopped work. Fooled around for a while. They went through the science books looking for a volcano picture. After gathering materials for a volcano they started work.

I didn't have time to help them with the spaceship, wasn't sure whether I should, and wanted them to "stick to it." Remembering Marty's example of the kid who came back and solved a problem days later, I decided to acknowledge that they were still working on the spaceship (were they?) and asked them if they wanted me to put it on the shelf until they figured out how to attach it.

They worked on the volcano for a few days and seemed to have forgotten the spaceship. Covered with wheatpaste Danny exuberantly announced, "I have a beautiful idea. Give me my spaceship." He got some paper clips and bent them to fit. The focus switched to the spaceship and it was a successful run. The next work period they returned to the volcano and talked about how to make the ship faster, having races, curving the wire, etc.

I wondered if the result would have been different if I had pushed them into finishing it or helped them solve it. What kind of classroom accepts and encourages kids delaying finding the solution to a problem? Is A product more important than THE product? Does feeling a pressure to come up with a solution right away make kids "give up"?

Source: B. S. Engel, *A Handbook on Documentation* (Grand Forks: University of North Dakota, North Dakota Study Group on Evaluation, 1975), p. 59. Reprinted by permission of the University of North Dakota.

Observing

The process began with observing. In the hustle and bustle of teaching, this is a luxury. But for teachers who want to develop a greater understanding of what is happening in their classrooms, it is a necessity. A starting point might be to secure the opportunity to watch pupils — perhaps only one pupil — in someone else's classroom. Michael Armstrong (1980) spent a year doing just this. His book, *Closely Observed Children,* is in essence a series of fairly detailed studies of pupils in action. It throws considerable light on how different children undertake different tasks. I found his commentary on the way Robbie set about the task of making something "that worked" particularly charming.

Armstrong had joined Robbie as he was watching three boys building model boats. Robbie had told him of the task the teacher had previously suggested and Armstrong in turn suggested that he might like to make a cotton-reel tank powered by elastic (albeit that Armstrong couldn't remember how to build it himself!). In spite of a rather unpromising start, Robbie persisted:

> "All morning and right through the dinner break he worked on his tank, continually adjusting and revising the propelling mechanism, until at last, by early afternoon, he succeeded in getting the tank to crawl forward smoothly and slowly, as it should. It was only then, as I watched him demonstrate the tank's performance that, at last I remembered clearly how it had been in my own cotton reel tank racing days. Robbie spent the rest of the day confidently experimenting with his own particular something 'that worked', testing it out on different surfaces, seeing how far and how long it would run, how much time it took to cross a given area, how steep a slope it could climb and so on. At the end of that day I tried to account for Robbie's success, in my daily notes:

> 'Friday, September 3rd.
> In successfully completing his cotton-reel tank Robbie has resolved a whole series of mechanical problems, with little help from me, and some of that misleading, except for the initial idea and the one tip which I derived from Stephen. I, indeed, had given up at an early stage and was all for waiting until we could be told by someone else what we were doing wrong and how to put it right. I had shown little confidence in Robbie's own ingenuity. What then had helped him to persist and finally to succeed: his eagerness to get his machine working properly, his own mechanical aptitude, or a series of intuitions, guesses and happy accidents? All of these had helped perhaps, but above all what had mattered, I think, was his responsiveness to the materials, to toys and toy making, and to a certain kind of playing, fiddling, experimenting, making do and imagining.'"
> (pp. 171–72)

> *Source:* M. Armstrong, *Closely Observed Children* (London: Writers and Readers in Association with Chameleon, 1980). Reprinted by permission of the author.

Armstrong spends two pages describing Robbie's actions as he undertook the task of making something "that worked." The detail is fascinating, but I also found myself wanting to know how other children went about the task. In what ways was their behavior similar and in what ways different? Looking for similarities and differences is revealing. It helps us to conceptualize significant features of the pupils' actions.

To move from observing just one pupil in somebody else's classroom to observing many pupils in your own classroom is to take two steps at once. But it is possible! The Open University (1980) describes examples of teachers who responded to the challenge of answering the question, "What did the pupils actually do?" A teacher decided to observe his or her remedial science class whilst they were working on some new worksheets which involved looking at an earthworm and answering some questions about it. A summary of the teacher's observations is shown in Box 5.2.

Box 5.2 Summary of a Teacher's Observations

Observations were made over three five-minute periods.

First five-minute period: The teacher noted that at first the whole group took delight in showing fear of worms. One pupil, Linda, refused to go near the worm. Later, Pauline and Diane discussed with Linda, quite sensibly, other things they were frightened of. Mark and David worked intently and produced some very accurate drawings. Angela, who usually worked with Carol, moved to be by herself. A couple of minutes later Carol put her coat on.

Next five-minute period: The teacher noted that David had moved to another seat. Angela too had moved once more. But David continued to work hard and Angela began to ask questions about her work. Pauline and Diane had put their worms together and were fascinated by their curling round each other. Linda, who was standing by herself, continued not to work. Later, however, she joined Carol and Angela and went to look at worms and talk about them. Linda picked up her pencil but put it down without using it. Gary was finding it difficult to remain in his seat for more than a few minutes at a time.

Last five-minute period: Most had nearly finished the worksheets. Gary turned on a tap. There was much loud talking unconnected with the work. Linda eventually answered two questions. Russell finished and brought his book to show the teacher. In the concluding discussion of the worksheet questions, the teacher was pleasantly surprised by their answers.

At first sight there is nothing very remarkable about these observations, but the more you look, the more you see. Indeed the teacher who subsequently made a deliberate attempt to make sense of these observations found that a variety of interesting and provocative categories emerged: things the pupils did which I intended/things pupils did which I did not intend; things they did which disrupted the learning process/things they did which enhanced the learning process; things which related to pupils' social development/things which related to academic development; things the pupils found relevant (enjoyed)/things the pupils found irrelevant (annoying) (Inquiry 5.1).

Making Inferences

The teacher categorized pupil actions in a diverse number of ways. Sometimes they were seen from the teacher's perspective, for example, "things the pupils did which I intended." Sometimes they were seen from the pupils' perspective, for example, "things the pupils found relevant (enjoyed)." This latter type of grouping is particularly interesting because it contains within it an inference. The teacher did not know for certain if the pupils were enjoying the task, but the way the pupils behaved encouraged speculation that it could well have been the case. When observations cluster together in this way, they provide clues about the type of thinking and feeling the pupils might be having, clues about the pupils' covert experiences. If we are to fully describe the teaching process, we need to make inferences of this type and check them to see if they hold.

When reflecting on Linda's actions the teacher said, "I am uncertain as to whether she would have done more if I had interfered earlier or whether she would have totally withdrawn from the worms." To illuminate this, let us take a second look at Linda's actions in sequence:

> "Linda refused to go near the worm.
> Pauline and Diane discussed with Linda quite sensibly other things they were frightened of.
> Linda, who was standing by herself, continued not to work.
> Later she joined Carol and Angela and went to look at worms and talk about them.
> Linda picked up her pencil but put it down without using it.
> Linda eventually answered two questions."

What was going on in Linda's mind? It looks to me as if she was coming to terms with something she found repulsive. Maybe she was experiencing some support or social pressure from Pauline, Diana, Carol, and Angela. If this was the case, I believe the lesson might have been a very valuable one for Linda indeed. Had the teacher intervened, Linda might well have been deprived of the opportunity of coming to terms with worms.

In summary then, we might well enrich our understanding of what is going on in classrooms if we make inferences about the thoughts and feelings the pupils are experiencing. Inference making can be facilitated by grouping pupils' actions as if from their perspective, and by examining an individual's actions in sequence (Inquiry 5.2).

As well as watching what pupils do we can also observe what they say and what they write. The relationship between the language pupils use and the way they are thinking or feeling is a close one. Not only does the way pupils use language reflect their thinking, but language as such is a means by which pupils develop their thinking processes. This area has been the focus of an escalating research interest in recent years and the findings from this research have substantially contributed to the "language across the curriculum" movement.

Barnes' 1976 study, *From Communication to Curriculum,* is regarded by many as a landmark in this area. He tape recorded small groups of pupils working on selected tasks and interpreted their conversations (actions) in terms of the type of thinking they were using.

In the following extract, a group of four eleven-year-old girls talk about the poem

"The Bully Asleep" by J. H. Walsh. The poem (Table 5.1) describes the reactions of a teacher and her pupils when they find the class bully asleep during a lesson.

1. Well the teacher's bound to notice.
2. Yes really . . . because I mean . . . I mean if . . . .
3. Or she could have gone out because someone had asked her or something . . . she probably felt really sorry for him so she just left him . . . . The teachers do . . . .
4. What really sorry for him . . .so she'd just left him so they could stick pins in him.
5. Oh no she probably . . . with the "whispered" . . . said "whispered" . . . .
6. Yes.
7. Yes but here it says . . . um . . . (rustling paper) . . . oh "stand away from him, children. Miss Andrews stopped to see."
8. Mm.
9. So you'd think that she would do more really.
10. Yes . . . you'd think she'd um . . . probably wake . . . if she would really feel sorry for him she'd . . . .
11. She'd wake him.
10. (cont'd.) . . . wake him.
12. Oh no! . . . No, she wouldn't send him home alone . . . because . . . nobody's . . . . (pp. 26-27)

One pattern in the conversation which struck Barnes forcibly was that which he called the "hypothetical mode." This is characterized by the pupils' wondering, speculating, or toying with possibilities. It is clearly evident in the extract and he commented as follows:

"Consider number 10: 'Yes . . . you'd think she'd um . . . probably wake . . . if she would really felt sorry for . . . sorry for him she'd . . . wake him.' You may feel that as communication this leaves something to be desired. But, as I have already said, communication is not the only function of language. The hesitations and changes of direction have a different function: we usually call it 'thinking aloud'. Talking her way into the problem is enabling this girl to monitor her own thought, and reshape it. Talk is here a means for controlling thinking. So if a teacher is too concerned for neat well-shaped utterances from pupils this may discourage the thinking aloud. In this book I call this groping towards a meaning 'exploratory talk'. It is usually marked by frequent hesitations, rephrasings, false starts and changes of direction . . . . In this case you may have noticed that the exploratory talk is marked also by hypothetical expressions: 'she could have gone out', 'she probably felt', 'you'd think . . .', 'Might have to . . .'." (p. 28)

Source: D. Barnes, *From Communication to Curriculum* (Harmondsworth, Middx.: Penguin, 1976). Reprinted by permission of the author.

Table 5.1 The Bully Asleep by J. H. Walsh

One afternoon, when grassy
Scents through the classroom crept,
Bill Craddock laid his head
Down on his desk, and slept.

The children came round him:
Jimmy, Roger, and Jane:
They lifted his head timidly
And let it sink again.

"Look, he's gone sound asleep, Miss."
Said Jimmy Adair;
"He stays up all night, you see;
His mother doesn't care."

"Stand away from him, children."
Miss Andrew stooped to see.
"Yes, he's asleep; go on
With your writing, and let him be."

"Now's a good chance!" whispered Jimmy;
And he snatched Bill's pen and hid it.
"Kick him under the desk hard;
He won't know who did it."

"Fill all his pockets with rubbish —
Paper, apple-cores, chalk."
So they plotted, while Jane
Sat wide-eyed at their talk.

Not caring, not hearing
Bill Craddock he slept on;
Lips parted, eyes closed —
Their cruelty gone.

"Stick him with pins!" muttered Roger.
"Ink down his neck!" said Jim.
But Jane, tearful and foolish,
Wanted to comfort him.

Source: John Walsh, *The Roundabout by the Sea* (Oxford: Oxford University Press, n.d.). Reprinted by permission of Mrs. A. M. Walsh.

Relating Pupils' Actions to the Task

The nature of the task clearly influences the way pupils respond to it. The demands the task makes will make a difference. The way the teacher introduces it will make a difference. Whether or not there are concrete materials to work with will make a difference. How the teacher intervenes will make a difference.

Barnes, in his study of pupils talking, recognized this, and he was concerned to gain insights into the circumstances (characteristics of the task) which might encourage exploratory talk. Here are some of the hypotheses he arrived at:
Exploratory talk is encouraged
if the teacher indicates the pupils' contributions are valued;
if the teacher helps the pupils to focus on the task by verbalizing necessary preliminary knowledge;
if the teacher provides common ground for discussion, for example, in the form of apparatus or pictures or films;
if the pace is adjusted so as to provide pupils with plentiful opportunities to sort out the material.
These hypotheses are provocative. If you would like to probe them, you might find English's (1981) list of suggestions of "Ideas for small group talk" useful (Inquiry 5.3).

The way in which the teacher organizes the task also makes a difference. I found the inquiry made by Russell Clarke, a teacher, into this aspect revealing. Russell was interested in finding out more about how the size of the group influenced his pupils' actions. He decided to video record three groups of eleven-year-old pupils who were tackling the mathematical problem, the "Tower of Hanoi." Box 5.3 is an edited extract from his report.

Box 5.3   Extracts from "The Effect of Group Size on Group Performance" by Russell Clarke

Each group was given written instructions which were reviewed before they began their work.

"The object of the game is to transfer the rings from one peg to either of the two other pegs.

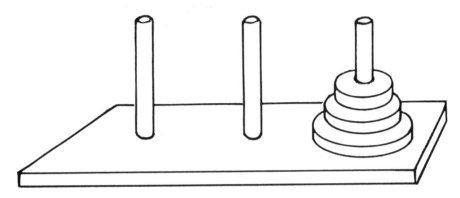

1. The rings must end up in the same order but on a different peg.
2. Only one ring may be moved at a time.
3. A larger ring may never be placed on top of a smaller one.

Begin with one ring and fill in the table below.
Repeat with two and three rings.
You are looking for the *least* number of moves needed.
Note that the answer for four rings is a minimum of 15 moves. Can you do it?

Number of rings	Number of moves needed
1	
2	
3	
4	15
5	
6	

As you work look for the number pattern. Can you predict how many moves it will take for 5 and 6 rings?"

Box 5.3 — continued

The groups had been chosen at random from volunteers, but in spite of this, the groups were not really typical. The single student was a low achiever with little background or interest in Math. The group of three, on the other hand, was made up of three girls of high ability and motivation who excelled in Math. Fortunately, the group of six showed a good cross section of abilities and interests. . . .

When first viewing the tapes, the large group made a striking impression. Their work was characterized by chanting aloud the number of moves to a definite beat. The members handling the rings seemed to be encouraged by this, to the point that they would often continue their moves long after it was obvious that they were not being successful. The smaller group seemed to lack this strong social interaction. They were quieter and less active. The single student showed nothing similar to this.

On subsequent viewing, however, a new pattern started to emerge. What seemed at first to be enthusiastic participation in the large group could now be viewed as an intense competition for the apparatus, and what was at first seen as a subdued effort on the part of the small group now seemed to be a reflective attempt to work out a competent strategy. Other things became more apparent, too.

There was unequal participation in the large group. Two people in the group (because of temperament or placing) soon abandoned any attempt to actually handle the rings and only participated in the counting. Later, two other brighter students in the group solved the math exercise while waiting their turn.

There was intense competition in the larger group. Students frequently interfered during a turn and, if a student paused for even a second, someone else would take over the sequence of the moves. In one particular sequence, for example, the control of the discs changed hands three times. Stopping the videotape at almost any point would show four or five hands reaching or pointing or helping to move the disc.

The smaller group, while still counting aloud, was more subdued and less rhythmical. The counting followed, rather than established, the pattern of the moves.

There was less competitive behavior in the small group and members felt free to stop and think over their next move.

The smaller group made predictions and doubled checked their results — a planning behavior that was absent in the larger group.

The comments were more constructive and supportive in the smaller group. ''It's your turn'', ''I think it goes there'', and ''We're making the same mistakes over and over'', were typical comments.

The single student gave the least desirable results in almost all aspects. He made little progress during his session and was the only group not to solve the math exercise. With no one to feedback, to make suggestions or to form plans with, he developed no coherent learning sequence. His was the only group, for instance, that did not seem to find the pattern in the first eight moves with the four discs.

Pupils' Actions in Perspective

In order to make sense of what the pupils are doing in the classroom, I have suggested that we should *deliberately* follow the process of (i) observing the pupils, (ii) categorizing their actions, (iii) making inferences about their covert experiences, and (iv) relating the pupils' actions to the task. It was this process that Danny and John's teacher intuitively followed when she was trying to make up her mind whether or not to help them with their spaceship.

Let us now put this in perspective. When discussing Danny and the spaceship (or Linda and the worms) we considered the pupil, the task he or she was given, his or her sequence of actions, and his or her product. This can be represented diagrammatically as follows:

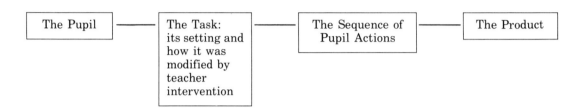

The diagram needs to be extended when looking at the actions of many pupils. Given a task, it is more likely than not that different pupils will respond in different ways and produce different answers or products. Suppose, for instance, that a class of pupils are invited to write a short story of their own choice. We would anticipate a wide variety of products and likewise would anticipate that pupils would go about producing these in different ways. Some might ask for clarification (for example, How long should it be? Has it got to be true?). Some might immediately put pen to paper. Some might talk over their ideas with their neighbors. Some might make notes or rough drafts. Some might ask the teacher for help. This can be represented as follows:

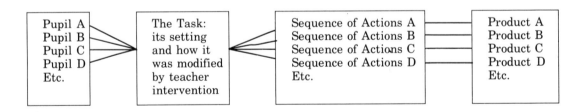

In the course of a number of lessons, a teacher may set many tasks. Again our diagrammatic representation needs extending. The enormous complexity of teaching is evident. And yet we are challenged to make sense of it! In spite of the complexity and the magnitude of the challenge, teachers do cope. Intuitively we find ways of making sense of our pupils' actions. How do we do it? If we knew, then we might be able to make the process deliberate. I suspect that sometimes we use a categorizing process similar to the one we considered earlier, that we characterize pupils, tasks, actions or sequences of actions, and products . We certainly talk in terms of characteristics. We talk about individual differences between pupils, types of task, patterns of action (or sequences of action), and qualities of products. Talking in terms like these helps to reduce the complexity and to make it manageable. The previous diagram is reduced to the one which follows:

Characteristics of the pupils	Characteristics of the tasks	Characteristics of the sequence of actions	Characteristics of the products
individual difference α	type α	pattern α	quality α
individual difference β	type β	pattern β	quality β
individual difference γ	type γ	pattern γ	quality γ
individual difference δ	type δ	pattern δ	quality δ
etc.	etc.	etc.	etc.

The sense-making process continues when we relate these characteristics one to another. When we interpret what we have perceived, we make hypotheses that there are links between specific characteristics of the pupil, task, pupils' actions (or sequences of actions), and product; for example, between individual differences α and task type γ, or between task type β and pattern of action δ, or between pattern of action α and quality of product β. This is what Barnes did when he hypothesized that exploratory talk (pattern of pupil action) is encouraged when the teacher provides common ground for discussion (type of task). In his study, Russell Clarke (Box 5.3) didn't take his analysis this far. He stopped at the stage of characterizing pupils' actions. You might find it interesting to have another look at his perceptions with a view to making some hypotheses.

At first sight this way of reducing the complexity with a view to making sense of what is happening may seem rather confusing. But it isn't really. We do it every day. Suppose, for example, you are choosing a location for a holiday. You might begin by talking about the general ways you would like to spend your time — eating out, playing golf, visiting art galleries. Then perhaps you would think in terms of types of locations — big cities, seaside resorts, camping sites. Finally, you might use a hypothesis such as, there are often plenty of places to eat out and plenty of art galleries in big cities, when making your choice. In essence, you would have simplified the problem by categorizing activities and locations and then linking one category with another (Inquiry 5.4).

To conclude this section, I'd like to put the literature on learning styles into this perspective. Dale (1958), in his pioneering work on learning styles, studied how trainee electricians went about finding a fault in an electrical circuit. In an experimental laboratory study he gave each trainee a circuit board and a tester. A simplified version of this is shown in the diagram (Figure 5.1). Their task was to find out between which two terminals the fault lay. Dale perceived that the trainees went about the task in many different ways; some adopted hit or miss procedures, some tried every hole in turn, others adopted more complex strategies. He categorized their strategies in different ways.

Given any task it is likely that different pupils will adopt different strategies. What is the best way of categorizing these? Applied psychologists find the con-

Figure 5.1   Board for training "fault-finders" in electrical work

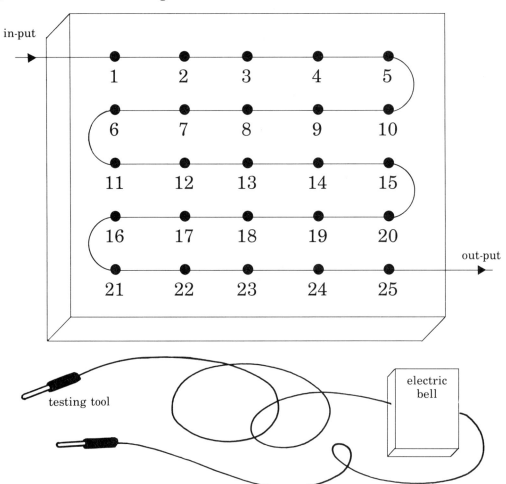

cept of learning style useful. This concept is a categorization of pupils' actions, not purely in terms of what they are doing, but in terms of the thinking strategies they are using. It may be useful to categorize pupils' actions as quick or slow, but significance is added if we try to describe these actions in terms of the thinking styles or strategies the pupils are adopting. For example, significance is added to quick/slow if translated into the categories "impulsive"/"reflective." Casting our minds back to the example of children writing a short story, it would be valuable to know who immediately put pen to paper and who were more naturally inclined to look for opportunities for reflecting, either by leaning back in their chairs, or by making a few jottings on a sheet of scrap paper, or by sharpening an already sharp pencil.

Applied psychologists have identified many different types of learning styles (see Open University, 1971, for an introduction). Pupils who prefer to see the task as a whole as opposed to being inclined to work through it step by step might be described as being at the holist end of the "holist/serialist" dimension. Pupils who prefer open-ended as opposed to close-ended tasks might be described as "divergers" rather than "convergers."

In discussing the teacher's pedagogical actions (chapter 4), we considered the ideas of dimensions (characteristics) of teaching methods and teaching routines.

Perhaps learning styles, dimensions of learning, could well be considered as a counterpart of dimensions of teaching. Perhaps, also, there is a counterpart to the idea of teaching routines, that is, learning rountines which refer to the sequence of actions a pupil takes when responding to the teacher.

Focussing on Pupil Participation

Teachers frequently categorize their pupils' behavior according to whether they are on task or off task, whether they are involved in their work. The teacher's aims of education are actualized in the tasks he or she initiates and in the actions the pupils undertake in attempting these tasks. If pupils are *fully participating* in tasks the teacher considers valuable, then one could argue that the teacher can do no more. To argue this case is useful insofar as it provides a different perspective for the critical appreciation of classroom events. But it is not without its problems and difficulties. Is it possible to agree on what we mean by participation? Is it possible to recognize it when we see it?

I would guess that arguments along these lines, coupled with the problems of measuring teacher effectiveness, have contributed to the rapid and fairly recent growth of interest in pupil participation. Harnischfeger and Wiley (1975) saw it as being at the heart of the teaching and learning process and devised a model of teaching around it.

Figure 5.2 Model Relating Pupil Activities to Achievement (after Bennett)

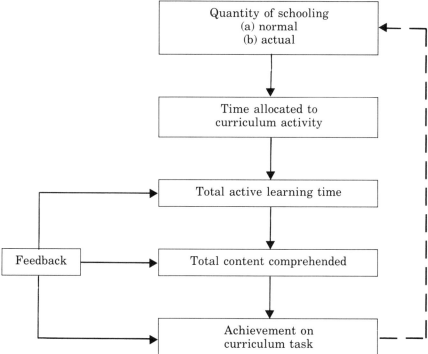

Source: S. N. Bennett, "Recent Research on Teaching: A Dream, a Belief and a Model," *British Journal of Educational Psychology* 48 (1978): 127–47. Reprinted by permission of the author.

Bennett (1979) in his comprehensive review of pupil participation highlighted the three major assertions on which their model was based:

> "(i) A pupil's activities are central to his learning, the effects of other aspects of the teaching/learning situation being mediated through the pupil's activities.
> (ii) The total amount of active learning time on a particular instructional topic is *the* most important determinant of pupil achievement on that topic.
> (iii) There is an enormous variation in time for learning for different pupils, their time devoted to specific learning topics and their total amount of active learning time." (pp. 128–29)

Recent American research following this line of thinking has attempted to establish the truth of some of these assertions empirically. Berliner (1979) and his co-workers made a quantative study of the relationship between participation and learning. They measured participation in terms of three sorts of time: allocated time, engaged time, and academic learning time. Allocated time is the time that the teacher has at his/her disposal. Engaged time is "the time the student is attending to instruction in a particular content area." And academic learning time is "the time a student is engaged in instructional materials or activities that are at an easy level of difficulty for that student." Berliner found the results of these studies supported the thesis

> . . . that the marked variability in allocated time, engaged time and academic learning time, between and within classes is the most potent explanatory variable to account for variability in student achievement — after initial aptitude has been removed as a predictor variable." (p. 125)

Pupil participation, conceived in terms of academic learning time, is thus put in a central position in the teaching learning process (Inquiry 5.5).

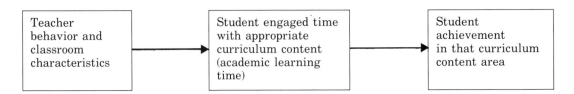

Reprinted by permission of the Publisher from Penelope L. Peterson and Herbert Walberg: *Research on Teaching, Concepts, Findings, and Implications,* Figure 6.1. © 1979 by McCutchan Publishing Corporation, Berkeley, Ca. 94704.

It is somewhat comforting to have one's hunches about the importance of participation supported by empirical evidence, but it does strike one — at least retrospectively — as being rather obvious. How could a student be learning unless he or she is engaged? To postulate otherwise would be a logical denial of our everyday experience. Moreover, it seems that some of the important problems which the studies raise are skated over rather hastily. In this respect, it is significant that Berliner and his co-workers considered it important to distinguish "academic learning time'' from ''engaged time'' in terms of the easiness of the task — a task is deemed easy when 20 percent or fewer errors are noted for a student engaged with work pages, tests, or classroom exercises. Although this figure of 20 percent has an empirical base (the correlation between achievement and academic learning time is high above this level of easiness), it does seem rather arbitrary in so far as insight about the magic of the figure is absent. Students encountering material for the first time might make a considerable number of errors, but if they are making considerable efforts to understand the material then surely one could claim that they are participating fully. On the other hand, a student making zero errors again and again on very similar materials might score highly in terms of academic engagement but be learning very little. The problem this raises is that of quality of participation.

The second problem, not fully dealt with by Berliner, is that of recognizing true participation. How does one know that the pupil looking out of the window, at first sight day-dreaming, is not actually working on a problem? Or how does one know that a pupil who is listening and watching, at first sight silently undertaking the same tasks as those more actively involved, hasn't his or her mind elsewhere? Can one recognize participation? In this respect there is perhaps an irony in the findings reported by Berliner. If the link between true participation and learning is as obvious as I have suggested, then the positive correlations obtained could be interpreted as evidence that it is indeed possible to recognize true participation!

In summary then, although it seems that one can make a case for participation being of crucial importance, two major problems remain: the problem of quality and the problem of recognition. Both these problems have the same thing in common. To recognize them is to declare that it is what is happening inside the pupil's mind, the covert experience of the pupil, which is important, rather than what we can see, the overt actions.

Assessing the Quality of Pupil Participation

A pupil is certainly active mentally when reciting his or her tables, but there comes a time when this exercise changes from being a struggle to remember to being a matter of routine repetition. The quality of participation changes as the demand made by the task changes. Unless a task is demanding or stretching, one could fairly conclude that its educational value is limited.

An interesting example of the sort of struggle, indicative of high-quality participation, is provided by Furlong. Furlong made an extended study of a difficult class of low-ability fifteen-year-old girls and sought to gain insights into what was happening from the pupils' points of view (see Box 5.4, page 90).

There comes a point, however, when the task is beyond the child, when it ceases to stretch him or her because of its difficulty. He or she might continue to participate in the sense of listening or even volunteering (guessing) answers to questions, but unless he or she is able to cope to some extent, then one cannot consider that he or she is participating in the full sense. If a task is too demanding, one should also conclude that its educational value is limited.

It seems to me that this discussion of participation is relevant to the attempts teachers make to match tasks to the abilities of their pupils. Since a well-matched

---

Box 5.4   High Quality Participation

''In lessons where the context enabled the girls to 'learn a lot', they would act as a unified group and the whole class was included in the same interaction set. Although they were not always in verbal contact, each girl was aware that the others defined the lesson as one where they could 'learn'. In these circumstances it was irrelevant whether the teacher was 'strict' or 'soft'. Mr. Marks was considered 'strict' and the whole class worked quietly and well. Miss Keen, on the other hand, was 'soft', yet in 'successful' lessons no-one took advantage of this fact. Consider this example of a typing lesson with Miss Keene.

Miss Keene is teaching the girls how to file alphabetically. It is a revision lesson, though evidently the girls do not understand the principles fully.

Miss Keene:	Carol, how would you file 'The Borough of East Hamilton'?
Carol:	Under H. (She obviously does not realize that the name is East Hamilton) . . . .
General Question:	How would you file Miss Mary Brown-Curtis?
Someone:	'C' (Not realizing it is a double-barrelled name).
Carol:	'M' (she is going by the other rule they have just learnt which says that if it does not go under the surname as a person, it must be the name of a company and therefore goes under the first name. She seems to be trying to apply the rules as she understands them, but is still confused) . . . .

Miss Keene goes around the room asking questions . . . .

Carol:	My turn now!
Miss Keene:	20th Century Films Limited.

Carol says 'C', then 'F', applying the rules she knows. But this is a new one. As 20th is short for twentieth it should go under 'T'.

Here the girls are willing to take risks, struggle to understand, and consistently keep applying rules to make sense of what they are being told, even though they make a lot of mistakes. They take into account that others are behaving similarly in choosing to act in this way. (pp. 36–37)

Source: V. Furlong, "Interaction Sets in the Classroom: Towards a Study of Pupil Knowledge," in M. Stubbs and S. Delamont, eds., *Explorations in Classroom Observation* (Chichester: Wiley, 1976), pp. 23–44. Reprinted by permission of John Wiley & Sons, Ltd.,

task involves stretching the mind of the pupil, then teachers might gauge whether a task is too easy or too difficult by looking for evidence of some struggling on the one hand and some coping on the other. Struggling and coping are indications of the quality of participation. We see them manifested in many ways: in tentative replies to a teacher's questions, in puzzled frowns and smiles of success, in crossing out and rewriting, and so on.

They are much in evidence in the following discussion between two boys (Barnes, 1976).

The boys had been given
the apparatus shown in the
diagram and instructed to
'Blow into the straw strongly
for as along as you can' and
then to observe what happened.
(The air pressure inside
the flask is raised and sends
a jet of water into the air.)

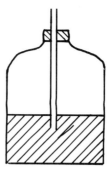

54.S	. . . I want to know though Glyn, when this . . . you know when this experiment three . . . .
55.G	Yes
56.S	You know when we blow down the straw . . .
57.G	Yes.
56.S (cont'd.)	. . . and the water comes up . . .
58.G	Yes.
56.S (cont'd.)	Well watch, and I'll do it again.
59.G	Not too much, then.
60.S	Yes, how come though, when it does come out . . . I think some comes out by this straw here?
61.G	Oh well, that's 'cos it's not been tightly fixed . . . most likely.
62.S	Yes. Well how come it doesn't make any bubbles at the bottom? Watch it, it doesn't.
63.G	Blow . . . it does make bubbles . . . look . . . see bubbles . . . coming up.
64.S	Mmm . . . yes . . . that's interesting.
65.G	Here, watch.
66.S	Yes . . . Now what? . . . Eee that's interesting.
66.G	That's because . . . aah — oah (clearing throat) . . . you've got no air pressure there to force the water out, so . . . (inaudible).
68.S	So what happens if you put both fingers on it? If you put a finger on each end what would happen? (p.46)

Source: D. Barnes, *From Communication to Curriculum* (Harmondsworth: Penguin, 1976). Reprinted by permission of the author.

Such struggling and coping may only become apparent over a period of time. Michael Armstrong (1980) provides a nice example of Paul's struggle to draw. Armstrong writes:

"He (Paul) returned to his drawings towards the end of the afternoon, partly at my instigation. I was anxious that he should achieve at least some success in his efforts to draw the mayfly larva. By clearing up time he had finally managed to complete a drawing of the larva though he was not really pleased with it . . . . Paul persistently refused to add the legs, however, complaining that he couldn't make out their proper shape and position; in the end I had to draw them for him myself." (p. 146)

Source: M. Armstrong, *Closely Observed Children* (London: Writers and Readers in Association with Chameleon, 1980). Reprinted by permission of the author.

And four days later,

"After a general look at the tank which revealed that one of the dragonfly nymphs was already dead, he fished out one of the large waterboatman and placed it in the small inspection jar. Then, without any suggestion from Stephen or myself, he drew it, considerably enlarged, filling most of a sheet of A5 paper as Monday's drawings had. There could not have been a more striking contrast between the way in which he set to work drawing the waterboatman today and the way in which he had tried to draw the mayfly larva at the start of the week. Today he drew quickly and confidently; nothing was torn up, little rubbed out, and there seemed few problems over the proportions of the drawing or the details of the creature being drawn. He didn't once summon Stephen or myself to his assistance and he was dismissive about my one suggestion, towards the end of his drawing, not so much because he disagreed with it — it was about the drawing of the waterboatman's front legs — as because I was interrupting him in a process of thought and action which he was perfectly happy to finish off for himself uninterrupted. By 10 o'clock or thereabouts the drawing was done: a very rapid piece of work for Paul." (Inquiry 5.6)
(pp. 155–56)

Recognizing Participation

It may well be that teachers are really quite good at recognizing whether or not pupils are participating. It would be interesting to know. Some evidence that they could would be gained if a group of teachers interpreted pupil's actions the same way. High inter-observer reliability would encourage one to be optimistic.

In order to probe this problem a group of twelve teachers first conceptually clarified the meaning of participation. Four different levels of participation were distinguished:

(1) Mind actively engaged in desired learning; for example, struggling to solve a problem.

(2) Mind casually engaged in desired learning; for example, listening, but not critically, to another student's contribution.

(3) Following the progress of the lesson *without* being engaged in desired learning; for example, getting out a book.

(4) Not following the progress of the lesson; for example, talking and thinking about the football game.

Retrospectively, very little attempt was made to further clarify these levels by adding to the list of examples of each and resolving borderline cases. Further, no training was given in using the scheme. We might, for instance, have viewed a recording of a pupil in action and discussed our interpretations of his or her level of participation.

The twelve teachers then viewed a video-recording of a seven-and-a-half-minute extract from a grade 6 math lesson on the subtraction of fractions. The camera had been focussed on a boy and a girl. At half-minute intervals the teachers noted the behavior of the students (for example, chewing lip, looking around, bent over work) and interpreted the level of participation of each. (At the twenty-five second mark, a five-second count down was called out and the teachers related their answers to the last second before the tape was stopped.) The results obtained are shown in the table (Box 5.5).

Box 5.5 Teachers' Estimates of Participation Levels

Participation of the boy

Time (min.)	Teacher's Initials											
	DM	GF	GM	MW	KF	HW	PH	KJ	DW	RC	RP	JR
½	4	2	2	3	1	2	2	?	4	2	2	2
1	2	3	4	4	3	2	2	3	4	2	3	4
1½	1	2	4	3	4	1	1	1	3	1	1	2
2	4	3	3	4	4	3	1	3	2	2	2	2
2½	4	3	2	2	2	1	1	1	2	1	1	1
3	1	2	2	3	1	1	1	1	2	1	1	1
3½	1	3	2	2	1	1	1	1	2	1	1	2
4	3	2	2	2	1	1	1 or 3	2	2	1	2	2
4½	1	2	2	2	1	1	1	1	3	1	2	3
5	4	2	2	3	1	2	3	2	3	4	4	3
5½	1	2	1	2	1	1	1	1	2	1	1	2
6	1	2	1	3	1	1	1	1	3	1	1	2
6½	4	2	2	2	2	3	2	1	3	4	2	4
7	1	2	1	3	1	1	2	1	3	1	2	2
7½	2	2	1	3	1	1	2	1	3	1	2	2

Box 5.5 — continued

Participation of the girl

Time (min.)	Teacher's Initials											
	DM	GF	GM	MW	KF	HW	PH	KJ	DW	RC	RP	JR
½	3	1	2	3	2	2	1	1	3	2	1	2
1	3	1	1	1	1	1	1	2	3	1	1	1
1½	1	1	1	4	2	1	1	1	2	1	2	2
2	3	2	1	3	1	2	1	2	2	2	3	2
2½	3	3	2	2	1	1	1	3	2	2	1	2
3	1	2	2	3	1	1	1	1	2	1	1	1
3½	4	3	2	3	2	2	1	2	3	3	4	3
4	1	2	2	3	1	1	1	1	2	1	1	2
4½	1	2	1	4	1	1	1	1	2	1	1	2
5	1	2	1	4	2	1	1	1	2	1	1	2
5½	1	2	1	2	2	1	1	1	3	1	1	2
6	1	2	1	3	1	1	1	1	3	1	1	2
6½	1	2	1	3	1	1	1	1	3	1	1	2
7	1	2	1	3	1	1	1	1	3	1	2	2
7½	4	2	2	2	1	2	1	2	3	1	2	3

We didn't find the results did much for our egos, but neither did we find them demoralizing. They did prompt a number of interesting conclusions, questions, and possibilities:

(i) On the whole there was a good level of participation. Threes and fours tended to be the exception rather than the rule. Most disagreement seemed to be between whether participation was at level 1 or level 2.

(ii) What were the pupils doing when the majority rated them as operating at levels 1 or 2? At 5 ½ minutes the boy was busy writing in his notebook (whereas at 5 he had been listening to the teacher and picking up his pencil). Some cues may be more strongly suggestive of participation than others.

(iii) It would have been interesting to have played the tape back to the pupils, stimulating recall of what was going on in their heads at the same points at which we stopped the tape. This might have gone some way to helping us to establish the validity of our interpretations (Inquiry 5.7).

Recognizing participation might be a particularly difficult problem in the case of the passive child. How does one know that the mind of a pupil, who is apparently listening and watching, at first sight silently undertaking the same tasks as those more actively involved, isn't actually elsewhere? Herrick (1981), in his review of communication apprehension, suggests that it is not uncommon for 20 percent of the school population to be anxious about communication — not only in words, but also non-verbally and in the written form. The teacher can gain little or no evidence as to whether these pupils are participating. The problem here then is not so much one of recognizing participation, but rather of recognizing those pupils who are suffering from communication apprehension. Herrick suggests that this might be done by looking for symptoms of communication apprehension or its absence:

- Are the student's vocabulary and pronunciation developed and clear?
- Does the student give an appropriate response in class or volunteer information?
- Does the student have friendships?
- Does the student participate in group discussion?
- Is the student able to describe rather than just express feelings?
- Does the student appear exceptionally nervous when speaking aloud? And so on.

Examining Some Factors Affecting Participation

Span of Attention: We are all aware that our attention waxes and wanes whilst listening to a lecture, watching a film, or writing some notes. Moreover, this personal experience of ours is strongly substantiated by hosts of psychological studies. Amongst these, I have always been most struck by this simple experiment of Trenaman (see McLeish, 1968). He randomly divided a class of adult students, who were studying astronomy, into three groups. They were to listen to a taped lecture by a distinguished speaker; the first group listened to the first fifteen minutes, the second group to the first thirty minutes, and the third group to the whole lecture which was forty-five minutes long. Immediately after hearing the recording, each group was given a sample recall test covering the content they had listened to. Their scores are shown in Table 5.2.

Table 5.2   Recall of Broadcast Talk; Trenaman's Data

Group Hearing	Amount recalled immediately, expressed as a percentage of material heard					
	First 15 mins.	Second 15 mins.	Third 15 mins.	Total	Possible Score	% age
45 mins.	20	24	15	59	300	20%
30 mins.	23	27	—	50	200	25%
15 mins.	41	—	—	41	100	41%

It would be inappropriate to apply generalizations about the span of attention to our own classrooms on the basis of our own experience and of studies such as Trenaman's. Nevertheless, they do sensitize us to the problem and alert us to the challenge of understanding the phenomenon in our specific contexts. In response to this challenge, a grade 5 elementary school teacher chose to make an exploratory study of her class during their silent reading time.

> "Each day after recess we take 15 minutes for silent reading. Sometimes a story from the children's reader is assigned or they may read their library books and the books and magazines available in the classroom. For this assignment on Day 1 and Day 2 no specific story was assigned. On Day 3 a reader story was assigned. (On each day 13 children were present.) A checklist of observable inattentive behaviour was made and the period broken into five 3-minute intervals. As inattentive behaviour was observed the child's name was written in the appropriate slot."

The checklist for Day 1 is shown in Box 5.6 and a graph showing the number of instances of inattentive behaviors recorded in each three-minute intervals is shown in Box 5.7. Amongst her comments and conclusions the teacher mentioned,

> "More inattentive behaviour during the first 9 minutes on Day 2 than on Day 1 and Day 3 . . . this could be due to the fact that the children had indoor recess on that day. Also the children seemed to be excited about the snow. . . . I might also add that the students appear to be more attentive when a story is assigned rather than when they are free to choose their own reading material."
> (Inquiry 5.8)

Holding-Power of the Setting: It is quite evident from the checklist (Box 5.6) that the pupils had different attention-spans: two scarcely embarked upon the reading assignment, two didn't show any signs of inattention. One wonders whether a similar pattern would have appeared had the task been different. The literature certainly suggests that the task does make a difference. Just as one associates attention-span with the individual, Rosenthal (see Kounin and Sherman, 1979, for an excellent summary of his and related work) associated "holding-power" with the setting. Holding-power is to a setting what attention-span is to a child; both describing duration of activity involvement. Rosenthal studied the behavior of preschool children where there was a wide choice of activity. He found that art, role play, books, and sand had highest holding power, and clothing, displays, and vehicles the lowest. These findings prompted speculation as to why this should be the case. Could it be that the appeal of art and sand lies in their containing within them indicators that the child has made some change or progress? Could it be that different settings have a different potential for social interaction? Children were found mostly working alone in the puzzle, clothing, and vehicle settings, but in small groups of two or three in the sand, science props, climber, and book settings. The quality of the social interaction certainly varied from setting to setting, "pro-social" (as opposed to anti-social) behavior occurring most in role play, prepare-clean up, and so on, and least in science props, displays, art, and puzzles. There seems to be no end of ways in which one can associate the holding power of settings with the behavior of the children engaging in them.

Box 5.6 Types of Inattentive Behavior at Different Times

Time Interval
(Minutes)

Type of Inattentive Behavior	0-3	3-6	6-9	9-12	12-15
Day dreaming					
Pencil tapping		Darren B.		Darren B.	
Talking out		Virginia		Darren B. Starr Carlis Mark	Darren B. Carlis Virginia Mark
Throwing things					
Doodling	Paul	Paul		Paul	Paul
Giggling					
Getting out of seats	Starr		Starr	Darren B. Carlis Leslie	Virginia Darren B Leslie Carlis
Cleaning desks					
Making sounds					
Moving in seats			Paul Tracy		Christine
Writing notes	Virginia	Leslie Virginia	Virginia Leslie	Virginia	Virginia
Yawning					
Sleeping					
Eyes wandering	April	Tracy	Darren A.		
Request to leave room	Darren B.				
Grooming					
Shuffling feet					
Spitballs					
Sharpening pencils					
Flipping through pages without reading					

98

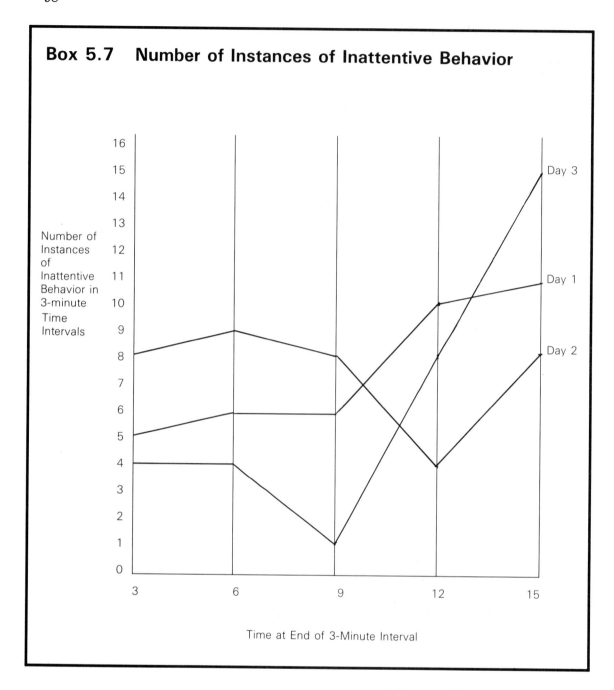

Box 5.7   Number of Instances of Inattentive Behavior

Signal Flow: In more formal settings other factors may well affect participation. Kounin and Gump (1974) made a study of these, again in preschools. They perceived that the children were stimulated by signals from the teacher, the materials, and other pupils, and their findings suggest that single, continuous, unfaltering sources of signals, together with insulation from distracting signals, lead to high levels of involvement (see Table 5.3 for a summary of their findings).

Table 5.3   Involvement in Different Types of Lesson

Lesson Type	Level of Involvement	Examples of Types of Lesson	Characteristics of Lesson Type
1	High	Making individual constructions. E.g., pupils cut out pictures from magazines and paste them to make collage.	Pupils receive a continuous source of signals from the pictures as it develops. They are "insulated" from distractions.
2	Average	Listening to teacher or records.	The teacher or the record provides a single continuous source of signals.
3	Average	Watching a demonstration. E.g., how pop corn is made.	High signal continuity provided by focus on the materials.
4	Low	Recitation. E.g., question and answer discussions dealing with concepts, categories, numbers.	Multiple, shifting signal sources. Continuity of signals sometimes falters.
5	Low	Role play. E.g., playing passengers and driver on a bus. Group discussion. E.g., general talk about community helpers. Group construction. E.g., making a group mural on felt board.	Multiple shifting signal sources. Continuity of signals often falters.
6	Low	Music and movement.	Continuous signal source (e.g., record) but intrusions (distractions) from other pupils' activities.

Intuition suggests that these findings will vary from classroom to classroom, particularly as the age of the pupil increases. However, the idea of relating pupil participation to the flow of signals received from the teacher, the materials, and other pupils could well prove illuminating.

Suggested Inquiries

Inquiry 5.1   Categorizing Pupils Actions

Select an area of the curriculum to study. Select a class or a group of pupils within the class to observe. Decide how best to carry out the observation — a number of options are available:

- setting aside a number of short periods for note making
- inviting a colleague to do the job for you
- audio- or video-recording the lesson

After you have collected the data, categorize it.

Inquiry 5.2   Making Inferences about Pupils Covert Experiences

Re-examine the data you collected in Inquiry 5.1.

Try clustering some of the pupils' actions together in ways which make inferences about the types of thinking and feeling that are going on in the classroom.

Examine the actions of one or two pupils in sequence. What inferences can you make about the thinking and feeling each was experiencing.

Discuss how you might proceed to check the inferences you have made.

Inquiry 5.3 Exploring Small Group Talk

Set up a small group task and record the conversation of two groups (you will need two tape recorders).

Ideas for small group talk (English, p. 50, 1981)

1. Two things to compare and contrast (listing similarities and differences); for example, two maps of the same area, printed at different times: describe all the changes in the landscape between the two. Other examples: two newspaper cuttings, two pictures, two circuits.

2. Something to make; for example, given an insect in a glass tube and some plasticine, make a model of it, with all the joints correct.

3. Finding the thread of an argument; divide a section of a relevant book into parts a few sentences long. Shuffle them so that they do not follow the author's intended sequence. The pupils try to work out the most coherent sequence.

4. Prediction; retype a relevant section of a textbook, leaving blank spaces one or two sentences long. At each stop the readers, in groups, try to decide what the author would have said next.

5. An unfamiliar object; ask them to decide what it is, how it works, what it's made of, etc., stating their evidence. (Examples: old-fashioned fire tongs, a wren's nest, a rosary, a sextant, an old manuscript such as a land contract.)

6. Devising questions; each group devises five questions on the topic they have studied, and decide what would make good answers to these questions. Let them swap and report.

7. Designing something; such as a room, flat, or house, for specified occupants (old people? babies?); how to decorate and furnish a flat for themselves, within a specified budget. (This might need several meetings, with time in between to visit shops, or you might provide old catalogues, or scale cutouts, of common items of furniture.)

8. Drafting a document; such as a manifesto, or a set of rules.

9. Describing games; one member of the group has an object in a box, which he alone sees (a yale key, a foreign coin, a blanket pin, a cup hook . . .?). Without naming it, he tries to describe it clearly to the others. They draw it. Take turns. Afterwards everybody discusses what makes a good description.

10. Imagining other people's points of view; give out a short description of a social situation, such as a parent–teenager row over whether a late night party should be held. Ask the group to describe how each person feels about it (father, mother, teenager).

Source: M. English, "Talking: Does It Help?" in C. R. Sutton, ed., *Communicating in the Classroom* (London: Hodder and Stoughton, 1981). Reprinted by permission of Hodder and Stoughton Educational.

Transcribe short extracts (five to ten minutes) from each group.
(a) Examine each for evidence of exploratory talk. To what can you attribute its presence or absence.
(b) Make a list of similarities and differences between the transcripts. To what features of the task would you attribute these.

Inquiry 5.4 Putting Pupils' Actions in Perspective

The discussion of characteristics of pupils, types of tasks, patterns of pupils' actions, and qualities of products sets the stage for a broadening exploration of their interrelationships.

In this chapter we have examined ways of characterizing pupils' actions (Inquiries 5.1 and 5.2). In the next chapter we examine the characteristics of pupils' work (Inquiry 6.5).

The present challenge is to design a simple inquiry which seeks to relate patterns of pupils' actions with *either* individual differences between pupils *or* types of task *or* qualities of products. On the one hand this might be carried out in the natural classroom setting, on the other it might be carried out under more experimental conditions. Russell Clarke's inquiry into the way in which group size — the way the task was organized — affected pupils' actions tends to fall into the latter category.

Inquiry 5.5 A Reconnaissance of Pupil Participation

This activity is a reconnaissance exercise into your pupils' participation. It is the sort of thing you might do if tackling an action research problem such as "Participation in my classroom is not as high as I would like. What can I do about it?" Invite an observer to monitor one of your classes with participation in mind. The observer might, for example, closely observe the behavior of six pupils. (To expect him or her to be able to observe more might be unrealistic.) Ask the observer to record once a minute what the pupils are doing (for example, by recording the dominant activity of each pupil, over a five-second period, in simple terms such as writing, sharpening a pencil, talking to a neighbor). It might be additionally revealing if you also devise a procedure which allows you later to correlate the pupil's activities with your activities. Alternatively — and preferably because you can review it again and again — set up a video tape-recorder and camera so as to focus on approximately six pupils/places.

There are many ways of processing this data. At a simple level you might compare the time on task for each pupil. You might look at periods in the lesson when there is most off task activity. You might try sorting out the different pupil actions. Perkins (1965), for example, sorted pupil actions into the following categories:

Liswat:	Interested in ongoing work: listening and watching — passive.
Rewr:	Reading and writing: working in assigned area — active.
Hiac:	High activity or involvement: reciting or using large muscles — positive feeling.
Woa:	Intent on work of non-academic type: preschool activity not assigned to be done right then.
Wna:	Intent on work of non-academic type: preparing for work assignment, cleaning out desk, etc.
Swp:	Social, work-oriented-peer: discussing some aspect of schoolwork with classmate.
Swt:	Social, work-oriented-teacher: discussing some phase of work with teacher.
Sf:	Social, friendly: talking to peer on subject unrelated to schoolwork.
Wdl:	Withdrawal: detached, out of contact with people, ideas, classroom situation; day-dreaming.

But other things and other questions may begin to emerge as you study the data — this is what reconnaissance is all about.

Inquiry 5.6   Appraising the Quality of Participation in a Lesson

Make a tape recording of one of your lessons with a view to appraising it in terms of the quality of participation of the pupils. If the lesson involves your moving from pupil to pupil or group to group, wear a neck microphone and carry the recorder with you over your shoulder.

Inquiry 5.7   Recognizing Participation

Review the section on "The Recognition of Participation" and refine the procedure used by the group of teachers. Repeat the process.

Inquiry 5.8   Factors Affecting Participation

Design a range of reconnaissance tasks which enable you to probe the factors which affect participation.

Suggested Readings

Open University. *Curriculum in Action*, Block 2, Unit 2, pp. 5–15. Milton Keynes: Open University press, 1980.

This provides an excellent introduction to the process of observing pupils and making inferences about their behavior. The following units (3 and 4) are also most interesting. They tackle the question, What were they learning? and, How worthwhile was it?

Barnes, D. *From Communication to Curriculum,* Ch. 2. Harmondsworth, Middlesex: Penguin, 1976.

Barnes takes a very close look at a number of small group conversations. This chapter is particularly rich for the inferences he makes.

Bennett, S. N. "Recent Research on Teaching: A Dream, a Belief and a Model." *British Journal of Educational Psychology* 48 (1979): 127–47.

This is a very useful review which emphasizes the work being done on pupil participation. It is a valuable source of reference.

Kounin, J. S., and Sherman, L. W. "School environments (as behaviours settings)." *Theory and Practice,* Vol. XVIII, No. 3 (1979).

An easy to read review of a number of studies concerned with work involvement. These were based on making analyses of video-recordings.

6

Pupils' Covert Experiences

The Meaning of Pupils' Covert Experiences

The phrase "the pupils' covert experiences" is meant to capture what is going on inside the pupils' minds: the thoughts and feelings taking place. It is not the same thing as a learning outcome; a pupil may be attempting to make sense of a paragraph in a book but fail to understand, a pupil may solve a problem but achieve this outcome by guessing.

Stephen Rowland (1984) provides a simple illustration of what I mean by the pupils' covert experiences in his field notes on Laraine writing a story. In these field notes one can distinguish what Laraine was visibly doing, her overt actions (working rapidly, stopping only occasionally), from the outcome of her efforts, her story, and from her mental processes, her covert experiences, which were revealed in the analysis of the interview and the product (see Box 6.1).

In a second example, I have presented my observations of Matthew doing a jigsaw puzzle (see Box 6.2).

Box 6.1 Field Notes and Analysis of Laraine Writing a Story (by S. Rowland)

I came across Laraine towards the end of the afternoon. She was starting a story. Beside her was a picture from a set of picture cards made by Chris Harris to be used as an occasional stimulus for writing. The picture showed a sailing schooner by a quayside. The quayside was deserted except for an old man sitting on an upturned box. He was smoking a clay pipe, with a bottle and glass of whisky at his side. The sun was setting over the sea . . . .

I asked her if she could tell me what was going to happen. She replied she didn't know yet but would find out as she went along.

She worked rapidly, stopping only occasionally to hear about the problems her friend Karen was having with her sewing. I sat with her quietly during most of the writing, and, by the end of the afternoon, she had finished.

Box 6.1 — *continued*

The Sailer and his Stories
This story is called. The baby Seal.

Long ago said the sailer to the little boy I was on my boat called ''Merry Men.'' All of a sudden I could hear a little noise. So I looked around and saw a little baby seal, looking so sad and unhappy that I picked him up and took him to my little hut on the boat. I gave him my last drop of milk and a little bit of fish that I caught that day. We got on so well together that he stayed with me for 4 days on the fifth day we went ashore to get some food. All so we got some fresh fist for the baby seal. When I got back to the boat I called the seal because it was dinner time. No seal came So I called again, again no seal. So I looked around the boat Still no seal. I was so upset that I went to my hut. When I opened the door a hole lot of seals jumped on me. So you have found your friends. But there was no ansew. So off they went all in a line. I think they are all happy now.

the end.

* * *

The little boy, to whom Laraine's sailor tells his story, is not in the picture. When I asked her about this she said that really he was not telling his story to a little boy at all, he was just ''going over it in his mind.''

When she had finished the piece, I asked her at what stage had she thought up the ending. She replied that she had stopped to think for a long time after ''Still no seal'' before realizing what the ending would be . . . .

On reading the piece over in the classroom I was particularly struck by the ending. The man's being ''upset'' at not finding the seal, followed by his disappointment at the seal not answering his ''So you have found your friends'', then the transformation into a happy ending. Talking this part over with Laraine, it was quite clear that she intended the man to feel first this sorrow and then also the gladness that the seal would now be happy. One is left with a feeling not so much of sorrow suddenly transformed into unequivocal gladness, but rather with a kind of ''coming-to-terms'' with the two feelings — sorrow at losing the seal plus gladness at his happiness — as is demanded by the realization of the seal's right to freedom. ''So you have found your friends'' is the ''philosophical'' state of mind in resolution of the conflict.

The style of this last section fits in clearly with that of the rest of the story. The emotions are underplayed, particularly in the short sentences ''No seal came.'' The subject is not treated with the kind of sentiment which so often accompanies stories written for children concerning these feelings. While this lack of sentiment fits with the ''philosophical'' outcome of the story, it is also consistent with the context in which it is set. A hardened old sailor is likely to tell stories and to reflect upon his experiences with wisdom gained from these experiences rather than by an appeal to sentiment. Laraine's writing was initially stimulated by a picture. The climate of this picture was one of solitude and reminiscence. She absorbs this climate and soon becomes involved in considering the essentially solitary nature of the sailor's life (or, perhaps, of life in general). Where a relationship with another being begins to form, the sailor realizes that he must control his own possessiveness. Laraine did not set out to tackle this problem but, as the story developed, she was led to consider these fundamental aspects of human relationships and does so with considerable skill and insight. (pp. 112-14)

Source: S. Rowland, *The Enquiring Classroom* (London: Falmer Press, 1984). Reprinted by permission of Falmer Press Limited.

Box 6.2 Observations of Matthew Doing a Jigsaw Puzzle

Matthew is nearly four. He enjoys doing simple jigsaw puzzles and has a collection of about six. The other evening we decided to do a puzzle together. It contained about twenty pieces. Instead of participating, offering suggestions, picking up pieces, encouraging him, etc., I decided to observe.

He first selected a piece with a straight edge and placed the edge along the line of the inside of the lid of the box which he was using as a tray. This was a departure from his previous practice. He now seemed to have got hold of the rule that straight edges go on the outside. What interested me was the fact that he put it in the top right hand corner; it wasn't a corner piece. And moreover, it seemed to me as if it belonged to the bottom of the picture — it looked like grass. After fitting in a few pieces he realized this too and turned the box-lid around. It puzzled me that in the early stages it did not seem to worry him as to whether the picture was upside down or not. It certainly worried me — I have learned to look for clues for the way pieces are oriented and use ideas about the vertical and horizontal for help. (E.g. tree trunks go up and down and are thicker at the bottom.)

Next, he selected a corner piece. He placed it against the edge but centrally along the side!

Progress was rather slow and he invited me to join in. I made a token response and this seemed to be enough to encourage him to continue.

The last but one piece was like an octopus. Spontaneously he began to put it in the right spot but before slotting it in place, changed his mind and began turning it round and round. Strange really, because the color match made its orientation obvious. He seemed to have devised a way of recognizing which piece goes where (albeit that since he's done the puzzle before, he could have remembered it) and of recognizing the possibility of turning pieces around if they don't fit at first. But even though we had on previous occasions looked for red bits or blue bits which might go into the red or blue spot, this strategy doesn't seem to have taken root (at least it wasn't evident on this occasion with this puzzle). Upon finishing the puzzle, he seemed distinctly pleased with himself and suggested that we should do another. I agreed. He chose one and to my surprise scarcely used any of the rules he had earlier employed. He seemed to do it from memory.

In this instance the child was successful in completing the puzzle. However, it is my contention that this overall outcome is of less significance than some of the processes that he was using. There is evidence that he was trying to use the rule that pieces with straight edges go along outside the puzzle, and that he thinks turning a piece round and round is a good way of finding out if it fits. He also showed a little lack of confidence in his own ability to complete the puzzle.

The boundary line between processes and outcomes sometimes seems rather hazy. Nevertheless, I think it is important to try to distinguish between mental events (processes) and learning (changes in the mental structure). According to Neisser (1976), "perceiving is the basic cognitive activity out of which all others must emerge," and he postulates that learning takes place as a child moves through the perceptual cycle shown in Figure 6.1.

Figure 6.1   The Perceptual Cycle

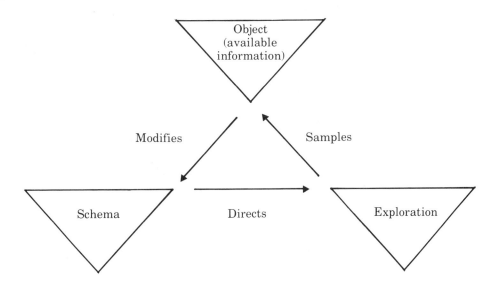

Source: From *Cognition and Reality* by Ulrich Neisser. W. H. Freeman and Co. © 1976.

If one applies this to the case of Matthew, we can see evidence of his "schema" *directing* his actions. He initially chose the piece with the straight edge, a strategy which he had presumably learned from earlier explorations. He then appeared to continue the exploration by *sampling* different strategies; trying the corner piece along the outside, turning a piece round and round, etc. Sometimes the strategies worked, sometimes they didn't. It is possible, although we don't know for sure, that in *modifying* his strategies he might have modified his schema. This would seem to depend on the extent to which he was reflecting upon what he was doing as opposed to proceeding through random trial and error. Either way, I would suggest that the task of doing the puzzle could be considered educationally valuable, since in order to complete it he would probably have exercised a variety of mental processes. We have some evidence that he was exercising these, albeit that he might not have increased his competence.

To further distinguish between the pupils' covert experiences and learning outcomes, let us examine a study by Bloom (1953), in which he was concerned to evaluate the relative strengths and weaknesses of the lecture and the discussion methods. Traditionally, this problem had been approached by comparing the pupils' test performances, that is, measuring the learning outcomes attributed to the different teaching methods. Bloom, however, considered this approach insufficiently sensitive and proceeded to examine the pupils' thinking in the two different types of situations using the technique of stimulated recall. Shortly after a lecture or discussion, the pupils were invited to relive their experiences by listening to recorded extracts. They were then interviewed about their thought processes. The results are illuminating. For example, during discussions, the pupils thought more about themselves, particularly with regard to those thoughts which were expressive of feelings of adequacy or inadequacy. During lectures, more thoughts were directed towards trying to comprehend the subject matter at a simple level. During lectures, there were twice as many irrelevant thoughts. And during discussions there were eight times as many thoughts trying to solve problems and synthesize the subject matter.

I hope this not only makes the distinction between the pupils' covert experiences and learning outcomes clearer, but also provides some indication of the value of exploring what is going on in pupils' minds.

The Emergence of Interest in Pupils' Covert Experiences

Of all the processes which constitute the core of the teaching and learning, the pupils' covert experiences probably remain the most mysterious, the least well defined, and the least researched. Yet I sense that this area is emerging as a new focus for inquiry.

John Holt in 1967 sharpened the focus in his book *How Children Learn*. Here is an extract from the foreword.

> "This book is more about children than about child psychology. I hope those who read it will come to feel, or feel more than when they opened it, that children are interesting and worth looking at. I hope that when they look they will notice many things they never noticed before, and in these find much food for thought. I want to whet their curiosity and sharpen their vision, even more than to add to their understanding; to make them sceptical of old dogmas, rather than give them new ones.
>
> The human mind, after all, is a mystery, and in large part, will probably always be so. It takes even the most thoughtful, honest, and introspective person many years to learn even a small part of what goes on in his own mind. How, then, can we be sure about what goes on in the mind of another?" (p. 9)

He then proceeded to advocate careful observation and suspended judgment as two essential ingredients of inquiry.

> "My aim in writing it is not primarily to persuade educators and psychologists to swap new doctrines for old, but to persuade them to *look* at children, patiently, repeatedly, respectfully, and to hold off making theories and judgements about them until they have in their minds what most of them do not now have — a reasonably accurate model of what children are like . . . . We must clear them [our minds] of preconceived notions, we must suspend judgement, we must open ourselves to the situation, take in as much data as we can, and wait patiently for some kind of order to appear out of the chaos." (p. 160)

Throughout the book, Holt describes his observations of people, young and old, and from them makes inferences in terms of thoughts and feelings they are experiencing. I found this example particularly charming.

"Recently Lisa has started to play fierce games. She bares her teeth, growls, roars, rushes at me. I pretend to be afraid, and cower behind a chair. It can go on for some time. From this, and many other things she does, it seems as if she feels a *Me* inside her, growing stronger, doing things, demanding things. Any game that makes that *Me* seem more powerful must be a good game." (p. 20)

Source: Excerpted from the book *How Children Learn* by John Holt. Copyright © 1983 by John Holt. Reprinted by permission of Delacorte Press/Seymour Lawrence.

In 1970, Rothkopf coined the phrase "mathemagenic behaviors." In his terms, these are the behaviors which give birth to learning; in ours, they roughly correspond to the pupils' covert experiences. For example, the pupil, when learning through reading, may undertake a variety of mathemagenic behaviors: scanning the material, translating it into interval speech, segmenting it, processing it by relating one sentence to another, and so on.

During the seventies, there was a surge of interest in such "mediating processes" as those identified by Rothkopf. Mediating processes were defined by Levie and Dickie (1973) as "the implicit human processes that mediate instructional stimuli and learning outcomes." The scope of the interest in them was evident in Doyle's (1977) review, and the importance of research into them was underlined by Winne and Marx (1977):

"Specifically we see the mental life of both teachers and students in classrooms as critical items to be studied if we are to understand the process by which teaching influences students' learning." (p. 670)

Winne and Marx portrayed their concern in diagram form (see Figure 6.2).

Figure 6.2   An Expanded Conception of Research on Teaching

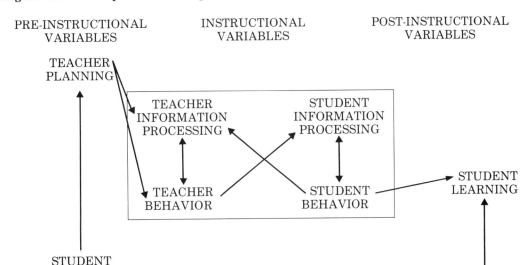

Source: P. H. Winne and R. W. Marx, "Reconceptualizing Research on Teaching," *Journal of Educational Psychology* 69 (1977): 668–78. Copyright © 1977 by the American Psychological Association. Reprinted by permission of the authors.

The central portion of this diagram resembles the central concern of this book: the relating of the teacher's frame of reference to the teacher's actions to the pupil's actions to the pupil's covert experiences. They drove their point home in no uncertain terms:

> "The point of this discussion is that without a better understanding of the unobserved and, heretofore, undescribed internal events in the teaching-learning environment, generating an accurate and efficient pattern of research on teaching is too chancy. The body of prior research must now take account of the mediating phenomena such as teacher decision-making strategies and student cognitive processes and structures to achieve a sufficiently accurate description of what happens in teaching and learning from teaching. Otherwise, the distance to be spanned in inferential leaps about teacher effects would be too great for generating sufficiently accurate and generalizable statements about teaching." (p. 671)

Now in the eighties, the momentum continues. A substantial part of the Schools Council's Programme Two — Helping Individual Teachers to Become More Effective — is applying action-research methodology to the study of pupils' covert experiences. It will be interesting to see what emerges from Rudduck and Hull's work at the Centre for Applied Research in Education, University of East Anglia, England, and from Rowland's continued work with the Leicestershire Insights into Learning Project.

Procedures for Uncovering Pupils' Covert Experiences

So far, I have tried to clarify what I mean by the phrase "the pupils' covert experiences," and to give some indication of the growth of interest in this area. But how can the concept be applied in the analysis of teaching? The immediate challenge is to observe classes in action with a view to recognizing different types of thinking and feeling taking place.

As a preliminary to undertaking some field research, small groups of about four teachers video recorded their own behavior when tackling some of the problems in de Bono's (1967) *The Five Day Course in Thinking.* (One set of problems is shown in Box 6.3.)

Subsequently, the teachers replayed the video-recordings and tried to identify the thought processes which were taking place. Evident in the discussions they had was the interplay between what they evidently said and did and what they said was going on inside their minds — the interplay between observation and introspection.

de Bono made explicit some of the types of thinking which he anticipated the problem-solving task demanded: logical thinking, modifying previous ideas, establishing general principles, original thinking, choosing an approach, visualizing, becoming confident, feeling desolate. We found it valuable to view the recording that we had made again, using these categories as a checklist, and noting clear examples of each. This procedure raised two interesting issues:

Box 6.3 Problems in "Sequential Thinking" (after de Bono)

Each problem requires that six blocks of equal size be arranged in accordance with certain requirements. These requirements consist of the way in which the blocks touch one another.

1. A block is said to touch another block when some **flat** surface or part of a flat surface of one block is in contact with a **flat** surface or part of a flat surface of the other block. Contact through an edge or corner does not count. In the diagram below the two blocks are **not** considered to be touching.

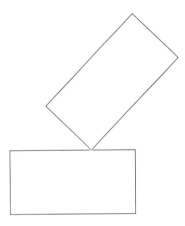

2. The arrangement must be self-supporting.
In order to be sure that the solutions are absolutely correct, it is suggested that each block be taken in turn and its contacts counted.

Problem 1:   Arrange the six blocks so that each touches two and only two other blocks. There are several possible solutions. If one solution is found with ease, then the other solutions can be sought.
Problem 2:   Arrange the six blocks so that each touches three and only three others.
Problem 3:   Arrange the six blocks so that each touches four and only four others.
Problem 4:   Arrange the six blocks so that each touches five others.

Source: E. de Bono, *The Five Day Course in Thinking* (Harmondsworth: Penguin, 1967). Reprinted by permission of the author.

1. The ability of teachers (de Bono in this case) to anticipate the demands which would be made by a task.
2. The desirability of approaching observation and analysis with preconceived categories, as opposed to allowing the categories to emerge from the data.
Following this preliminary exercise, the teachers undertook a variety of small-scale observation exercises in their own classrooms (Inquiry 6.1).

Good teachers often find themselves making inferences about how pupils are thinking and feeling. A pupil doesn't seem to understand something; the teacher tries to explain it another way and watches the reaction. A pupil gets stuck with a problem; the teacher asks a few questions to try to find out where the sticking point is. A pupil gives up trying to tackle a task; the teacher tries to simplify it. A pupil makes light of a task; the teacher suggests something more demanding. Such exchanges, I would maintain, are fundamental to good teaching. Each involves the teacher trying to read the pupils' mind and acting in response. Frequently each involves just one pupil and is often very quick. Through experience, over the years, teachers build up an intuitive understanding of what is difficult, what seems to interest pupils, and so on. In short, they develop an understanding of how pupils think, that is, of their covert experiences when they undertake certain tasks.

But what exactly is involved in gaining this understanding? If the procedures used by teachers were made explicit, if these were developed and extended, and if these were used deliberately, then it might result in our understanding being enhanced. This section focusses on this process of diagnosing pupils' covert experiences and discusses four types of procedures which might be of use to teachers who wish to stand back somewhat from the give and take of classroom interaction and reflect upon what might be happening inside their pupils' heads. I have grouped these procedures under the following headings:
- Observing pupils' actions
- Identifying problems and difficulties which the pupils encounter
- Examining pupils' work
- Interviewing pupils

Observing Pupils' Actions

I would guess that many inferences are made from the simple close observation of the pupils' verbal and non-verbal behavior. What pupils say may be a true articulation of how they are arranging ideas in their heads. Tones of voice, and other ways of saying something, may reflect feelings they have. The expressions on their faces may be indicative of what is going on inside. At the beginning of chapter 5 we discussed how pupils' actions can be categorized in order to throw light on the pupils' covert experiences. Here we are challenged to extend this procedure by setting out to make inferences about their thinking and feeling. As teachers, the thoughts and feelings which concern us most are those related to learning. It is a rewarding exercise to monitor the actions of a group of pupils and then to ask about each action, "What might the pupil have been learning?" (Open University, 1980) (Inquiry 6.2)

Identifying Problems and Difficulties

In introducing these procedures I suggested that teachers learn about their pupils' thinking by being sensitive to the problems and difficulties they have. If this is true, you might be able to learn a lot about your pupils' thinking from systematic studies. Ganshow (1981) set out to show how much could be discovered about children's learning strategies for spelling through error pattern analysis. She began by listing the errors present in a sample of pupils' scripts. Her data for one pupil is shown in Table 6.1.

Table 6.1 Pupil's Spelling Errors

Misspelled word	Correct Spelling
coff	cough
boul	bowl
here	hear
resight	recite
two	too
their	there
highbirnate	hibernate
tuff	tough

The next step involved looking for patterns. A number are evident in the data. Once the patterns of errors have been identified, one is in a good position to speculate about the child's thinking. For example, in this case, she might have thought that her memory of sounds of known words will always help her attack new words, such as hibernate. Error pattern analysis has been used in a variety of situations and it could conceivably be a valuable tool for teachers in many others.

The same sort of procedure could be applied to what pupils say. It would be interesting to tape record a lesson and to list instances where pupils were making mistakes or otherwise experiencing some difficulty. Applying pattern analysis to this data might provide the basis for fruitful inference-making (Inquiry 6.3).

In their studies of pupils' progress in learning science, Harlen and her co-workers (1977) carefully recorded pupils' tackling a variety of tasks. The pupils often worked in pairs so that inferences could be made from what they said to each other as well as what else they did. The researchers were particularly concerned to identify differences between pupils when engaged on such tasks as building a paper bridge across two bricks strong enough to hold a toy car.

By comparing the pupils with each other, focussing on the problems and difficulties they encountered, the researchers mapped out the pupils' thinking along a number of dimensions: curiosity, originality, willingness to co-operate, perseverance, open mindedness, self-criticism, responsibility, independence in thinking, observing, problem solving, raising questions, exploring, finding patterns in observations, communicating verbally, applying learning, cause and effect, classification and the concepts of weight, length, area, volume, time, and life cycle. Subsequently, they proceeded to relate typical problems and difficulties to a developmental sequence along each dimension. For example, they perceived perseverance as proceeding through three major stages:

Stage (i)   Gives up a task at the first sign of difficulty, or if his first attempt does not succeed.

Stage (ii)   Sticks at a task as long as there is some external incentive in the form of encouragement or ready help. Keeps to the same approach even when it is clearly unsuccessful, using more effort than thought.

Stage (iii)   Persists despite difficulties or the amount of effort required, as long as there is evident chance of progress towards a goal. Changes his approach if unsuccessful but does not give up.

In problem solving, they noted the following stages:

Stage (i)   Generally unable to approach a problem without help.
Stage (ii)   Tries one or more ways of tackling a problem without much forethought as to which is likely to be relevant.
Stage (iii)   Identifies the various steps which have to be taken and tries to work through them systematically.

Further studies along these lines in other subject areas with other pupils could well provide teachers with greater insight into how their pupils think (Inquiry 6.4).

Examining Pupils' Work

It is possible to examine what the pupils have done and to make inferences about the type of thinking they used in doing it. Armstrong (1980) does this when he writes extended sympathetic critiques of pupils' work. In the following discussion of Simon's story, "My rabbit's adventures," his style resembles that of a critic in a literary magazine (see Box 6.4).

In adopting the style of a critic, Armstrong is in essence comparing the skills of the pupil with those of the community of practitioners and scholars. His commentary examines the gap between the two. Each piece of work is characterized by the presence of some qualities and the noticeable absence of others. This procedure is a useful way of pinpointing the type of thinking and sensitivities the pupil is employing. Moreover, considerable insight might be gained if this form of criticism is extended to cover the work of a number of pupils within the same class.

An alternative and somewhat easier procedure for examining pupils' work is to make comparisons between them. Let us suppose that you set a group of pupils a task. Select any three of the products and ask yourself, "In what way are two similar and the third different?" (You might, for example, be struck by two being neat and the other being untidy.) Examine the three again and ask the question once more. (On second viewing, you might notice one developing his or her ideas more logically than the other two.) Repeat until nothing else of consequence strikes you. Now select another three scripts and review these in the same way. More features of the pupils' work might catch your attention. This procedure is called "triadic elicitation" and was developed by Kelly (1955) in order to discover the constructs people use to make sense of the world. Constructs are bipolar concepts, such as neat–untidy or logically developed–without logical flow. If you employ the procedure to examine the products of pupils' work, you could discover the constructs you use to make sense of their products. It should then be possible to make inferences from these constructs about the type of thinking and feeling the pupils were experiencing when engaged with the task (Inquiry 6.5).

In passing, I imagine Britton (1971) might have used a similar procedure to this when he categorized the language of two thousand pupils' scripts as having one of three major functions: the transactional, the expressive, and the poetic. He later proceeded to speculate about the role of language in education and saw expressive language as having a key role to play. Expressive language is one which people naturally use when presenting their view of things, and when they are rehearsing the growing points of their formulation and analysis of experience.

Box 6.4 A Critique of a Pupil's Work

''My rabbit's adventures.

I'm Tufty the snow rabbit and I'll tell you the adventure I had one winter's morning last year when I was collecting carrots. I saw Farmer Brown walking down the field with his shotgun! I was so scared I picked up all my carrots and ran into a cave. I accidentally ran through a passageway and tripped over and hurt my little foot, but luckily another rabbit came hopping up, a black rabbit, and he said ''I'm Simon's rabbit''. I said ''Who's Simon?''. ''Simon W,'' Messy said. Just then I heard footsteps. ''Don't be afraid'' Messy said, ''it's only Simon.'' I said ''Let's go and meet him then.'' Simon said ''Got yourself a friend, then?'' ''What a shame, you've hurt your little paw'' he said and took a handkerchief from his pocket and wrapped it round my paw and tightened it so it wouldn't fall off. ''We better get going. I've got a trolley with a box of hay on.'' He picked my carrots up and put them in the box, then he picked me up and put me in the box, then he picked Messy up and put him in with me, and we all went home.''

*   *   *

The more I thought about it the more Simon's story intrigued me. I had not expected it to end as and when it did but on reflection the ending was both natural and necessary; for the most striking feature of the story is the way in which Simon manages to convey so much in so little space, a complete adventure in a bare 200 words. As Simon had suggested when describing to me the plot, the story is about making friends. It is told by a rabbit but its concern is with human feelings and human relationships. After introducing his narrator he sets the scene with a simple, exact detail, ''one winter's morning last year when I was collecting carrots''. The panic flight follows, its cause made more dramatic by the device of punctuating the word shot gun with an exclamation mark, originally two marks. One thing leads to another in quick succession, the flight to the fall, the fall to the chance encounter with the black rabbit and thereby to the introduction to Simon whose kindness is at once confirmed by the care with which he binds up the damaged paw with his handkerchief. It is a sign of Simon, the author's, attention to detail that at this point he should add that Simon, the character in the story, ''tightened'' the handkerchief ''so it wouldn't fall off'', a detail which succinctly expresses the character's tender concern. That is the end of the adventure, the act of bandaging signifying the establishment of friendship. All that remains is for the three characters to return home together, a resolution which Simon achieves neatly in the long, slow final sentence with its cumulative ''thens'' and ''ands''.

I do not wish to overstate Simon's achievement. The story was slight, yet it was also skillful and its skill was not accidental or unaccountable. Simon pondered the story as he wrote; its form and its language reflect the care with which he composed it. (pp. 32–33)

Source: M. Armstrong, *Closely Observed Children* (London: Writers and Readers in Association with Chameleon, 1980). Reprinted by permission of the author.

Interviewing Pupils

It is common for teachers to stop and talk to individual and groups whilst they are working in their seats. And for their part, pupils accept this as being a perfectly natural part of the classroom routine. Much can be gained from recording these exchanges. When doing so, I have found it helpful to use a radio-microphone. It is less obtrusive than a cassette recorder. A tiny microphone is clipped to your clothing and leads to a transmitter, the size of a cigarette carton, which can be held or simply slipped into a pocket. The sort of questions you might want to ask may be rather more open and personal than usual: instead of "What's the capital of France?," it might be more revealing to ask "Do *you* remember the capital of France?"; instead of "Why didn't Hitler invade England?," it might be more revealing to ask "What do *you* suppose Hitler's reasons for not invading England were?"

All the procedures outlined so far simply involve making deliberate and extending common classroom practice. However, interviewing pupils can go beyond this. You might wish, for instance, to discuss openly certain features of a lesson with your pupils so as to get their view on what was happening. Stimulated recall is a powerful way of doing just this. It involves playing back a recording (audio or video) of the whole or parts of a lesson and inviting pupil discussion of it. The discussion itself is recorded.

Another valuable procedure, currently being used by Rudduck and her co-workers in the Schools Council Programme 2, is to invite pupils to critically discuss their own performance. The pupils, for example, might be asked to rate their musical performance or their separate performances in tasks such as solving a problem or writing a report. In doing so, it is anticipated that they will reveal some of the thoughts that were passing through their heads when they were undertaking the tasks. In some respects, the procedure resembles stimulated recall, but it is less formal and more natural (Inquiry 6.6).

Perspective on Pupils' Covert Experiences

If you use any of the procedures described in the previous section, then you will likely identify a wide range of thinking and feeling processes. Here, we will put these findings in perspective by trying to answer two questions:
(i) How valid are the findings?
(ii) How can they be used in making appraisals?

Validity

We can never know for sure what is on someone else's mind. We need to be cautious and circumspect. John Holt's (1969) delightful anecdotes underline this need. Pupils' actions can be misleading.

> "This fear leads her to other strategies, which other children use as well. She knows that in a recitation period the teacher's attention is divided among twenty students. She also knows the teacher's strategy of asking questions of students who seem confused, or not paying attention. She therefore feels safe waving her hand in the air, as if she were bursting to tell the answer, whether she really knows

it or not. This is her safe way of telling me that she, at least, knows all about whatever is going on in class. When someone else answers correctly she nods her head in emphatic agreement. Sometimes she even adds a comment, though her expression and tone of voice show that she feels this risky. It is also interesting to note that she does not raise her hand unless there are at least half a dozen other hands up.

Sometimes she gets called on. The question arose the other day, 'What is half of forty-eight?' Her hand was up; in the tiniest whisper she said, 'Twenty-four'. I asked her to repeat it. She said, loudly, 'I said,' then whispered 'twenty-four.'" (p. 27)

Source: Excerpted from the book *How Children Fail* Revised Edition by John Holt. Copyright © 1964, 1982 by John Holt. Reprinted by permission of Delacorte Press/Seymour Lawrence.

Seeking corroboration, checking up, can help to increase our certainty. One of the most powerful ways of doing this is to use a procedure called triangulation. Triangulation is a procedure used by surveyors to locate a point on a map. In classroom research it is used to substantiate the validity of a point of view. If an observer, the teacher, and the pupils perceive an event in the same way, then we can be reasonably certain that their viewpoint is the true one.

Elliott (1976-77) provided the neat example of triangulation shown in Box 6.5 on page 118 (see also Figure 6.3 on page 123). A teacher and his pupils have been discussing the results of experiments into plant growth. Data about the classroom interaction was collected by tape recording the lesson. This was supplemented by field notes made by an observer. Data about the teacher's intentions (the teacher's frame of reference) and data about pupils' covert experiences were gathered by the observer in two separate interviews. Triangulation is a discomforting procedure, particularly if it dwells upon discrepancy and involves an outside observer. But this is a nettle to be grasped by the teacher who is concerned to extend his or her professionalism through the monitoring of his or her own practice (Inquiry 6.7).

There is a second aspect to validity which is important. This arises from the way in which we come to understand and talk about people's thoughts and feelings. When we make inferences about others' thoughts and feelings we often associate their behavior in a situation with the thoughts and feelings we have had in a similar situation. Our understanding of them often reflects the understanding we have about ourselves — one which has been developed through introspection. When we discuss their thoughts and feelings, we use the language of our culture. We have developed words and phrases which we use to describe the intangible. Language provides a means of sharing our inner experiences.

The subculture of the psychologists, whose concern is to study the mind, has developed a specialist or technical language. This aims to refine and enhance everyday talk: psychologists are careful to define what they mean by understanding; complex processes like problem solving are analysed into components. Hence some of the subjectivity may be removed and some precision may be added if we relate what we say to what they say. It may be useful, then, to compare our inferences about the thoughts and feelings of our pupils with those described in the literature of educational psychology.

Box 6.5 Example of Triangulation

Extract from observer's notes (written during lesson)

Look at old tables of results. "What's happened?" Teacher asks specific pupils questions. When he disagrees, raises his voice quizzically as if he disagrees. Question and answer. Hints. When right answer is given, it is reinforced by the teacher. "Right" (guessing game). Do you all agree with that? Reply by one boy, "M". When boy responds in a way which doesn't fit what teacher wants, it is chopped. People not encouraged to elaborate on ideas. Wants to get them critical of John Innes, compost manufacturer. John Innes made by pupils promotes growth better than commercial product. Asks why paper pots are better than plastic pots. Often makes an interpretation. Asks pupils if it is a "reasonable guess." Someone murmurs again, "yes."

Excerpt from tape-recorded lesson

Teacher: Yeh, do you all agree with that?
Pupil: Mm.
Teacher: What do you think Derek? I mean are you bothered? . . . Would that be the only thing you want to know about a plant?
Pupil: How to condition it, sir.
Teacher: Yeh, do you all agree with that?

Interview with Teacher

Observer: Do you know that you use the words "Do we all agree?" quite a lot?
Teacher: No, I didn't. (pause) Okay — I know I use that a lot.
Observer: Three or four times.
Teacher: I am asking for assent.
Observer: Are you? Is that what you are asking?
Teacher: I think probably I am. I think possibly I use that when I don't get . . . if I make a statement and I haven't got a . . . I don't know sometimes if it is a rhetorical question, or whether it is a question I want an answer to, or whether it is just a statement, but I make a statement and I hope the response will come from it. If a response doesn't come from it, you either repeat it in a different way to a single individual and put them on the spot, or you perhaps get over it by saying "Okay" or "Do you all agree with that?" I suppose they can possibly con me by saying yes and carry on. It is something I hadn't thought of.
Observer: Do they all say yes?
Teacher: Well, they didn't all say no. I reckon if you take a non-negative approach to be an affirmative, which is perhaps a big thing to do. I don't think you ought to do that really. Yes, that's naughty, isn't it!
Observer: Well, the thing is, I suppose when you say "Do we all agree?" they can say no.
Teacher: I give them the opportunity to say no.
Observer: They can say no, but how do they see it. If they see it as your seeking agreement . . . .
Teacher: I think a lot of the time one must be seeking agreement. . . what I am trying to put forward is what I feel to be a reasonable statement; a true statement. Although I didn't today, I do in fact sometimes put forward draft statements and you do usually find that they disagree if there is something stupid. It was a bit tame today — I mean you

Box 6.5 — continued

were coming in part way through a situation which wanted finishing and therefore I finished it. In terms of them going away and doing things — and I thought you would be more interested in discussion because of the material you had got — your recording technique . . . .

Interview with Pupils

Pupil: But he wouldn't ask you what you think your conclusions were. He'll put his own conclusion up on the board, and you have to write it. He says do you agree. Not always, but he don't want to rub it off, so you just say yes to keep him quiet?

Observer: You say yes to keep him quiet?

Pupil: Keep him happy . . . .

Observer: There was a time when he said he was making a guess and he asked you if you agreed whether it was a reasonable guess. I don't know if you remember that?

Pupil: Yes.

Observer: And one person said yes and everbody else kept quiet. Now what I want to know is whether the person who said yes really did agree with him or just said yes because they thought he wanted them to say yes, and why everybody else kept quiet?

Pupil: Well, he would have liked us to say yes, really, 'cause I mean you could see it.

Pupil: If you'd said no, you'd waste time arguing wouldn't you.

Pupil: He'll keep on 'til you come to his way of thinking.

Pupil: So it's best to say yes to start with.

Observer: So even if you did disagree when he said ''Do you all agree?'' you wouldn't.

Pupil: If you said no, he'd keep on to you until you said yes.

Pupil: And if you argued with him, he'd come round to the same point where you left off.

Pupil: Back to his way of thinking.
(pp. 11–12)

Source: John Elliott, "Developing Hypotheses about Classrooms from Teachers' Practical Constructs: An Account of the Work of the Ford Teaching Project," *Interchange* 7/2 (1976–77): 2-22. © 1976, The Ontario Institute for Studies in Education.

The most well-known classifications of ways of thinking is probably Bloom's (1956) *Taxonomy of Educational Objectives. Handbook I: Cognitive Domain.* For me, the tone of Bloom's work is nicely captured in this extract from the introduction:

"It is especially intended to help them (teachers, administrators, professional specialists, and research workers) to discuss these problems with greater precision. For example, some teachers believe their students should 'really understand', others desire their students to 'internalize knowledge', still others want their students to 'grasp the core or essence' or 'comprehend'. Specifically what does a student do who 'really understands' which he does not do when he does not understand." (p. 1)

Bloom proceeded to divide all types of thinking into six major categories and arranged these hierarchically: knowledge, comprehension, application, analysis, synthesis, evaluation. Each successive category builds upon the previous one in terms of its complexity.

Guildford (1956), at about the same time as Bloom, having attempted to distill the wide-ranging research on intelligence, produced a theoretical model describing the "structure of the intellect." This model distinguished five broad types of cognitive operations: cognition, memory, divergent production, convergent production, and evaluation. The emphasis given to convergent and divergent thinking is the most obvious difference between Guildford's and Bloom's categories. Guildford saw convergent thinking as one which "proceeds toward one right answer, that is to say, a determined or conventional answer," and divergent thinking as "the kind that goes off in different directions. It makes possible changes of direction in problem solving and also leads to a diversity of answers, where more than one answer may be acceptable." For a more comprehensive view of Bloom's and Guildford's categories and for a survey of findings when they are applied in teacher effectiveness studies, see Dunkin and Biddle (1974).

Taba (1966) was concerned to categorize thinking according to its level. I find her categories particularly interesting because they bear some resemblance to Piaget's developmental stages (see Table 6.2).

Table 6.2 Categories, Levels of Thought, and the Concrete-Abstract Dimension
(Adapted from Taba, by Dunkin and Biddle)

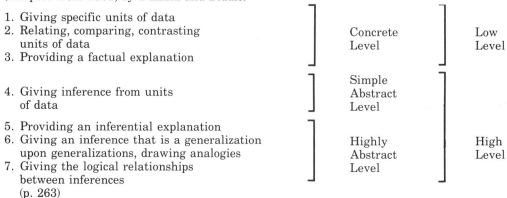

1. Giving specific units of data
2. Relating, comparing, contrasting units of data — Concrete Level — Low Level
3. Providing a factual explanation

4. Giving inference from units of data — Simple Abstract Level

5. Providing an inferential explanation
6. Giving an inference that is a generalization upon generalizations, drawing analogies — Highly Abstract Level — High Level
7. Giving the logical relationships between inferences
(p. 263)

Source: From *The Study of Teaching* by Michael J. Dunkin and Bruce J. Biddle. Copyright © 1974 by Holt, Rinehart and Winston, Inc. Reprinted by permission of CBS College Publishing. Reprinted also by permission of San Francisco State University.

Bloom's, Guildford's, and Taba's categories have been the most widely used in monitoring pupils' covert experiences in the cognitive domain. What about the affective domain, which is concerned with the development of feelings? To simplify matters, I would like (at least initially) to distinguish between feelings about objects or distant events from feelings about oneself. There seems to be quite a difference, at least superficially, between the feelings one has about poverty in the Third World to the feelings one has when being reprimanded for being late for an appointment. The distinction I am making relates to the formation of a value structure on the one hand (namely, feelings about poverty) and to the formation of a self-concept on the other.

First, let us consider pupils' covert experiences which relate to their development of values. Just as Bloom produced a taxonomy of educational objectives in the cognitive domain, so Krathwohl and his co-workers (1964) produced one in the affective domain. Their categories are as follows: receiving, responding, valuing, organization, characterization by a value, or value complex. These categories are arranged along a dimension of progressing "internalization"; from receiving, which describes a pupil's willingness to attend to a particular phenomena, to the development of a value complex, which is so embedded as to govern a pupil's life-style.

It is interesting to compare Krathwohl's categories with the processes which Raths, Harmin, and Simon (1978) considered as collectively defining valuing:

Choosing: 1. freely,
             2. from alternatives,
             3. after thoughtful consideration of the consequences of
                each alternative,
Prizing: 4. cherishing, being happy with the choice,
             5. enough to be willing to affirm the choice to others,
Acting: 6. or doing something with the choice,
             7. repeatedly in some pattern of life.

The most widely known studies of the growth of children's values are probably those of Kohlberg (see Turiel, 1973). Kohlberg's studies involved his presenting moral dilemmas, in anecdotal form, to children of different ages. For example, he would question them at length about the case of the penniless man who was faced with the decision of stealing medicine for his wife or letting her die. From their replies he would make inferences about the thought processes they were using in resolving the dilemma. Subsequently, he would seek to place these inferences in categories. Longitudinal studies of children's responses to dilemmas of this sort led him to suggest that development proceeds through three major stages:

1. In the first stage (the preconventional level), the child makes judgments of right and wrong according to how he or she would be affected, or by copying the values of those who have physical power.
2. In the second stage (the conventional level), the child makes judgments on the basis of conforming to or actively maintaining the social order.
3. In the third stage (the post-conventional level), the child makes judgments on the basis of values and principles which have a validity apart from the authority of groups holding them.

I would like to conclude this discussion of categories of feelings which pupils experience by considering the feelings they might have about themselves. Throughout their lives, pupils are building up pictures of themselves: knowledge of their strengths and weaknesses (their capacity to differentiate); confidence in themselves (their sense of potency); self-awareness (salience); self-acceptance (acceptance of the disparity between the self they recognize, the picture which they think others have of them, and their idealized view of how they would like to be); and so on. There is evidence that pupils develop part of this picture whilst at school. For example, a study by Staines (1958) suggested that pupils can be helped to become well adjusted in the above respects by a teacher who positively emphasizes skills, makes few negative comments, and who offers pupils opportunities for self-determination. It is unfortunate that his study leaves a gap between the teacher's actions and the pupils' learning. However, given his cue, there is no reason why individual teachers shouldn't explore the gap.

In summary, then, I have briefly reviewed the categories of thinking and feeling produced by a number of prominent authors. If one of their category systems or components of it relates to a matter about which you are particularly concerned, then it would seem appropriate to use it to monitor one of your lessons. For example, Aschner and Gallagher et al. (1965) used Guildford's model as the basis for designing their classroom observation schedule. Wade (1981) used his own version of a category system to compare the effects of the presence and absence of the teacher on small group discussions of a poem (Inquiry 6.8).

Appraisal

The most obvious question to ask about a lesson is probably, "Was it worth doing?" This is to ask if the pupils' covert experiences were valuable. The teacher is challenged to say why particular types of thinking or feeling are highly valued.

The Open University (1980) posed the same question when it asked how worthwhile certain types of thinking were. The answers teachers gave were thoughtful and provocative. For example, one teacher cited a number of reasons for valuing what the pupils were learning when they worked with clay,

> "Because children are learning skillful manipulation with their fingers.
> Because of the pure enjoyment and satisfaction of creating something out of a shapeless mass without any artificial aid.
> Because of learning patience and discipline."

These reasons are provocative because they invite one to ask why, again. The teacher answered,

> "I value the adoption of hobbies and interests out of school, now and later.
> I believe it is important for children to become aware of otherwise undiscovered pleasures and talents."

But values are usually relative. In addition, teachers might be challenged to ask further questions such as,

- To what extent should I be concerned with preparing pupils for the careers they might choose?
- Have I paid sufficient attention to the affective domain?
- Am I making an important contribution to pupils' developing their self-pictures?
- Have I got the balance right between lower and higher level thinking in the cognitive domain?

At this point the teacher is invited to rejoin the debate about the aims of education.

In chapters 3 to 5 we considered how information might be gained about the teacher's frame of reference, teacher's actions, and pupils' actions. Here we have been considering the pupils' covert experiences. We are now in a position to see whether or not there is harmony between these four elements.

Does the teacher orchestrate the educational process successfully? As well as asking was the job worth doing, we can also ask was it done well? The technique of triangulation, focussing as it does on these different elements (see Figure 6.3), may be of considerable value in helping answer these questions.

Figure 6.3 Triangulation

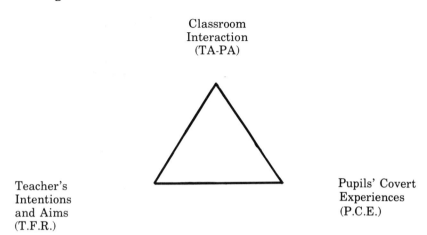

Classroom
Interaction
(TA-PA)

Teacher's
Intentions
and Aims
(T.F.R.)

Pupils' Covert
Experiences
(P.C.E.)

In his discussion of the technique, Elliott (1976–77) had this to say,

> "Triangulation involves gathering accounts of a teaching situation from three quite distinct points of view; namely, those of the teacher, his students, and a participant observer. Who in the 'triangle' gathers the accounts, how they are elicited and who compares them depends largely on the context . . . . The teacher is in the best position, via introspection, to gain access to his own intentions and aims in the situation. The students are in the best position to explain how the teacher's actions influence the way they respond in the situation. The participant—observer is in the best position to collect data about observable features of the interaction between teachers and students. By comparing his own account with accounts from other standpoints, a person at one point of the triangle has an opportunity to test and perhaps revise it on the basis of more sufficient data." (p. 10)

Conclusion

One could argue that the process of education is the process of developing and refining ways of thinking and feeling. To accept this argument invites us to accept the challenge of paying particular attention to the pupils' covert experiences.

If you pause for a moment to compare the work of a cabinet maker with a teacher, it becomes very evident what a difficult job teaching is. The cabinet maker begins to work with a product, such as a table, in mind; the teacher is challenged to help individual pupils develop their capacities to their potential. The cabinet maker is always in touch with the materials and can fashion an approach to match the needs of the moment; the teacher cannot even see what is going on inside the pupils' minds.

The problems of uncovering the pupils' covert experiences are central to the difficulty of the teacher's job. It has many facets. We have discussed how we can never know for sure what is on another's mind, how our understanding of how others think and feel is shaped by our own introspection about how we think and feel, and how our communication with others about thinking and feeling is hampered by linguistic barriers. Nevertheless, the challenge remains, and although these problems may never be completely overcome, the gap may be narrowed.

Suggested Inquiries

Inquiry 6.1 Making Inferences about Pupils' Thinking
Stephen Rowland (1981) wrote:

> "A classroom is like a laboratory in which thirty or so people are engaged in a variety of activities. Even when occupied on similar tasks, they each have their own trains of thoughts, their own sets of experience to draw from and their own skills to apply to it .... The point of the kind of classroom analysis I have in mind is this: If we can scrutinize just a small fraction of this plethora of activity in some depth, then experience suggests that this will increase our sensitivity, develop our awareness and sharpen our intuition. The detailed study of a few paintings by a child may give us insight into how art exploits and develops a child's intellect; the analysis of half an hour's play with sand and water may give rise to an increased understanding of the beginnings of scientific thought; consideration of a tape recording of our conversation with a child working on a project of his own, may help us to examine our own contribution and the ways in which we influence a child's thinking." (p. 1)

These comments provide the background for this activity.

Choose a small part of the curriculum which interests you–such as a task which you consider particularly valuable. Restrict your observations to one pupil or to a small group, making field notes, recordings, and so on. If the problem of organizing and managing the class at the same time causes too many difficulties, you might consider inviting a colleague to come and help you. Alternatively, conscious of the artificiality of the situation, you could do worse than to make a recording of your teaching just one pupil in a quasi-experimental situation (interacting as far as possible as you normally would). Collect any work which the pupils produce.

Afterwards, analyse your notes/recordings/pupils' work. Prepare a commentary, grounded in the data, on the types of thinking and feeling which you infer were taking place.

Finally, if you judge it appropriate, you might interview the pupil with a view to checking up on your findings.

Inquiry 6.2 What Might the Pupils Be Learning?
Monitor the behavior of a group of pupils (field notes, video tape recording, and so on). List each of their actions on a separate line. Afterwards, alongside each action, write down what you think they might have been learning. An extract

from observations and inferences made in an elementary school art and craft class is shown in Table 6.3 (Open University, 1980). Finally, discuss how you might seek corroboration of your inferences.

Table 6.3 Some Observations in Art and Craft Class

What did the pupils actually do	*What might they have been learning?*
Children covered tables with newspaper and plastic covers. Put on overalls. Put out paint, water, glue, etc.	Organizational skills. (Learning in progress) Responsibility for possessions, keeping tables in good order, looking after their clothes, preserving their own clothes. (Learning in progress) Social skills: working together, considering the caretaker, parents, etc. helping each other. (Learning in progress) Independence. (Learning in progress)
(Nicola) (She is making a bee. It has two wings stuck on the top of the balloon.) "It needs those things that stick out." "Feelers," says Ashton.	What a bee looks like. (New learning)
"Antennae," says Lee. "Would a straw do?" says Nicola.	Specialist language "antennae". (New learning)
(Nicola) Brings back the bee. "We need a sting. I will use this card." She sits and cuts a little piece of card to stick to his bottom.	Biological information about a bee and its sting. (New learning)
(Alison) "Can I have some stronger glue to stick these egg cartons? Just one first." She holds it in place.	Manipulative skill. (Learning in progress) The properties of some glue. It is quick drying. (New Learning)

Source: Open University, *Curriculum in Action: An Approach to Evaluation* P 232 Block 2, Unit 3, p. 6. Copyright © 1980 The Open University Press.

Inquiry 6.3   Using Error Pattern Analysis

The purpose of this inquiry is to identify common problems and difficulties which your pupils experience when learning. I would suggest that you begin by *either* collecting a sample of your pupils' work *or* alternatively tape record a lesson. Then apply error pattern analysis:

- list the errors, problems, or difficulties
- search for patterns or recurring features
- make an inference about the pupils' thinking, which explains how the error pattern might have arisen

Subsequently, you might like to check up on some of the inferences you made. Often pupils will willingly tell us what was on their minds.

Inquiry 6.4 Identifying Pupils' Difficulties in Thinking

Over the course of a few periods, keep a diary, noting the problems and difficulties which you observe your pupils encountering. With these in mind, design a short task, which you might typically use in your teaching, for selected pupils to carry out.

Video record three pupils or three groups of pupils carrying out the task. There might be some advantage in giving the task to pairs of pupils since interaction between them can be very revealing. Compare and contrast the behaviors of the pupils, focussing in particular on problems and difficulties they encounter. Identify dimensions of thinking and feeling which describe these problems and difficulties. Specify how these pupils vary with respect to these dimensions.

Inquiry 6.5 Examining Your Pupils' Work

The immediate object of this task is to help you identify the constructs which you personally use when appraising pupils' work. Collect together a sample of about nine pieces of work. You might, for example, choose pieces they have written, drawings they have done, or models they have made. Label them arbitrarily, 1, 2, 3, 4, 5, and so on. Prepare a repertory grid like the one in Figure 6.4. Along the top write the labels.

Figure 6.4 Repertory Grid Form

Similar Features ✔ (Construct Pole)	1	2	3	4	5	6	7	8	9	Different Features × (Construct Pole)
A	0	0	0							
B				0	0	0				
C							0	0	0	
D	0			0			0			
E		0			0			0		
F			0			0			0	
G										
H										
I										
J										

Proceed as follows:
 (i) Select the first three pieces.
 (ii) Identify them in the grid by placing a large circle in the corresponding box of row A.

(iii) Ask yourself which two pieces seem most alike and different from the third. Put a tick within the circle of those which are alike and a cross within the circle of the one which is different.

(iv) Identify the feature (construct pole) which the two alike have in common and write it opposite A in the similar features column.

(v) Identify the feature (construct pole) which makes the third distinct and write it in the different feature column.

(vi) So far, by comparing and contrasting the first three pieces, you have identified construct A. Repeat for the next three pieces, 4, 5, and 6, but search for a different construct which distinguishes them.

(vii) Repeat for the next three pieces 7, 8, and 9, and so on until you have covered a wide range of combinations.

In carrying out this process you will have discovered a variety of constructs which you use when making sense of pupils' work. These describe some of the qualities of pieces of work which you perceive as important. Review these constructs and relate each one to the thinking and feeling which your pupils might have experienced when they undertook the task you set.

Finally, you might try to find out which constructs are associated with your regarding a piece of work highly (Fransella and Bannister, 1977). This could help you to pinpoint types of thinking and feeling which you value highly.

Inquiry 6.6 Interviewing Pupils

Either record the conversations you have with individuals or small groups of pupils as they work on a common task. In these conversations, try to discover the types of thinking and feeling they were experiencing. Prepare a digest of your findings.

Or video record one of your lessons. Afterwards, invite a group of three or four pupils to view the recording and to discuss it with you. Replay the recording stopping it at any points which either you or the pupils thought significant. Record your discussion. Prepare a digest of your pupils' thoughts and feelings during the lesson.

Or select four pieces of pupils' work. Invite the four to read or examine each and then discuss them. At a simple level, you might ask them to grade them. Record their discussion. Prepare a digest of your interpretations of the thoughts and feelings these pupils had whilst preparing their pieces. If you carried out Inquiry 6.5, an interesting comparison between their viewpoints and your constructs might be made.

Inquiry 6.7 Towards Triangulation

Make a recording (audio or video) of one of your lessons. From it, select two short sequences, one which you were pleased about, and another which left you less than satisfied. If appropriate, transcribe each sequence. Closely examine the transcript of each sequence and make a list of the thoughts and feelings that you infer your pupils were experiencing in each. The next day, play each of the sequences to your pupils and ask them what was going on in their minds at the time. Write up a short account of each sequence, comparing your view with the pupils' views.

Inquiry 6.8 Categorizing Pupils' Responses

Tape record part of one of your lessons. Select one of the category systems (Bloom, Guildford, Taba, and so on) with a view to analysing your pupils' responses. Alternatively, you might use them as a basis for devising your own categories. For example, you might choose to examine the balance between cognitive thinking, affective thinking related to objects, and affective thinking related to self.

Before carrying out the analysis, make a note of your reasons for selecting the system you chose. You might also make a note of the balance between the categories that would please you if this showed up in the subsequent analysis. Then proceed with the analysis.

Comment on your findings. What is your response to them? How do they compare with your ideal? In your opinion, did the categories satisfactorily reflect the thinking and feeling that the pupils were experiencing during the lesson?

Suggested Reading

Bloom, B. S. "Thought-Process in Lectures and Discussions." *Journal of General Education* 7 (1953): 160–69.

This article may help to make clear the distinction between what the pupils learn and what the pupils are thinking, their covert experiences. In addition, it provides a good example of the use of the stimulated recall technique.

Ganshow, L. "Discovering Children's Learning Strategies for Spelling through Error Pattern Analysis." *The Reading Teacher* (1981): 676–80.

This article describes clearly the technique of error pattern analysis and the assumptions underpinning it. It could well stimulate teachers to use the technique in their own subject areas.

Open University, "The Pupils and the Curriculum," *Curriculum in Action: An Approach to Evaluation,* Block 2, Units 3 and 4. Milton Keynes: Open University Press, 1980.

Unit 3 focusses on the question, "What were they (the pupils) learning?" and Unit 4 on, "How worthwhile was it?" Both units are rich in examples of studies teachers actually made.

PART II:
Implementing and Monitoring Change

7

Improving Teaching: The Professional Role

This book started by asking the question, "What makes good teaching?" It rapidly emerged that, not only are there no definitive answers, but that there is disagreement about how one should proceed to go about finding answers. Chapter 2 introduced one way of finding answers, which in the light of past experience looked as though it might be fruitful. This envisaged a detailed study of four closely related aspects of the teaching and learning process: the teacher's frame of reference, the teacher's actions, the pupils' actions, and the pupils' covert experiences. The following chapters contained invitations to teachers to examine what was happening in their classrooms under these four headings, so that they might begin to make a personal appraisal of their own teaching.

The latter part of this book begins with the question, "How can teaching be improved?" This question similarly does not presume that there are definitive answers and is concerned to examine how teachers can go about the process of introducing worthwhile changes. The dimension of change is added to appraisal. The chapter following this one contains invitations to teachers to follow a process which is designed to lead to improvement of what is happening in their own classrooms.

The problem of curriculum evaluation and curriculum implementation, which are closely related to questions about appraising teaching and changing teaching respectively, have been the focal points of concern for some years now. A substantial literature has accumulated around them. To put the matter of changing teaching into a historical perspective, I will begin by examining a few interesting and pertinent ideas from the literature surrounding curriculum implementation. Following this, I will examine in some detail the teacher's role in change and associate it with professionalism. The footnote on accountability at the end of the chapter leads into an exercise designed to be of value to teachers concerned with extending their professionalism.

Some Aspects of the Problem of Change

The sixties and early seventies will be remembered as the years of curriculum development. There was an explosion of activity in the design of new courses, new teaching approaches, new materials, and so on. Many commentators (see, for example, Travaglini, 1975) have associated the beginning of this activity with the launching of Sputnik in 1957. It is certainly true that this event was followed by much soul-searching in the United States, and this in turn was followed by enormous governmental support for extensive curriculum development in science. Not long afterwards, in 1962, the Nuffield Foundation in England followed suit by making a huge investment in its Science Teaching Project. And shortly after that, the newly formed Schools Council began wide-ranging sponsorship of a variety of projects right across the curriculum. By 1970, a vast amount of new material had been developed and still more was in process. New journals, such as the *Journal of Curriculum Studies,* were launched (1969) to provide a forum for the exchange of ideas amongst those who were concerned with innovation.

Curriculum development had become a booming business and there was widespread optimism that the new materials would revolutionize education. However, by 1970, many doubts had begun to creep in. New materials were readily available, but things didn't seem to be changing. There was no revolution; both the speed and the extent of the uptake of the new materials was lacking. As early as 1964, Mort had estimated that there was a fifty-year lag between the appearance of a need and an innovation to answer it. Tales of woe began to appear in the literature. Here are a few extracts from Wastnedge's (1972) plaintiff article, "Whatever Happened to Nuffield Junior Science?" (Box 7.1)

Box 7.1 Whatever Happened to Nuffield Junior Science? (Ron Wastnedge)

In 1968 WHERE produced a special supplement which aimed to tell parents all about the exciting school work being done as part of the Nuffield Junior Science Project. It explained the what, the why and the how for parents whose children were lucky enough to be involved, or who might become involved in the future. But the vision didn't materialize. Not many children now get the chance to work the Nuffield Junior Science way.

Inevitably, controversy raged around the flags which the project nailed to the mast. For instance, over our insistence on the importance of children solving the problems that they themselves raised. . . .

We were repeatedly under pressure . . . to produce kits or sets of cards. . . .

Others pressed us to treat science as a subject on a timetable. . . .

Like other projects we suffered from communication problems. Written words frequently remained unread or were often misunderstood or misinterpreted. Letting children solve problems they have raised themselves was too often taken as meaning 'turn them loose and they'll teach themselves', or 'teacher opts out'. Letting children write freely became 'don't give them any help at all, not even discussion about what they might write'. . . .

Box 7.1 — continued

> Like other projects, we pinned much faith on the written word. . . .
>
> We also pinned a great deal of faith on courses for serving teachers. . . .
>
> I suppose that Nuffield Junior Science was essentially like all other national ventures. It created an enormous initial splash and the ripples became progressively weaker and modified with time and distance. . . .
>
> There is perhaps only one showplace for the project — an area where you can visit the schools and see the Nuffield Junior Science Project in action. But it is a long way away — over three thousand miles. A group of enthusiastic and influential educationists in Ontario were deeply impressed by the work and ideas of Nuffield Junior Science. . . .
>
> It is called the Early School Environment Study, and is organized by Paul B. Park, based on Althouse College of Education, Ontario.
>
> Nuffield Junior Science has not entirely vanished. It is alive and well and living in Canada.

Source: Open University, *The Curriculum: Context Design and Development* E283 Unit 13, p. 35. Copyright © 1972 The Open University Press.

Why wasn't change taking place? What was going wrong? The shape of curriculum projects, sensing a problem, began to change. Many began to employ specialist evaluators and it seems that they were beginning to give almost as much attention to the dissemination of the materials as to the design of them (see, for example, Rudduck and Kelly, 1976). The emphasis of articles in the literature began to veer away from reflections about the process of design and development towards the process of change. The process of change became the object of scrutiny: not only change involving the implementation of new curriculum materials, but also change involving organizational innovations and policies, such as mixed ability teaching. At first, it was common to analyse the change process into a number of component parts, such as research, development, diffusion, adoption, and implementation (see, for example, Open University, 1972). Later, it became more common to see the whole process described in terms of political and cultural perspectives (see, for example, House, 1979).

One of the earliest studies of the process of innovation, and probably the most influential, was made by Havelock (1971). Havelock reviewed a very large number of innovations and perceived three major types: the research, development, and diffusion model (R.D. and D.), the social interaction model (S.I.), and the problem-solving model (P-S). As Becher (1971) pointed out, the change agent takes a very different role in each:

> "In the research and development and diffusion model, the external change agent is concerned mainly with preparing and disseminating packaged solutions. In the social interaction model, he concentrates on identifying and strengthening communication networks and promoting the exchange of ideas. And in the problem-solving model he acts as a resource consultant, working in a non-directive relationship with his clients."

The change process becomes progressively more teacher-centred as one moves from the R. D. and D. model to the S.I. model to the P-S model.

Many of the early projects, such as the Nuffield Science Teaching Project, were of the R. D. and D. type. They were characterized by extensive centralized planning, heavy spending, and catered for the passive consumer. They didn't seem to be very effective in promoting change (see House, 1979). As time went by, projects organized along the lines of the S.I. model became increasingly common. I personally acted as a "coordinator" of a project, which aimed at improving the quality of teacher education through the collection, sharing, and evaluation of a bank of ideas within a community of about two hundred tutors. The social interaction model was deliberately adopted in this project (see Haysom and Sutton, 1974). But the S.I. model evidently wasn't the elusive panacea, as is apparent in the growth of popularity of the P-S model. The Schools Council's Humanities Project, directed by Stenhouse, was of this type. Stenhouse (1975) favored the P-S model, but later went a stage beyond this, envisioning the teacher as the researcher. In a nutshell, then, there was discernable movement away from the R. D. and D. model towards the S.I. model and then towards the P-S model.

It seems then, that the search for effective models of change increasingly put the teacher at the centre of the stage. Fullan (1972) concluded his overview of the role of the user in the process of educational change as follows:

> "A radical restructuring of the role of the user and a complete reversal of the direction of influence in the process of change are required if effective innovations are to occur."(p. 1)

He arrived at this conclusion after reviewing the findings of a number of authors which pinpointed and emphasized the diverse range of problems facing teachers: the lack of clarity about the proposed changes, the problem of learning new roles, the lack of time and other resources, the lack of motivation, the inability of their students to respond, and so on.

But there is more to the matter than efficiency of getting change to work. Reid (1979) began his paper with this quotation from the Washington Post:

> "The issue in the D. C. teachers' strike . . . is the deskilling of teachers. . . . In many cases, teachers are being forced to become mere parrotters of packaged curricula. . . ." (p. 325)

He comments as follows:

> "There seems to be something rather implausible about the assumption that people occupying certain social or organizational roles can view objectively what teachers are doing and then explain it in mechanistic terms or in terms which allow them only very limited possibilities for autonomy or altruism in the choice they make." (p. 333)

He goes on to assert:

> "What we additionally need to do as well as drawing on a variety of insights in order to fashion a perspective on curriculum change, is to reimpose the idea of the teacher as a rational person, capable of making informed choices, and still more capable of formulating or helping to formulate what those choices should be between." (p. 335)

Change and Professionalism

The previous discussion of the chequered history of curriculum development and of our understanding of the process of change suggests that if the quality of teaching is to improve, then, on both practical and moral grounds, the teacher should move towards centre stage. The aspirations of the eighties and nineties would seem to be pinned upon teachers exercising more autonomy, sharing more responsibility, and developing the qualities they need in order to act as effective change agents. In short, it seems likely that extensive demands will be made on the teachers' professionalism.

What does professionalism mean in the context of improving teaching? It certainly doesn't mean blind acceptance or rejection of curriculum materials or other innovations. Rather, the professional would regard them as a concrete recommendation as to how a range of ideas — educational aims, principles of procedure, and hypotheses about interaction — might be operationalized. Stenhouse (1975) was keen to emphasize the importance of the teacher being critically aware of the tentative nature of curriculum proposals. He put it this way:

> "The crucial point is that the proposal is not to be regarded as an unqualified recommendation, but rather as a provisional specification claiming no more than to be worth putting to the test of practice. Such proposals claim to be intelligent rather than correct. . . . It is a way of translating any educational idea into a hypothesis testable in practice. It invites critical testing rather than acceptance."
> (p. 142)

In this respect, it might be considered unfortunate that some new materials are presented bald. Ideas for activities and materials supporting these activities are sometimes not accompanied by a detailed, well-argued, and justified rationale, closely linked to their design. When this is the case, the developers can scarcely grumble if they are not fully appreciated by the user. Failure to make the design considerations explicit places the additional burden on the teacher of speculating about what the designer had in mind.

I have been emphasizing two components of curriculum innovations: their rationale, that is, the curriculum designer's frame of reference, and their concrete form, that is, the curriculum designer's view of the practice which best translates the rationale into action. In passing, I should perhaps note that sometimes designers cannot decide upon *the* best way of translating a rationale into action. This was evident in the Nuffield Chemistry Project which produced two alternative "Sample Schemes."

Previous to deciding whether or not to try out any innovation, it would seem reasonable to expect the teacher to carry out some form of preliminary evaluation, involving:

(i) examining the rationale: extracting the aims, principles of procedure, and hypotheses about interaction; reviewing the justifications used to support these claims; critically appraising these justifications;

(ii) juxtaposing the rationale and the recommendations for action in order to assess whether or not the recommendations truly reflect the rationale;

(iii) assessing the practicality of the recommendations in terms of time, resources, and so on. This might involve considering how the recommendations might be adjusted to meet available provision.

The decision itself would then involve the teacher in perceiving the innovation to have advantages over existing practice. This seems terribly simple at first sight, but I believe it is just the opposite, for it implies that teachers are fully aware of both their frames of reference and their classroom actions. This would be an idealized state of affairs. How else can they compare?

Logically, one can distinguish four different polar states of affairs in this respect: the teacher may or may not be aware of his or her frame of reference; the teacher may or may not be aware of his or her actions. These four states of affairs are represented in the following diagram.

	Unawareness of Actions	Awareness of Actions
Unawareness of Frame of Reference	(i)	(ii)
Awareness of Frame of Reference	(ii)	(iv)

(i) Little needs to be said about the teachers who are unaware of both their frames of reference and actions! Could such people be considered professionals? It is salutary to note though, that all of us will be unaware to some extent!

(ii) Teachers who are aware of their actions, but unaware of their frames of reference, might be tempted to idealize their actions.

(iii) Teachers who are aware of their frame of reference, but unaware of their actions, might be tempted to rationalize their actions.

(iv) This is an interesting case. The teachers' responses will conceivably vary according to the extent of the match they see between their frames of reference and their actions.

The Ford Teaching Project (see Elliott 1976-77) was concerned with assisting teachers, who perceived a gap in their aspirations, to adopt an inquiry approach and their practice in implementing it. The assistance provided took the form of helping teachers to reflect about their practice (actions), that is, to develop their capacity to self-monitor. At the beginning of the project, they estimated that only one of the forty teachers was self-monitoring to any significant extent. At the end, twenty-five teachers were estimated to have made some progress in self-monitoring. As a second order task, the project researched its own activities. Here are some of the hypotheses which emerged.

> "The less teachers' personal identity is an inextricable part of their professional role in the classroom, the greater their ability to tolerate losses in self-esteem that tend to accompany self-monitoring. . . .
>
> The more teachers value themselves as potential researchers, the greater their ability to tolerate losses of self-esteem. . . .
>
> The more able teachers are at self-monitoring in their classroom practice, the more likely they are to bring about fundamental changes in it." (pp. 18–20)

Teachers who are aware of both and who perceive a reasonable match between them might respond by either trying to dot "i's" and cross "t's" or might deliberately explore, *prima facie*, worthwhile alternatives such as those embodied in curriculum proposals. This latter response has the attraction of extending the teachers' capacities to choose on the basis of first-hand experience.

To return to the main argument then, any rational decision to try out an innovation would seem to require the teacher to examine and appraise the rationale and recommendations for action contained in the innovation, to reveal his or her own frame of reference and current classroom practice, and then to make a judgment in the light of the interplay between these factors.

So far, I have been developing notions about professionalism by considering the way teachers might relate to curriculum proposals. Now, I will broaden the discussion by considering teachers' roles as change agents more generally.

First, not all invitations to change will take the form of new curriculum ideas and materials. Sometimes teachers will be invited to respond to organizational and policy changes: changes in the length of the class periods, changes in the way pupils are grouped, changes in class size, changes in the way curriculum content is divided or integrated, changes in school entrance and leaving ages, and so on. Some of these changes will be initiated by the teachers themselves. (I believe that the respective roles of teachers and management in initiating change is an important part of professionalism, but will not consider it here.) All such changes will likely affect what transpires in the classroom. In varying degrees, these changes will be accompanied by a rationale, but it is unlikely to be complete. For example, one school I know recently decided to double the length of the class periods. I presume the reasons for doing so, or at least the enthusiasm with which they were expressed, outweighed the reasons for not doing so. However, it would be surprising if further reasons, both for and against, didn't emerge after the change had been introduced. Either way, the school's frame of reference would have likely been spelled out to some extent. In contrast with curriculum innovation, however, it is very unlikely that the change would have been supported with ready-made ideas for action. Such organizational changes invite a response from teachers. In the first place, they are entitled to question the rationale and in the second, they are challenged to modify their actions. They might respond by searching for alternative curriculum ideas, or devising their own, and at the same time find new demands made on their skills.

Second, not all ideas for change take the form of curriculum ideas and materials, or organizational and policy innovations. The literature contains a vast wealth of theoretical ideas, some of which bear directly on the teacher's aims, principles of procedure, and hypotheses about interaction. What characterizes the relationship between the professional and the literature — between practice and theory? The relationship can work in either of two directions. It can begin with the literature and finish with the teacher (theoretical idea → teacher's frame of reference → teacher's action), a direction implicit in the majority of teacher education courses. Or alternatively, it can begin with the teacher and finish with the literature (teacher's actions/teacher's frame of reference → theoretical idea), a direction which conceives of the teacher's role as a researcher of his own practice.

When the direction is from theory to practice, the literature may be viewed as an invitation to the teacher to examine his frame of reference and enter into a discussion about it. It is conceivable that subsequent to this discussion, the teacher may decide to try to make some changes. At first sight, there doesn't seem to be anything objectionable to a teacher entering into this sort of relationship with the literature. However, Fenstermacher (1978) has pointed out some possible pitfalls in doing so. He was concerned that the teacher should not fall victim of the "triple-play" latent in some writings. The nature of the "triple-play" is as follows. Let us suppose a researcher finds a positive relationship between the use of praise and pupil work involvement. The first mistake would be to conclude that praise causes work involvement. It might be the other way around, or it might be that other factors such as carefully structured worksheets produce work involvement, and that the teacher uses praise a lot when the pupils are using worksheets. The second mistake would be to follow the first by saying, because praise produces work involvement, teachers should be trained to use praise. Fenstermacher pointed out that the empirical study of teaching does not contain any moral imperatives which compel the teacher to apply findings, and moreover, to train the teacher to apply findings is not educative.

Fenstermacher concluded that the dialogue between the teacher and the literature is more meaningful if it begins with the teacher. This view was developed by Elliott (1982). In discussing self-evaluation and professional development, he emphasized the value of the teacher making explicit his or her tacit practical knowledge and deliberating upon it. For me, the word deliberation evokes the idea of formative tension, an intrinsic motivation for change. Such tensions may be stimulated when teachers compare their actions with their frames of reference, or their actions with someone else's, or their frames of reference with the literature.

By way of summary, then, this discussion of the teacher's role in the context of change has yielded a variety of qualities which I have associated with professionalism:

- Professionals consider curriculum ideas and materials as potentially valuable and seek them out. They are concerned to understand their rationale. They are concerned to relate concrete recommendations to this rationale. If *prima facie* consideration endorses the materials, professionals respond by being prepared to test them with a view to determining whether or not the hypotheses embodied within them can be substantiated in their specific teaching situations.
- Professionals are concerned to develop their awareness of their own frames of reference and their own practice. This requires them to study systematically their own teaching and their rationale for it.
- Professionals seek to develop their competence, that is, to improve the match between their frames of reference and their classroom practice.
- Professionals seek to develop their versatility, that is, to increase the range of options available to them.
- Professionals are active in promoting and responding to organizational and policy changes.
- Professionals are researchers of their own teaching and are concerned to relate their findings to the literature.

These statements, which may sound rather forbidding, are offered as the basis for a critical discussion of the qualities of the professional. You might find it worthwhile reviewing them in the light of the findings of one piece of research on change and three different views of the meaning of professionalism (Inquiry 8.1).

Eichholz and Rogers (1964) examined teachers' reasons for rejecting electromechanical teaching aids and categorized them according to the way shown in Box 7.2. Which forms of rejection do you find compatible with the view of professionalism presented?

Box 7.2 Rejection of Electromechanical Teaching Aids (Eichholz and Rogers)

Form of Rejection	Rejection	State of Subject	Anticipated Rejection Responses
1. Ignorance	Lack of dissemination	Uninformed	"The information is not easily available."
2. Suspended judgment	Data not logically compelling	Doubtful	"I want to wait and see how good it is, before I try."
3. Situational	Data not materially compelling	1. Comparing	"Other things are equally good."
		2. Defensive	"The school regulations will not permit it."
		3. Deprived	"It costs too much to use in time and/or money."
4. Personal	Data not psychologically compelling	1. Anxious	"I don't know if I can operate the equipment."
		2. Guilty	"I know I should use them, but I don't have time."
		3. Alienated (or estranged)	"These gadgets will never replace a teacher." ("If we use these gadgets, they might replace us.")
5. Experimental	Present or past trials	Convinced	"I tried them once and they aren't any good."

Reprinted by permission of the publisher from G. Eichholz and E. M. Rogers, "Resistance to the Adoption of Audio-visual Aids by Elementary School Teachers" in Matthew B. Miles, ed., *Innovation in Education* (New York: Teachers College Press, © 1964 by Teachers College, Columbia University. All Rights Reserved.), p. 310.

Eggleston (1976), when faced with considering the "Evaluation of Professional Components in the New B. Ed. Degree Programmes," had the following to say (see Box 7.3 on page 140). To what extent do his views match those presented earlier.

Box 7.3   Teacher Education: Professional Components (Eggleston)

''The products of a course in professional studies are teachers, capable of engaging effectively in the activity of teaching not according to prescription or the dictates of fashion, but as an intentional activity rationally based on accepted principles. This implies that trained teachers can give an account of:

1. *Curriculum Considerations*
   (a) how they decide what to teach,
   (b) how they determine the sequence and level of both subject matter and individual demands they make of their pupils,
   (c) how they recognize the potential of subject matter for developing a range of intellectual skills and its power to generate useful concepts and generalizations.

2. *Teaching and Learning Strategies*
   (a) how they attempt to optimize the conditions for learning of individuals and groups of pupils,
   (b) how they decide the strategies of teaching and their interactions with their pupils in classroom transactions,
   (c) how they conceptualize pupils' characteristics and learning strategies,
   (d) school and classroom management, discipline, etc.

3. *Assessment of Learning*
   (a) Educational measurement and psychometrics,
   (b) Observations, evaluation and recording of pupils' attainment and progress.

It is highly unlikely that students will make much progress towards these goals if exposed only either to lectures in professional studies or the traditional block teaching practice. New learning experiences for students born out of new working relationships between Colleges and Schools must be subjected to systematic enquiry as part of an on-going evaluation of new course structures.

The assessment of students' progress in professional studies in these new courses can no longer be subject to vague 'high inference' impressionistic judgements of tutors on one dimensional scales, but requires a more searching analysis of students' intentions, decisions and actions when preparing for, and engaging in the process of teaching.''

Source: J. F. Eggleston, "Evaluation of Professional Components in the New B.Ed. Degree Programmes," Internal Document, University of Nottingham, 1976. Reprinted by permission of the author.

Hoyle (1972) introduced the notions of the restricted and extended professional. He saw the restricted professional as having these characteristics:

"A high level of classroom competence;
Child-centredness (or sometimes subject-centredness);
A high degree of skill in understanding and handling children;
Derives high satisfaction from personal relationships with pupils;

Evaluates performance in terms of his own perceptions of change in pupil behavior and achievement;
Attends short courses of a practical nature."

The extended professional has these characteristics in addition:

"Views work in the wider context of school, community and society;
Participates in a wide range of professional activities, e.g. subject panels, teachers' centres, conferences;
Has a concern to link theory and practice;
Has a commitment to some form of curriculum theory and mode of evaluation."

Whilst criticizing Hoyle's notions, Stenhouse (1975) incorporated elements in building his view of the extended professional. He concluded:

"The critical characteristics of that extended professionalism which is essential for well-founded curriculum research and development seem to me to be:
The commitment to systematic questioning of one's own teaching as a basis for development;
The commitment and the skills to study one's own teaching;
The concern to question and to test theory in practice by the use of those skills.
To these may be added as highly desirable, though perhaps not essential, a readiness to allow other teachers to observe one's work — directly or through recordings — and to discuss it with them on an open and honest basis.
In short, the outstanding characteristics of the extended professional is a capacity for autonomous professional self-development through systematic self-study, through the study of the work of other teachers and through the testing of ideas by classroom research procedures."
(p. 144)

Accountability

Recently, there has been a growing concern to hold teachers accountable. As I see it, accountability adds a public dimension to professionalism. Within a democracy, this is in itself not a bad thing. However, if agencies assuming the responsibility for holding teachers accountable have a naive view of professionalism, they may easily fall into the trap of using simplistic procedures to "measure" it. In passing, I would hope that teachers themselves would take some initiatives in this respect. Many professions have, after all, assumed some responsibility for monitoring their practice.

Professionals (doctors, lawyers, engineers, teachers, and so on), providing a public service, can quite legitimately be expected to answer questions from their clientele about their practice. A little girl fell off her bicycle and badly grazed her face. She was taken to hospital for treatment. Her mother, who was previously a nurse, was very concerned lest her face be permanently scarred. Her anxiety increased when a very young doctor took responsibility for treating her. "Will her face be scarred?" "How will you know if you have got all the dirt out?" "Have you done

142

all you can to stop infection?" "Should you stitch the wound or not?" These questions seemed to be prompted by the mother's concern to assess the young doctor's professionalism. Indeed, she was holding him accountable.

Although they may be reluctant to ask teachers such questions, I suspect many parents would very much like to do so. How would you respond if a parent asked you the questions in Box 7.4 at a parents' evening? (Inquiry 7.2)

Box 7.4   A Parent's Questions

Q.1   What I really want to know is, is my child getting the best? (Are the conditions you provide for learning optimal?)

Q.2   Can you tell me a bit more about this? (What are these optimum conditions that you have established?)

Q.3   How can you be sure about this? (On what do you base your answer? What evidence, research data, etc., supports your claim?)

Q.4   Are you really sure? (What kind of a base is that? Is the data, etc., sound and reliable?)

Q.5   Do other teachers do the same thing? (Can the arguments, data etc., be applied to other schools in the district?)

These questions were explored by a group of teachers who were concerned to begin examining their own practices. They first role-played the situation and because they were not satisfied with their responses, they decided that it would be a valuable exercise if they each prepared written answers.
A French-language teacher gave these answers:

> "1. Yes, despite 30 plus enrolment per class and despite 40 minute periods which I feel are too long for oral language instruction. Also the French Department is affluent — every resource is available and cheerfully provided. Curriculum development is maximal.
> 2. Physically, seating is arranged for maximum student participation. Group work encourages participation and increases active oral exchanges. Privacy corners are screened for private lab work. I have set up work and interest centres to eliminate 'dead' time and promote independence. Furthermore, negative reinforcement is non-existent which sets, I believe, a healthy mental atmosphere and discourages fear of failure. Fortunately it is possible to test students on a one to one basis when they are ready, further negating 'failure syndromes' or expectancies.
> 3. I can cite no data; I rely on the success my students have generally enjoyed and the ease with which they have been able to continue in the program. . . .
> 4. Yes — but only subjectively.
> 5. Yes."

A mathematics teacher gave these answers:

> "1. The learning environment in my classroom is established with a particular group's needs in mind. Since the child has special needs in mathematics, a special learning environment has been established in the classroom. The teaching environment is good, but could improve with fewer students in the classroom.
> 2. Within a classroom, where the students are weak in the basic skills of the subject, activity is of great importance. The "hands-on" approach to mathematics is used. The noise level is higher in this type of class; however, good planning and high interest activities channel the students' energy in the right direction. A well decorated and bright classroom is of great importance. If a positive feeling for the subject is established learning will take place.
> 3. The personal experiences I have had teaching and discussions with others in our sub-system strengthen my belief that a positive attitude towards subject matter acts as a catalyst for learning. It is a policy of the county school board at the present time to use as many concrete examples as possible. Teaching guide #13 stresses this point. A bright and meaningful physical environment in the class has always been a priority.
> 4. The data which is meaningful for my use comes from a very reliable source: the interaction and cooperation with our sub-system has been the one greatest source of the data which I have made use of in my classroom.
> 5. I believe it is important to meet the needs and desires of particular students at particular times. Therefore, what may be right for your classroom may not be right for mine. Classroom strategies must constantly be redeveloped to meet the needs of students."

A survey of teachers' answers to these questions yielded some interesting findings. Answers to question 3, "On what do you base your answer?," usually mentioned experience. Here are some examples chosen at random:

> "Past experience. In general terms, what noted educators have been claiming for years."
> "Personal experience. What has worked in the past. Success in tests based on previous experience."
> "Experience and advice and general reading of material made available."
> "Experience and instinct only I think. Haven't had chance to do any research other than to observe what seems to work and what doesn't.
> "Own teaching experience. Moffat's ideas on curriculum and learning process. Research from language across the curriculum on how students' language develops."

It was the phrase *optimum conditions* (Q.2) which probably caused the most difficulty. Answers frequently were very generally phrased. For example:

> "A variety of teaching/learning situations."
> "A positive attitude."
> "A pleasant, fairly relaxed learning situation."
> "Gear the program to the students' ability, needs and interests."

Subsequent to this survey the same teachers produced a list of specific questions which they thought needed to be answered in order to help a teacher decide whether or not conditions were optimal:

- Is participation maximized?
- Is allowance for individuals maximized?
- Are the students talking too much/too little?
- Do I talk too much/too little?
- Are my mannerisms distracting/involving?
- Is the way I mark producing a favorable/unfavorable response?
- Are my instructions too prescriptive/too vague?
- Should able students work with the less able or should they be grouped by ability?
- Do I set too much/too little written work?
- Do I achieve the optimal balance between individual work, small group work, and whole class activity?

My reason for describing this exploration at such length is twofold. First, it prompts one to ask questions about the teachers' replies; for example,

- As a parent, would you be happy with the replies of the French and the mathematics teacher?

What supplementary questions would you like to ask?
- Is the appeal to experience satisfactory?"
- Are the questions, which the teachers thought needed to be answered, valuable?

And second, I think this sort of exploration might help teachers to identify some of their concerns about their own practice. It can provide a focus or a starting point for some of the inquiries outlined in the next chapter.

Suggested Inquiries

Inquiry 7.1 The Meaning of Professionalism

Examine the view of the meaning of professionalism developed in this chapter by comparing and contrasting it with the findings of Rogers and Eichholz and the opinions of Eggleston, Hoyle, and Stenhouse. Prepare a critique which makes your position clear.

Inquiry 7.2 Beginning a Study of Your Own Practice

Prepare your answers to "A Parent's Questions" (page 142). Beforehand, in order to set the stage, you might try role-playing the parent–teacher interview. Afterwards, exchange your answers with those of other teachers with a view to elaborating upon them and making them more meaningful.

This activity may develop in a number of directions, but in my view, it can yield two important outcomes:

(i) It can provide you with the beginnings of an overview of your teaching which is quite explicit.

(ii) It can help you identify some features of your teaching which you think deserve further attention.

The first two parent's questions invite you to make explicit some of the significant features of your classroom interaction, the next one, your frame of reference with respect to these features, and the last two, your justifications for the items in your frame of reference which you cited. You might find it helpful to display your answers in three columns: Significant features of interaction, item in frame of reference, justification.

This activity will remain a paper exercise unless it is related to what is actually going on in your classroom. Make a video-recording of yourself in action. Compare it with your answers to the parent's questions. List any matters which cause you concern and which you consider warrant further investigation.

Suggested Reading

Elliott, J. "Developing Hypotheses about Classrooms from Teachers' Practical Constructs: An Account of the Work of the Ford Teaching Project." *Interchange,* Vol. 7, No. 2 (1976-77), pp. 2-22.

This article is a landmark. It describes how a research team tried to help a group of teachers tackle the problem of trying to implement inquiry teaching into their classrooms. It is rich in insights and charted new methodological directions.

8

Improving Teaching: Some Procedures

This chapter contains descriptions of and comments on three different types of procedures which teachers have used in order to study and improve their teaching. The first is a simple study of questioning techniques; the second, a simplified inquiry into an aspect of teaching; and the third, action-research into a problem of concern. In my view, these studies become progressively more revealing as greater and greater demands are placed on the teachers' observational, analytical, interpretative, and reflective capacities.

A Study of Questioning

A group of teachers each made a simple tape **recording** of one of their classes; one which they each thought was reasonably **typical**. Without exception, the posing of questions featured prominently in every class. Questioning evidently has a major pedagogical function, and a study of it could feasibly reveal much about classroom processes. With this in mind, the teachers each selected a five-to-ten-minute extract and transcribed it. To provide a context for the extract, they wrote a brief one-page descriptive account of the lesson. Subsequently, they worked through the sequence of operations outlined in Figure 8.1.

The first step in analysis involves looking for characteristic features. This is not as simple as it sounds. Seldom is one struck by anything particularly remarkable and it is often necessary to proceed more formally either using pattern analysis or by making comparisons between different transcripts.

Pattern analysis (see also chapter 4) involves looking for recurring features within a sequence. Each question, response, or element in the dialogue is carefully examined with a view to identifying similarities with others. Within any transcript, many patterns are often evident and different analysts often spot different ones.

For example, in the transcript shown in Box 8.2 (Russell, 1984), the teacher identified different patterns from the observer.

Figure 8.1 Outline of a Study of Questioning

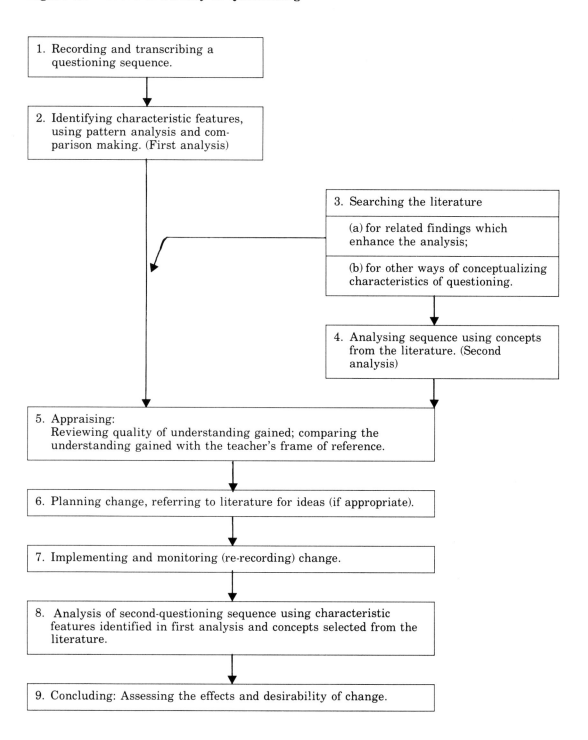

Box 8.2 Transcript of a Questioning Sequence

Teacher: Now one of the methods that form mountains is folding. We talked about that yesterday. Could someone tell us about folding? Would you raise your hand if you can tell us how mountain building occurs, sorry how folding occurs, how it happens, why it happens, what happens? O.K., Karen, do you want to start off? (1)

Karen: (Inaudible) (2)

Teacher: All right, that's pretty simply stated, more or less what happens. There are a few details that I think we can add. One thing I'd like to clarify is the idea of what was underneath the water. What did it look like when it was under water? (3)

Jeff: Sedimentary. (4)

Teacher: Right. And what does sedimentary rock look like? We have them around Ottawa. They're along the Queensway on the way to Kanata or at Hogsback. You can see really good examples of it.(5)

Bryan: Layers of rock. (6)

Teacher: Right. O.K., limestone, shale, those are examples of it, sandstone too. Right, now we have this sedimentary rock. At the bottom of the ocean, usually it's at the bottom of the ocean and that's why it's covered with water. Does the water exert much pressure on this rock? Is there any pressure built up by the water or does the rock just lie there sort of flatly and calmly? (7)

Cathy: (Inaudible) (8)

Teacher: Does the water exert any pressure on the rock? (9)

Cathy: (Inaudible) (10)

Teacher: Does the water exert any pressure on anything? If you have a large body of water, let's say an ocean and you were sitting at the bottom of the ocean, would you feel any pressure? (11)

Cathy: Yes. (12)

Teacher: Do you think the ocean would exert pressure on the sedimentary rock? (13)

Cathy: Yes. (14)

Teacher: All right, good. Now there are frequently pressures from above, in other words from the water on the sedimentary rock. There are other pressures that can occur. And how can these occur? And where do they come from? What is their source? (15)

Ian: Well like sometimes you can get storms underwater, like if you get a big tidal wave or something there's pressure under the water, and like it just builds up on the sedimentary rock. It just adds more and more pressure. (16)

Teacher: Well, not exactly. The only pressure you would have would be coming from below. But there are also pressures coming in from the sides. When, what would be an example of pressure coming in on these sedimentary rocks?. . . When would you have pressure coming in from the sides? Remember we talked yesterday of ''bumper'' cars at the Ex? Remember if you've ever been on ''bumper'' cars, how does this pressure come about? Bryan? (17)

Box 8.2 — continued

Bryan:	Well, it usually comes from an earthquake. (18)
Teacher:	Good point, there's a possibility. Now can you tie in something else? (19)
Bryan:	Underwater mountains. (20)
Teacher:	O.K., Stuart. (21)
Stuart:	He said it. (22)
Teacher:	O.K. Yesterday David was talking about something. Ah, David and Jim were talking about a time when the continents were together. Now they're not together any more. What do we call that? What is that all referring to? (23)
Jeff:	Continental . . . (24)
Teacher:	Continental. (25)
Chris:	Drift. (26)
Teacher:	Right. We'll be studying this in more detail. We'll be having film strips about it. Basically, it is the idea that the continents were all together and they floated apart. And what happens when sometimes . . . .

Source: T. Russell, "Developing Teachers' Analytical Skills," in H. Munby et al., eds., *Seeing Curriculum in a New Light: Essays from Science Education* (Lanham, Maryland: University Press of America, 1984). Reprinted by permission of University Press of America.

The patterns identified by the teacher were: teacher uses adult words previous to simpler language, lack of variety in the teacher's responses, teacher uses "O.K." previous to saying something new, teacher refers back to previous lessons, teacher rephrases a question if a pupil doesn't get it, teacher repeats questions at times. Those identified by the observer were: teacher talks longer than pupils talk, teacher elaborates on correct answers, teacher selects illustrations, some of the teacher's questions call for "yes" or "no" responses, pupils' responses are brief (often labels or brief descriptions). Ultimately, questions have to be asked as to whether or not the different patterns are interdependent and a decision has to be made as to which combinations are the most significant.

When teachers' co-operate in the analysis task, the making of comparisons between transcripts can usefully complement pattern analysis. Whereas pattern analysis tends to focus on identifying similarities within a sequence, comparative analysis tends to focus on identifying differences between different sequences. Pattern analysis and comparative analysis are semi-formal techniques designed to help reveal perceptions of characteristic features. The findings are usefully described in the form of an "analytic memo." Sometimes, these perceptions will be original to the extent that they have not been documented in the literature.

Much, of course, has been written about questioning. Researchers have examined the technique from many points of view. Synopses of a few selected examples are displayed in Box 8.3 on page 150. Every year more studies, new ways of perceiving questioning, ways of quantifying perceptions and numerical data relating question type to other features of the classroom appear in the literature.

Box 8.3 Synopses of Some Studies of Questioning

1. Douglas Barnes

In his study *Language, the Learner and the School* (1969), Barnes worked with a group of teachers in a similar way to that described in this chapter:

> "they tape recorded first year lessons taught by friends, transcribed them and analysed them according to a scheme I supplied. The teacher participating found this an enlightening and disturbing task."

The scheme Barnes supplied for analysing the teachers' questions consisted of four major categories:

(1) factual questions, which elicited recall of information;
(2) reasoning questions, "How?" and "Why?" questions as opposed to "What?" questions;
(3) open questions, as opposed to closed questions: questions having more than one acceptable answer;
(4) social questions, which exercise control or seek concurrence.

It was perhaps the large proportion of factual questions and the low proportion of open questions which disturbed the teachers.

2. B. S. Bloom

Many people (see, for example, Sadker and Sadker, 1982) have used Bloom's *Taxonomy of Educational Objectives* (1956) as a way of categorizing teachers' questions. Bloom challenged us to recognize that there is more to thinking than just recalling facts. He perceived six different types of thinking (cognitive activity):

(1) knowledge: remembering.
(2) comprehension: understanding concepts, making inferences, and so on.
(3) application: problem solving, using understanding in a new situation.
(4) analysis: sorting out an argument or communication.
(5) synthesis: creating, speculating.
(6) evaluating: making a judgment based on criteria.

Bloom and his co-workers did not confine themselves to the cognitive domain. They were also concerned with the affective. These matters are developed in chapter 6.

3. Mary Budd Rowe

If the teacher waits after asking a question or after a pupil answers, then the length of the answers increases dramatically. This was just one of the effects of introducing "wait-time." Amongst the other effects Rowe (1978) observed were an increase in the number of unsolicited responses, fewer failures to respond, fewer inflected responses indicating greater confidence, more speculative thinking, an increase in the number of questions asked by pupils, more contributions by "slow" pupils, and a decrease in disciplinary moves.

Box 8.3 — continued

4. John Holt

In his book *How Children Fail* (1969), Holt portrays, through a delightful series of anecdotes, strategies which children use to avoid answering questions: ''the mumble strategy,'' vigorous hand-waving, nodding in emphatic agreement, and so on. Alerted to this phenomenon, a group of teachers set about trying to identify other examples. They pinpointed vague responses, partial responses, requests for clarification, repetition of the question as well as a variety of non-verbal behaviors.

5. John Elliott

In his studies of the inquiry approach in action, John Elliott (1976-77) contrasted two questioning sequences. In one sequence the questions were personalized; for example, ''How do you know?'' ''So how can you overcome the problem?'' He suggested that in this exchange, the teacher wanted the pupil to reflect on his/her own problems, decisions, beliefs, and so on, whilst in the other, the teacher's concern was for the subject matter.

Access to many of these studies may be simply gained by the computerized searching of the ERIC (Educational Resources Information Centre) data base. Descriptors, information categories used by the system, such as questioning techniques, classroom observation techniques, interaction process analysis, are fed in and the number of articles held in each category or combination of categories is displayed. The computer will provide further details, ranging from the reference numbers of articles to full abstracts, upon request. However, computer time is costly and skill is required in gaining the information at the appropriate level of detail. A computer print out from a simple search is shown in Box 8.4 on page 152.

The first instruction given to the computer was search (s) for the articles in which "questioning techniques" was listed as a descriptor. There were 1683 articles in this category. In the category "classroom observation techniques," there were 1726 articles. When these categories were combined, there were only 28 articles. This is quite a manageable number to examine. However, further focussing was obtained by finding out how many of these 28 were concerned with "interaction process analysis" — just 8. The computer was instructed to print out the full reference and the abstract of the first item, the basic reference (authors, title, and source) for the second, and the reference numbers for items three to eight inclusive.

The full reference and the abstract can be looked up in the appropriate ERIC catalogue using the reference number, and money can be saved that way.

Reference number, beginning with EJ, such as EJO86700, relate to journals, and those beginning with ED, relate to documents. Documents are stored on microfiche.

The full reference includes the descriptors used for categorizing it. The asterisked descriptors are major descriptors, that is, they refer to particularly important characteristics of the article. If a relevant article is already known, it is often useful to find out what descriptors are used to categorize it and to use these to conduct the search.

Box 8.4　Computer Print Out from a Simple Search

Filel*:ERIC: — 66-82/Aug

    Set Items Description
? s questioning techniques

   1 1683 QUESTIONING TECHNIQUES (METHODS USED FOR CONSTRUC
? s classroom observation techniques

   2 1726 CLASSROOM OBSERVATION TECHNIQUES (PROCEDURES USED
? s combine 1 and 2

   3　28　1 AND 2
? s interaction process analysis

  4 3614 INTERACTION PROCESS ANALYSIS (METHOD OF STUDYING
? combine 3 and 4

   5　8　3 AND 4
? type 5/5/19 type 5/3/2; type 5/1/3 − 8

5/5/1
EJ086700　SE509430
   The Smallest Meaningful Sample of Classroom Transactions
   Rosenshine, Barak
   Journal of Research in Science Teaching, 10, 3, 221−226　1973
   Language: ENGLISH
Discusses the number of observations necessary to obtain a trustworthy sample of classroom transactions by reanalyzing existing data. Eleven to twenty observations appear necessary for teachers' questions which required students to hypothesize. The reliability of a single observation was zero for four other questioning types. (CC)
   Descriptors: *Classroom Observation Techniques; *Elementary School Teachers; *Lesson Observation Criteria; *Questioning Techniques; *Teacher Characteristics; General Science; Interaction Process Analysis; Research Methodology; Science Education

5/3/2
ED150161
   Texas Teacher Effectiveness Study; Classroom Coding Manual.
   Brophy, Jere E.; Evertson, Carolyn M.
   Texas Univ., Austin, Research and Development Center for Teacher Education
   57p; For related documents, see TM 006 782, and 785　1976
   EDRS Price — MF01/PC03 Plus Postage.

5/1/3 − 8
ED150159　ED150158　ED150157　ED079260　ED050031　ED049143

? logoff
   23aug82 13:31:05 User 2650
$0.93 0.037 Hrs Filel* 3 Descriptors
$0.30 Telenet
$1.23 Estimated Total Cost

Finally, it is worth noting that the total time taken for this search was 2 minutes 9 seconds and the cost, $1.23.

Reference to the literature may contribute to developing our understanding of what is happening in the classroom, in this instance, the teacher's questioning technique. Characteristic features identified through pattern analysis or comparison may find a responsive echo that refines, extends, or gives perspective to them. Additionally, the literature might draw our attention to certain features of our questioning which we would value, and thus alert us to establishing the extent to which these are present or absent.

At this stage, having developed some understanding of what's happening, the individual teacher should be in a position to work towards making an appraisal or judgment of his or her practice. In the first place, the quality of the understanding gained might valuably be checked by asking such questions as,

- Are the features of my questioning, which have been identified, really significant?
- Why are they significant?
- How might they be related to other classroom processes?

And secondly, this understanding of actual practice might be compared with ideas about good practice, that is, the teacher's frame of reference.

Making explicit his or her frame of reference, in this case, with respect to questioning, is not an easy matter. However, a useful start can be made by simply posing the question, "What makes good questioning?" In answer, one teacher had this to say:

> "(i) There should be a wide range of questions, ranging from the factual type to evaluation (think of Bloom's Taxonomy).
> (ii) The questions should allow for participation, response from various students.
> (iii) The questions should not be directed to the smarter students.
> (iv) The questions should be posed so as to initiate class discussion.
> (v) The questions should be dependent upon the type of class being taught (streamed or non-streamed, general or academic).
> (vi) The questions should be linked to some degree, especially if trying to develop a concept.
> (vii) The questions should not be shot in 'rapid fire'; allow for 'think-time'."

This useful beginning may then be developed by seeking justification for each of the assertions made. Moreover, sometimes such assertions prompt reanalysis of original data with a view to ascertaining the extent to which desired features are present. For example, in response to the assertion that "questions should not be directed to the smarter students," the teacher would be challenged to examine the way in which he or she does indeed distribute questions.

It is hard to conceive that this strategy of analysis and appraisal would not yield some possibilities for making changes or improvements. Again, the literature might have certain suggestions to make. The task now facing the teacher is to specify these. Some changes are sensibly expressed in hypothetical form; if X is done, then Y will likely follow. It should be recognized that if X is done, Z may also follow; that is, there may be some unanticipated effects. Indeed, the more radical the change, the more one should expect unanticipated effects to emerge.

Following the planning of change, the next task is to implement and monitor it. The first step in monitoring is a simple matter and merely involves making

154

a recording in a similar way to the first. Subsequently, this second recording is analysed for the same features that were identified in the earlier analysis.

At this point, there may be some merit in quantifying the data so as to provide a numerical comparison between the situations before and after change. I found the following checklist (Box 8.5) developed by a teacher, who was interested in John Holt's descriptions of the avoidance strategies used by pupils, potentially useful in quantifying change.

Box 8.5   Checklist–Verbal Strategies Developed by Children (after Holt)

Pupils' responses to teacher's questions:

- Whispering
- Vague responses
- Asks questions
- Mumbling
- Requests repetition
- Requests explanation
- Makes background comments
- Partial response, seeking teacher's reaction.

Teacher's behavior:

- Repeats student's mumbles, whispers
- Clarifies hazy responses
- Completes responses
- Implies correct response through question
- Directs question to particular pupil
- Directs question to specific group
- Ignores willing pupils
- Early short comments, for example, ''right on.''

Finally, the stage of drawing tentative conclusions is reached. The change made may have produced desired effects or it may not. Whatever the case, I would maintain that the study will likely have enhanced the teacher's professionalism: it will likely have provided an understanding of what is happening in the classroom, developed the ability to employ and recognize the strengths and weaknesses of alternative procedures, and enhanced the capacity of the teacher to make intelligent choices.

However, the study is not without its limitations. Scant attention is given to the pupils' view of the classroom — any inferences made about their covert experiences should really be checked upon. More serious perhaps is the danger that the study will remain at a superficial level. For example, a teacher may be able to satisfy his concern to distribute questions well without tackling the more fundamental problem of treating pupils equally.

Nevertheless, I would maintain that this is a useful exercise, capable of being extended in a number of directions:

(1) Instead of focussing on questioning, teachers might select components of their teaching which are significant in terms of frequency of use — a type of task or activity frequently employed, for example, discussion, explanations, homework, groupwork, lesson introductions, experiments, helping individuals in seatwork (Inquiry 8.1).

(2) The data base and analysis can be broadened by making a video recording of a lesson and then asking the question, "What are the characteristic features of my teaching?" (Inquiry 8.2).

In the following section, another type of study free from these limitations is described.

A Simplified Inquiry into an Aspect of Teaching

A group of teachers carried out a variety of simplified inquiries into an aspect of teaching which each was particularly interested in. I will illustrate the procedure they used with five examples of these inquiries with a view to discussing its features.

Inquiry 1 What Are the Significant Features of My Teaching?

Five teachers decided to launch an inquiry into the major similarities and differences between them as they went about teaching a small section of the science syllabus.

They decided that they would each design and teach a thirty-minute lesson on the concept of "heat transfer by conduction." They agreed that this concept would include the following items of content: insulators, factors affecting the amount of heat conducted (type of material, length or thickness of material, area of cross section, and so on), conductivity, good conductors (for example, copper, iron) and bad conductors (for example, glass, plastic). These items were arranged in this random order so as not to prescribe the order in which they should be taught. They agreed that it was reasonable to cover a substantial number of these items in the lesson but that they would not feel obliged to do so.

In order to separate the design stage from the teaching stage, the teachers were invited to list the most important guiding principles which they used in planning the lesson. Some chose to speak aloud into a tape-recorder as they planned, previous to preparing the list. They completed this part of the exercise prior to teaching and did not share their ideas as to how they proposed proceeding until the inquiry was complete.

The teaching situation was simplified by teaching one student only. Each taught a twelve-year-old pupil of average ability. Before being taught the pupil was asked if he or she would be prepared to help the teacher with an inquiry being made into ways of teaching science. During the teaching, the teacher switched on the video-recorder.

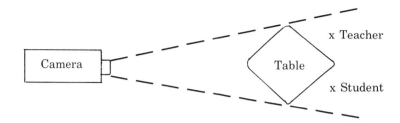

After the teaching, the teacher invited the pupil's comments. "Were there any things you didn't understand very well?" "Which were the best parts of the lesson?" — open questions designed to enable the pupil to give a free response. Subsequently, the teacher and student reviewed the videotape recording, each stopping it at places deserving a comment. All these comments were recorded on audiotape.

Inquiry 2 How Do I Adjust to Individual Pupils?

A teacher made plans to teach similar material separately to four different pupils in the same grade level for thirty minutes. The pupils were chosen to be widely "different" from one another. Previous to teaching the students, the teacher prepared a brief one-paragraph "pen-portrait" of each.

Previous to teaching the first student, the teacher outlined his plans in the form of a short list of actions he *might* take ("might" is accentuated since the teacher did not feel constrained to follow his plan). He reviewed these plans between each teaching session. When he varied them, he made a note of why he did so.

Each teaching session was video-recorded. To help make the situation more relaxed and natural, the teacher had selected only those pupils who were willing to help him make inquiries into ways of improving his teaching. The teacher operated the video-recorder himself.

After each lesson, the teacher interviewed the students in a similar way to that described in the previous example.

Inquiry 3 How Is Interaction Influenced by the Size of Pupil Groups?

A teacher selected the problem "The Tower of Hanoi" for his grade 6 class (eleven year olds) and prepared a simple instruction card, giving the pupils the details of the problem.

During the course of a day, he invited three groups to tackle the problem. The pupils remained in the class whilst doing so. The groups contained a single pupil, three pupils, and six pupils. They were selected from volunteers and given some choice as to which groups they wished to be in. The video-recording equipment was operated by a technician.

Inquiry 4 How Is Interaction Influenced by My Teaching Approach?

A teacher was interested in comparing the heuristic and didactic approaches to teaching. In order to make the comparison, she video-recorded herself teaching "Haiku poetry" to two different pupils who were of roughly similar ability. Each class was about thirty minutes long.

Before beginning the inquiry, she attempted to outline her conception of the two approaches. In addition, she attempted to list the strengths and weaknesses of each approach. Through this task she was making explicit her own frame of reference.

This done, she prepared short lesson outlines in the form of a simple list of actions she *might* take ("might" is accentuated since she was not inclined to be bound by these plans).

After teaching, she invited each pupil to comment openly on the lesson. They viewed the tape together with teacher or pupil stopping the tape whenever they wished to ask questions or comment. This discussion was audio-recorded so as to provide evidence about the pupils' covert experiences which might prove valuable in the subsequent analysis.

Inquiry 5 How Do I Modify My Approach when Teaching Classes of Different Sizes?

A teacher was concerned to find out how he varied his approach when teaching the same content to different size classes. The content he chose to teach was a modern poem. The length of the class was about thirty minutes. He subdivided his class of twenty-nine pupils into four groups of seventeen, seven, four, and one. The composition of these groups was determined by scheduling considerations. They were told about the inquiry and their help solicited. The classes with the large group were scheduled at the regular time and the smaller groups during free time. Each class was video-recorded, the largest with the help of a technician.

Prior to teaching the different classes, the teacher outlined his plan in the form of a list of actions he *might* take. After each class, he invited volunteers to help him analyse the recording.

What then are the features of this procedure? The essence, as I see it, is the facilitating of comparison through simplification. Simplification is often achieved in two ways: by reduction in scale and by control of conditions. Reduction in scale frequently takes the form of the teacher instructing just one pupil. This is the case in three of the five examples cited. There is some degree of control with respect to four broad features affecting interaction: the teacher, the pupil(s), the content, and the approach. In some of the examples, the teacher is the same person; in others, the content is kept similar; in others, the approach is broadly maintained. However, control is not tight. The science teachers exercised some freedom with respect to the content they selected. The teachers who chose to examine how they adjusted their approach when teaching different pupils possibly modified it in the light of the experience they had gained with the previous student, that is, in some respects they were not the same person.

The raw data which emerged from using these procedures was in the form of video-recordings. The sound and picture quality was very good relative to the quality usually obtained in classrooms, the technical problems being so much less demanding. The analysis began with the simple question, "How does the interaction in the first recording differ from the second and third, etc.?" The number of recordings made for each individual inquiry ranged from two to five. When two recordings were made, only one comparison was possible; when three recordings were made, three were possible; and when four were made, six.

After significant differences had been identified, many teachers sought to interrelate them so as to form hypotheses.

These are the bare bones of the procedure. In practice, however, the teachers made efforts to collect additional data designed to add meaning to the observations of the teacher's actions (TA) and the pupils' actions (PA).

The teachers, who were trying to find out how they adjusted to individuals, wrote "pen-portraits" of each pupil. They compared and contrasted them with a view making explicit their constructs relating to individual differences. Some followed a similar procedure to that used by Nash (1973), who applied Kelly's Repertory Grid Technique. After each teaching session, these teachers noted what they had learned from their previous experience, since they thought that this, as well as the pupil they were about to teach, should be considered when trying to account for differences in their behavior. In this way, the teachers were able to relate what was in their minds, their frames of reference (TFR), to the interaction which took place.

In addition, the teachers interviewed the pupils after teaching them. For example, the teacher who was examining the influence of different approaches afterwards interviewed the pupils and used the stimulated recall technique with a view to throwing light on what was going on inside their minds, their covert experiences (PCE), whilst they were learning.

In this way, as well as identifying significant features of what happened overtly, the teachers built "pictures" of how the teachers' frame of reference was related to the covert experiences of the pupils (TFR — TA — PA — PCE). Through such a process of triangulation a more complete picture is obtained (see Adelman, 1981).

The main strength of this procedure lies in the way the process of analysis is facilitated. The inquiries are designed and the data collected with the subsequent task of analysis in mind.

However, there are two major weaknesses arising from the simplification of the classroom situation through reduction in scale and control. In reducing the scale it is probable that some significant features of the natural classroom setting will be eliminated, and in imposing control, it is probable that some features will be added. Hence, it is necessary to ask whether or not any findings are valuable. The answer to this question would seem to depend on whether or not the findings can be generalized to the natural setting. On the one hand, one could argue that since the setting has been changed (for example, in the majority of cases, there is no possibility of pupil–pupil interaction), generalization is nonsensical. On the other hand one could argue that certain characteristics of teacher, pupil, and task are not affected by the procedure, and hence generalization in these respects is feasible. This issue, however, becomes a non-issue if the findings are regarded as genuinely hypothetical. They can provide a focus for further inquiry which seeks to establish whether they do indeed hold in the natural setting, to what extent, and why. The teachers who undertook these inquiries seemed to appreciate the problem:

> ". . . although I will hypothesize that certain features are typical of or likely to be manifested in small groups, clearly, I would not claim this must necessarily be."

> "As a result of this enquiry, I realize I must carry it one step further and use the didactic and enquiry methods with a whole class group. The students especially brought this to my notice. Diana explained how she enjoyed my teaching on a one to one basis, but may not have been absorbed in a group setting . . . ."

Action-Research

Although there are many views about what classroom-based action-research actually is, much contemporary thinking (see Grundy and Kemmis, 1981) associates it with the involvement of teachers in studying classroom practice with a view to improving the quality of interaction in it. Not only does action-research aim to improve practice, but it also aspires to improve the situation within which the practice takes place and to help teachers extend their professionalism.

In this section, I shall outline one conception of the action-research process. This follows closely the procedure used by teachers in the Schools Council Programme 2 Project, Teacher–Pupil Interaction, and the Quality of Learning (see Elliott 1981).

Stage 1. Identifying and Clarifying the Problem

A problem, or an area of concern, is a natural starting point for action research. Since problems are often not readily identified, it may be necessary to undertake some form of review of one's teaching in order to heighten one's consciousness of them. Some of the activities described earlier in this chapter and at the end of the previous one may be particularly useful in this respect. In particular, I favor Bailey's procedure, where the teacher reviews a video-recording of a lesson and notes the positive and negative feelings experienced in it (Inquiry 8.2).

At this point, it would be useful to sharpen the focus of a problem with a view to translating the vague into the specific and then to link it with action. For example, one might translate a vague concern, that the pupils are not as attentive as they might be, into terms such as, "Pupils seem to waste a lot of time." An action dimension is added if one appends, "How can the time they spend on a task be increased?"

Stage 2. Reconnaissance

Stating the problem in specific terms is valuable insofar as it prompts one to collect further information which describes the facts of the situation: information in answer to questions about who, what, where, and when.

- "Which pupils are wasting time?"
- "Is it always the same pupils?"
- "What are they doing when they are not on-task?"

- "What is the teacher doing when the pupils are wasting time?"
- "Is time wasting associated with some tasks rather than others?"
- "At what points in the lesson is off-task activity greater?"
  (For another example of reconnaissance questions, see chapter 4, "Understanding Difficult Behavior.")

The product of reconnaissance is a collection of raw data which describes more fully the facts surrounding the problem being examined.

Stage 3. Developing an Understanding of the Situation

Meaning is added to the facts of the situation if they are tentatively related. For example, let us suppose that certain tasks are accompanied by more inattention than others. Understanding the situation here would involve hypothesizing that certain characteristics of the task cause inattention (or even a certain type of inattention). This understanding may remain somewhat superficial unless further explanation is sought. Why? Is it because the pupils find the tasks irrelevant? Is it because the instructions are inexplicit? Is it because . . .?

The aim at this stage, then, is to generate a number of hypotheses which not only relate the facts of the situation, but which seek to explain the relationships as well. For example, one might arrive at a hypothesis such as, "When the instructions for tasks are given verbally (rather than in written form), pupils are initially inattentive, since they are uncertain about what to do." Findings of this sort are usefully recorded in an analytic memo.

As well as providing the basis for explanatory hypotheses, the data may also yield other matters of note: new perceptions of what is happening, shifts away from the original conception of the problem, the emergence of related problems, the demand for data not initially anticipated.

Stage 4. Planning, Implementing, and Monitoring Action

Having gained some understanding of the situation, one is now in a position to plan change. It is useful to detail the plan in writing so that reference can be made to it when the time comes to assess the extent to which change has been made. In the simple example that has been developed, the teacher might be prompted to introduce tasks in different ways. When monitoring the effects of the change, it is important to look for the unexpected as well as those anticipated. You only begin to understand a situation when you try to change it!

Stage 5. Reporting

At the end of an action-research cycle, it is worth distilling the process and the findings in report form. The case study is a common vehicle for such a report. This might include:

- a statement of the problem; how it was identified and its clarified form;
- the reconnaissance tasks and the data collected from them;
- the analytic procedures used and the hypotheses developed;
- further evidence sought and gathered;
- the details of the planned change;
- data collected in monitoring the extent and effects of change;
- interim conclusions, which not only draw on the study made, but which reflect on other related studies.

Presentation of the case study as a blow-by-blow account is not necessarily the most desirable format. The reader may be confused by the detail and fail to follow the line of thinking developed. In this respect, I find Stenhouse's (1978) distinction between case study, case record, and case data useful. He sees the case data as the assembly of the data collected: transcripts of lessons and interviews, field notes, documents (for example, cards, copies of pupils' written work, syllabuses, examination papers), questionnaires, observation schedules, and so on. The case record contains the researcher's notes, analytic memos, and other material, and these draw upon the case data to which they are cross-referenced. Finally, the case study is the coherent presentation of the inquiry, grounded in the case record and the case data (which are sometimes appended).

Stage 6. Extending the Action Research Cycle

The process I have outlined is seldom as straightforward as I have suggested: the concept of the problem may shift, the demand for information changed and extended. But action-research does not stop here. I have merely described the first cycle. Action-research proceeds in spiral fashion, one cycle following another. Progressively, the teacher develops a greater and greater understanding of the situation and a greater capacity to act responsively.

Methodological Review

The cyclical action-research process of observing, reflecting, planning, and implementing change (see Figure 8.2) embraces the procedures I have outlined in this chapter.

Figure 8.2 The Action-Research Cycle

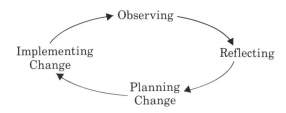

I have elaborated on this simple diagram in Figure 8.3. This expands upon the process of reflecting (incorporating a cycle of progressive focussing or extended reflection), and indicates a number of entry points into the cycle.

Reflecting can be a more deliberate process than simply thinking about what is observed. I see it beginning with the task of making sense of raw data, examining it for significant features, perceiving some order or regularity in it, perhaps using a technique such as pattern analysis. This would be followed by different types of interpretation: relating significant features and patterns to one another, adding meaning by making inferences about the thinking of the participants, and so on. Subsequently, it may be decided to narrow the focus of investigation (Parlett and Hamilton, 1972, use the idea of progressive focussing), or alternatively to extend it so as to put the findings in broader perspective. Either way, more observa-

Figure 8.3 Expanded Action-Research Cycle

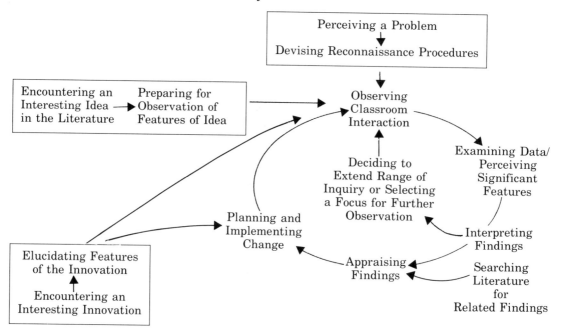

tions will be required. The final stage of reflecting involves appraising. Appraising seeks to resolve the tension inherent between the observed (and interpreted) events, the teacher's frame of reference, and the thinking of the community of other teachers and educators as made public in the literature.

The diagram (Figure 8.3) shows three entry points into the cycle: perceiving a problem, encountering an interesting innovation, and encountering an interesting idea in the literature.

Some teachers may be readily able to identify a problem of concern to them, in which case, they may immediately proceed with the task of devising reconnaisance procedures. Others may have identified areas of interest when studying other chapters of this book (see, for example, Inquiry 7.2). But for some, little of concern or interest may spring to mind. A number of possibilities remain open to these people:

- Carrying out an initial study based on Bailey's procedure (Inquiry 8.2).
- Keeping a daily diary of noteworthy events. If, on average, three events a day are noted, then this would yield thirty entries over a two-week period. These entries may then be analysed for recurring features.
- Using pattern analysis to study video-recordings of one or two lessons or of frequently used tasks or activities (Inquiry 8.1).
- Characterizing frequently employed methods using the repertory grid technique and then observing the classroom with one important characteristic in mind (Inquiry 4.1).
- Identifying the tasks set to a class of pupils over a series of lessons and then categorizing them (Inquiry 4.4).
- Observing pupils' actions with a view to categorizing them (blending Inquiries 5.1, 5.2, and 6.2).
- Examining pupils' work (blending Inquiries 6.3, 6.5, and the third part of 6.6).
- Asking the pupils to list the major strengths and weaknesses of the course, possibly using the nominal group technique (see Inquiry 2.3 for procedure).

My purpose in making these suggestions is to offer ideas for starting points. The suggestions are designed to reveal significant features of the teaching situation. Each suggestion approaches the teaching situation from a different perspective: some emphasize the teacher's thinking (TFR), some the teacher's actions (TA), some the pupils' actions (PA), and some the pupils' covert experiences (PCE). From a research viewpoint each has its strengths and weaknesses.

From time to time in conversation, at an in-service meeting or through subject journals, an interesting innovation is encountered. For instance, inside the front cover of the journal *The History and Social Science Teacher* (1977), the editors wrote:

> "The History and Social Science Teacher is designed as a vehicle to promote comment on the relationship of significant educational ideas to the curriculum in history and the social sciences. It is also intended to encourage the exchange of ideas among history and social science teachers and to improve classroom practice at all levels of education."

Many professional magazines and journals provide a forum for the exchange of ideas between the members of the professional community they serve. And some interesting ideas have certainly appeared in this journal:

- Cartoons in the classroom: a largely untapped resource.
- "Free-vote": role-playing parliament in action simulation.
- Games in moral education.
- Involving the student's "self" through a reflective log.
- Practical suggestions for improving class discussion.
- Teaching with artifacts.
- Pioneer skills — How grandmother did it.
- A role play of native Indian–white differences.
- Economics and the daily newspaper in the elementary classroom.

More often than not these types of articles tell you what you could do. They vary in the extent to which they articulate why you should do it or what might happen in the classroom if you did. If such an innovation is to be used as a starting point for breaking into the action-research cycle, then clearly it is important for the key features to be elucidated beforehand so that they can be monitored during implementation (see chapter 7 for a fuller discussion).

Whilst discussing innovations, I should mention a remarkable book written by Bruce Joyce and Marsha Weil, *Models of Teaching* (1972). Joyce and Weil set themselves the task of drawing together the work of more than eighty theorists, schools of thought, and curriculum projects, looking for commonalities that could be rationalized. The results of their efforts, published in the first edition of their book, was the characterization of sixteen distinct models.

Each model was carefully defined procedurally and the underpinning thinking made explicit. Joyce and Weil thus challenge teachers to select models they find themselves in accord with, and to extend their versatility by implementing them on an experimental basis. The detail they provide lends assistance in selecting features to monitor.

The final entry point shown in the diagram is an encounter with an interesting idea or argument in the literature. For the teacher to find an idea interesting, it is likely to find harmony with his teaching or frame of reference. However, ideas are frequently expressed on an abstract level and thus need to be made more concrete before they can be related to action. Munby (1984), in his essay "Analysing

Teaching for Intellectual Independence,'' provides an example of how this can be done. Early in the essay he seeks to clarify the meaning of intellectual independence. He then proceeds to develop a classroom observation instrument so that practice can be monitored. Where observation instruments are not available, teachers might find it worthwhile developing their own.

In conclusion, the action-research process involves the teacher as researcher. It fosters self-evaluation and leads to professional development. The teacher-researcher's task is

- to make explicit the teacher's frame of reference;
- to portray accurately classroom events; and
- to relate these to the thinking of other professionals made public in the literature (for example, see Inquiry 8.1).

Such research sets the stage for a three-way dialogue (see Figure 8.4 and cover design).

Figure 8.4 Dialogues Leading to Professional Growth

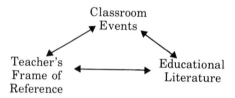

As I see it, it is these dialogues that naturally prompt self-evaluation and lead to professional growth. Heightened awareness of any discrepancy between classroom events and the teacher's frame of reference can be intrinsically motivating. Dialogue between the teacher's frame of reference and the literature can help the teacher to extend and develop his or her rationale. And dialogue between the literature and classroom events can lead to an enhanced appreciation of what is happening in the classroom.

Inquiry 8.1 Appraising a Component of Your Teaching

Choose to study a type of task or activity which you frequently employ, for example, discussion, explanations, homework, groupwork, lesson introductions, experiments, helping individuals in seatwork.

Make an appraisal of your practice by juxtaposing the following:

- An analysis of your practice. You might make recordings and then proceed to identify significant features.
- An analysis of your frame of reference. As a basis for analysis, you might put yourself in the position of an author writing an article reviewing important considerations or the chosen type of task or activity.
- A review of the literature.

Inquiry 8.2 Identifying Significant Features of Your Teaching

Teachers often find the task of identifying significant features of their teaching from a video-recording of one of their lessons a tantalizing one. However, the following procedure, based on that suggested by Bailey (1982), can be used to attack it.

After you have made the video-recording, replay it and proceed to map your feelings. There will be those which signify pleasure or satisfaction (such as successful, happy, autonomous, delighted, benevolent, warm, fulfilled) and those which signify unhappiness or dissatisfaction (such as irritated, frustrated, angry, malevolent, vulnerable, threatened, anxious). Display these along a time line as illustrated in the following figure.

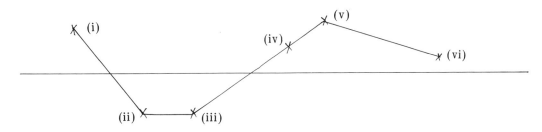

The peaks represent positive feelings and the troughs, negative ones. Prepare a table which relates the peak or trough of your feeling at the time, your frame of reference, your actions, and the pupils' actions.

Bibliography

Adams, R. S., and Biddle, B. J. *Realities of Teaching: Explorations with Video Tape.* New York: Holt, 1970.

Adelman, C. (1981) "On First-Hearing." In *Uttering Muttering: Collecting, Using and Reporting Talk for Social and Educational Research,* edited by C. Adelman. London: Grant McIntyre, 1981.

Adelman, C. ed. *Uttering Muttering: Collecting, Using and Reporting Talk for Social and Educational Research.* London: Grant McIntyre, 1981.

Armstrong, M. *Closely Observed Children.* London: Writers and Readers in Association with Chameleon, 1980.

Aschner, M. J.; Gallagher, H. J.; et al. *A System for Classifying Thought Processes in the Context of Classroom Verbal Interaction.* Urbana, Illinois: University of Illinois, 1965.

Bailey, B. J. *Starting Points for Self Appraisal.* Teacher Self-Appraisal of Classroom Practice, Schools Council Programme 2 Project, Interim report. Cleveland Local Educational Authority, U.K., 1982.

Barnes, D.; Britton, J.; and LATE. *Language, the Learner and the School.* Harmondsworth, Middlesex: Penguin, 1969.

Barnes, D. *From Communication to Curriculum.* Harmondsworth: Penguin, 1976.

Becher, A. *The Dissemination and Implementation of Educational Innovation.* Annual Meeting of the British Association for the Advancement of Science, 1971.

Berliner, D. C. "Tempus Educare." In *Research on Teaching: Concepts, Findings, Implications,* edited by P. L. Peterson and H. J. Walberg. Berkeley: McCutchan, 1979

Bennett, S. N. *Teaching Styles and Pupil Progress.* London: Open Books, 1976.

Bennett, S. N. "Recent Research on Teaching: A Dream, A Belief and A Model." *British Journal of Educational Psychology* 48 (1978): 127–47.

Bishop, A. J., and Whitfield, R. C. *Situations in Teaching.* Maidenhead: McGraw-Hill, 1972.

Bloom, B. S. "Thought-Processes in Lectures and Discussions." *Journal of General Education* 7, (1953): 160–69.

Bloom, B. S. et al. *Taxonomy of Educational Objectives. I: Cognitive Domain.* London: Longmans, 1956.

Borich, G. D., and Madden, S. *Evaluating Classroom Instruction: A Sourcebook of Instruments.* Reading, Mass.: Addison-Wesley, 1977.

Britton, J. "What's the Use?" *Educational Review* 23 (1971):205–19.

Brophy, J. E., and Good, T. L. *Teacher–Student Relationships: Causes and Consequences.* New York: Holt, Rinehart and Winston, 1974.

Bross, I. D. *Design for Decision.* New York: Crowell-Collier and MacMillan, 1953.

Clark, C. M., and Yinger, R. J. "Teachers' Thinking." In *Research on Teaching: Concepts, Findings, Implications,* edited by P. L. Peterson and H. J. Walberg. Berkeley: McCutchan, 1979.

Collinson, B. S., and Dunlop, S. F. "Nominal Group Technique: A Process for Inservice and Staff Work." *Staff Counsellor* 26 (1978): 18–25.

Cooper, J. M. ed. *Classroom Teaching Skills.* 2nd ed. Lexington, Mass.: Heath, 1982.

Cronbach, L. J. *Educational Psychology.* 3rd ed. New York: Harcourt Brace Jovanovich, 1977.

Dale, H. C. A. "Fault-Finding in Electronic Equipment." *Ergonomics* 1 (1958): 356–85. (See also Open University, 1971.)

de Bono, E. *The Five Day Course in Thinking.* Harmondsworth: Penguin, 1967.

Department of Education and Science. *Primary Education in England: A Survey by H. M. Inspectors of Schools.* London: HMSO, 1978.

Department of Education and Science. *Aspects of Secondary Education in England: A Survey by H. M. Inspectors of Schools.* London: HMSO, 1979.

Doyle, W. "Learning the Classroom Environment: And Ecological Analysis." *Journal of Teacher Education* 28 (November-December 1977): 51–55.

Doyle, W. "Research on Classroom Realities: Who Needs It?" Paper presented at the Annual Meeting of the American Educational Research Association, Toronto, 1978.

Doyle, W. "The Tasks of Teaching and Learning in Classrooms." Paper presented at the Annual Meeting of the American Educational Research Association, San Francisco, 1979.

Doyle, W. "Academic Work." *Review of Educational Research* 53 (1983): 159–99.

Dunkin, M. J., and Biddle, B.J. *The Study of Teaching.* New York: Holt, Rinehart and Winston, 1974.

Eggleston, J. F. "Evaluation of Professional Components in the New B. Ed. Degree Programmes." Internal Document, University of Nottingham, 1976.

Eichholz, G., and Roger, E. M. "Resistance to the Adoption of Audiovisual Aids by Elementary School Teachers." In *Innovation in Education,* edited by M. B. Miles. New York: Teachers' College, Columbia University, 1964.

Eisner, E. W. *The Educational Imagination.* New York: Macmillan, 1979.

Elbaz, F. "The Teacher's Practical Knowledge: Report of a Case Study." *Curriculum Inquiry* 11 (1981): 43–71.

Elliott, J. "Developing Hypotheses about Classrooms from Teachers' Practical Constructs: An Account of the Work of the Ford Teaching Project." *Interchange* 7 (1976–77): 2–22.

Elliott, J. *Action-Research: A Framework for the Self Evaluation in Schools.* Schools Council Programme 2: Teacher–Pupil Interaction and the Quality of Learning Project, Working Paper No. 1, Cambridge Institute of Education, U.K., 1981.

Elliott, J. *Using Nominal Group Procedures as a Basis for Cooperative Action-Research in Schools.* Teacher-Pupil Interaction and the Quality of Learning Project, Working Paper No. 6. Cambridge Institute of Education, U.K., 1982.

Elliott J. "Self-evaluation, Professional Development and Accountability." Paper Given at the Annual Conference of the Association for the Study of the Curriculum, Oxford, 1982.

Engel, B. S. *A Handbook on Documentation.* North Dakota Study Group on Evaluation. Grand Forks: University of North Dakota, 1975.

English, M. "Talking: Does It Help?" In *Communicating in the Classroom* edited by C. R. Sutton. London: Hodder and Stoughton, 1981.

Fenstermacher, G. D. "A Philosophical Consideration of Recent Research on Teacher Effectiveness." In *Review of Research in Education,* edited by L. Shulman. Itasca: Peacock, 1978.

Fiedler, M. L. "Bidirectionality of Influence in Classroom Interaction." *Journal of Educational Psychology* 67 (1975): 735–44.

Fransella, F., and Bannister, D. *A Manual for Repertory Grid Technique.* London: Academic Press, 1977.

Fullan, M. "Overview of the Innovative Process and the User." *Interchange* 3, 2–3 (1972): 1–68.

Furlong, V. "Interaction Sets in the Classroom: Towards a Study of Pupil Knowledge." In *Exploration in Classroom Observation,* edited by M. Stubbs and S. Delamont. Chichester: Wiley, 1976.

Gage, N. L., ed. *Handbook of Research on Teaching.* Chicago: Rand McNally, 1963.

Gage, N. L., and Berliner, D. C. *Educational Psychology.* Chicago: Rand McNally, 1979.

Ganshow, L. "Discovering Children's Learning Strategies for Spelling through Error Pattern Analysis." *The Reading Teacher* (1981): 676–80.

Good, T. L., and Dembo, M. "Teacher Expectations: Self-Report-Data." *School Review* 81 (1973): 247–53.

Graham M. J., ed. *Science Teacher Education Project: Film Review.* Maidenhead: McGraw-Hill, 1974.

Grundy, S., and Kemmis, S. *Educational Action Research in Australia: The State of the Art (An Overview).* Paper presented at the Annual Meeting of the Australian Association for Research in Education, Adelaide, 1981.

Guildford, J. P. "The Structure of the Intellect." *Psychological Bulletin* 53 (1956): 267–93.

Hamilton, D. et al., eds. *Beyond the Numbers Game: A Reader in Educational Evaluation.* London: Macmillan, 1977.

Harlen, W.; Darwin, A; and Murphy, M. *Match and Mismatch: Raising Questions.* Schools Council Progress in Learning Science Project. Edinburgh: Oliver and Boyd, 1977.

Harnischfeger, A., and Wiley, D. E. "Teaching/Learning Processes in Elementary School: A Synoptic View." *Studies of Education Processes,* No. 9, University of Chicago, 1975.

Havelock, R. *Planning for Innovation through the Dissemination and Utilization of Knowledge.* Ann Arbor, Michigan: Center for Research on Utilization of Scientific Knowledge, 1971.

Haysom, J. T., and Sutton, C. R. *Theory into Practice.* Maidenhead: McGraw-Hill, 1974.

Haysom, J. T., and Sutton, C. R. *Innovation in Teacher Education.* Maidenhead: McGraw-Hill, 1974.

Herbert, J. *A System for Analysing Lessons.* New York: Teachers' College Press, 1967.

Herrick, M. J. "Recognizing Communication Apprehension in the Classroom." *The Exceptional Child in Canadian Education,* Seventh Yearbook, Canadian Society for the Study of Education, 1980.

Hinely, R., and Ponder, G. "Theory, Practice and Classroom Research." *Theory into Practice* 18 (1979): 135-37.

Holt, J. *How Children Learn*. Harmondsworth, Middlesex: Penguin, 1967.

Holt, J. *How Children Fail*. Harmondsworth, Middlesex: Penguin, 1969.

House, E. R. "Technology versus Craft: A Ten Year Perspective on Innovation." *Journal of Curriculum Studies* 11 (1979): 1–15.

Hoyle, E. "Creativity in the School." Unpublished paper given at O.E.C.D. Workshop on Creativity of the School at Estoril, Portugal. Cited by L. Stenhouse (1975).

Hunt, D. E. "How to Be Your Own Best Theorist." *Theory into Practice* 19 (1980): 287–93.

Joyce B., and Weil, M. *Models of Teaching*. Englewood Cliffs: Prentice Hall, 1972.

Kelly, G. A. *The Psychology of Personal Constructs*. New York: Norton, 1955.

Knight, V. *Teaching for Control: An Action-Research Study*. Classroom Research Association, Occasional Publications No. 2. Halifax, N.S.: Saint Mary's University, 1984.

Knowles, M. S., and Knowles, H. *Introduction to Group Dynamics*. Revised ed. New York: Association Press, 1972.

Kounin, J. *Discipline and Group Management in Classrooms*. New York: Holt, Rinehart and Winston, 1970.

Kounin, J. S., and Gump, P. V. "Signal Systems of Learning Settings and Task-Related Behaviour of Pre-School Children. *Journal of Educational Psychology* 66 (1974): 554-62.

Kounin, J. S., and Sherman, L. W. "School Environments as Behaviour Settings." *Theory into Practice* 18 (1979): 145-51.

Krathwohl, D. R.; Bloom, B. S.; and Masia, B. B. *Taxonomy of Educational Objectives. Handbook II: Affective Domain*. New York: David McKay, 1964.

Levie, W. H., and Dickie, K. E. "The Analysis and Application of Media." In *Second Handbook of Research on Teaching*, edited by R. M. W. Travers. Chicago: Rand McNally, 1983.

McCutcheon, G. "Of Solar Systems, Responsibilities and Basics: An Educational Criticism of Mr. Clement's Fourth Grade." In *Qualitative Evaluation: Concepts and Cases in Curriculum Criticism*, edited by G. Willis. Berkeley: McCutchan, 1978.

McFadden, C. P. "Barriers to Science Education in Canada: A Case in Point." In *World Trends in Science Education*, edited by C. P. McFadden. Halifax, N.S.: Atlantic Institute of Education, 1980.

McFadden, C. P., ed. *World Trends in Science Education*. Halifax, N.S.: Atlantic Institute of Education, 1980.

McLeish, J. *The Lecture Method*. Cambridge: Cambridge Institute of Education, 1968.

Medley, D. M. "The Effectiveness of Teachers." In *Research on Teaching: Concepts, Findings, Implications,* edited by P. L. Peterson and H. J. Walberg. Berkeley: McCutchan, 1979.

Miles, M. B., *Innovation in Education*. New York: Teachers' College, Columbia University, 1964.

Mitzel, H. E. "A Behavioral Approach to the Assessment of Teacher Effectiveness. Division of Teacher Education, College of the City of New York (mimeographed), reported in A. Morrison and D. McIntyre (1973).

Morrison, A., and McIntyre, D. *Teachers and Teaching*. 2nd ed. Harmondsworth: Penguin, 1973.

Mort, P. R. "Studies in Educational Innovation from the Institute of Administrative Research: An Overview." In *Innovation in Education*, edited by M. B. Miles. New York: Teachers' College, Columbia University, 1964.

Munby, H. "Analysing Teaching for Intellectual Independence." In *Seeing Curriculum in a New Light: Essays from Science Education*, edited by H. Munby et al. Lanham, Maryland: University Press of America, 1984.

Munby, H.; Orpwood, G.; and Russell, T. *Seeing Curriculum in a New Light: Essays from Science Education.* Toronto: OISE Press, 1980.

Nash, R. *Classrooms Observed.* London: Routledge and Kegan Paul, 1973.

Neal, M., and Tyrrell, F. "Sharing Meanings: An Introduction to the Repertory Grid Technique." *Industrial and Commercial Training* 11 (1979): 327–34.

Neisser, U. *Cognition and Reality: Principles and Implications of Cognitive Psychology.* San Francisco: Freeman, 1976.

Nuffield Combined Science. *Teacher's Guide 1.* London: Longman, 1970.

Open University. *Learning Styles.* Course E281, Units 1 and 2, Bletchley: Open University Press, 1971.

Open University. *Problems of Curriculum Innovation I.* Course E283, Unit 13, Bletchley: Open University Press, 1972.

Open University. *Curriculum in Action: An Approach to Evaluation.* Milton Keynes: Open University Press, 1980.

Parlett, M., and Hamilton, D. (1972) "Evaluation as Illumination: A New Approach to the Study of Innovatory Programmes." Reprinted in D. Hàmilton et al., *Beyond the Numbers Game: A Reader in Educational Evaluation* (London: Macmillan, 1977).

Perkins, H. V. "Classroom Behavior and Underachievement." *American Educational Research Journal* 2 (1965): 1–12.

Peters, R. S. *Authority, Responsibility and Education.* 2nd ed. London: George Allen and Unwin, 1963

Peters, R. S. *Ethics in Education,* Ch. 10. London: George Allen & Unwin, 1966.

Peterson, P. L., and Walberg, H. J. eds. *Research on Teaching: Concepts, Findings, Implications.* Berkeley: McCutchan, 1979.

Piaget, J. *The Child's Conception of the World.* Translated by Jean and Andrew Tomlinson. London: Routledge and Kegan Paul, 1929.

Raths, L. E.; Harmin, M.; and Simon, S. B. *Values and Teaching: Working with Values in the Classroom.* 3rd ed. Columbus, Ohio: Charles E. Merrill, 1978.

Reid, W. A. "Schools, Teachers and Curriculum Change: The Moral Dimension of Theory-Building." *Educational Theory* 29 (1979): 325-36.

Reynolds, J., and Skilbeck, M. *Culture and the Classroom.* London: Open Books, 1976.

Robertson, J. D. C. "An Analysis of the Views of Supervisors in the Attributes of Successful Graduate Student Teachers." *British Journal of Educational Psychology* 27 (1957): 115–26.

Robertson, J. *Effective Classroom Control.* London: Hodder and Stoughton, 1981.

Rogers, C. R. *Freedom to Learn.* Columbus, Ohio: Merrill, 1969.

Rosenshine, B., and Furst, N. "The Use of Direct Observation to Study Teaching. In *Second Handbook of Research on Teaching,* edited by R. M. W. Travers. Chicago: Rand McNally, 1973.

Rosenthal, R., and Jacobson, L. *Pygmalion in the Classroom: Teacher Expectations and Pupils' Intellectual Development.* New York: Holt, 1968.

Rothkopf, E. Z. "The Concept of Mathemagenic Activities." *Review of Educational Research* 40 (1970): 325–36.

Rowe, M. B. *Teaching Science as Continuous Inquiry.* 2nd ed. New York: McGraw-Hill, 1978.

Rowland, S., ed. *Teachers Studying Children's Thinking.* Leicestershire Classroom Research Inservice Education Project. Berwal, Hose, Melton Mowbray, England (mimeo), 1981.

Rowland, S. *The Enquiring Classroom.* London: Falmer Press, 1984.

Rudduck, J., and Kelly, P. *The Dissemination of Curriculum Development.* Slough: National Foundation for Educational Research, 1976.

Runkel, P. J. "A Brief Model for Pupil–Teacher Interaction." In *Handbook of Research Teaching,* edited by N. L. Gage. Chicago: Rand McNally, 1963.

Russell, T. "Developing Teachers' Analytical Skills." In *Seeing Curriculum in a New Light: Essays from Science Education,* edited by H. Munby et al. Lanham, Maryland: University Press of America, 1984.

Sadker, M., and Sadker, D. "Questioning Skills." In Classroom Teaching Skills, 2nd ed., edited by J. M. Cooper. Lexington, Mass.: Heath, 1982.

Schools Mathematics Project. *Teachers' Notes, Cards 1.* Cambridge: Cambridge University Press, 1973.

Sharp, R., and Green, A. *Education and Social Control.* London: Routledge and Kegan Paul, 1975.

Shulman, L., *Review of Research in Education.* Itasca: Peacock, 1978.

Simon, A., and Boyer, E. G., eds. *Mirrors for Behaviour: An Anthology of Classroom Observation Instruments.* Philadelphia: Research for Better Schools, 1970.

Smith, L. M., and Geoffrey, W. *The Complexities of an Urban Classroom: An Analysis Toward a General Theory of Teaching.* New York: Holt, Rinehart and Winston, 1968.

Staines, J. W. "The Self-Picture as a Factor in the Classroom." *British Journal of Educational Psychology* 28 (1958): 97-111.

Stake, R. E. "The Countenance of Educational Evaluation." *Teachers College Record* 8 (1967): 523–40.

Stenhouse, L. "Some Limitations of the Use of Objectives in Curriculum Research and Planning." *Paedagogica Europaea* 6 (1970): 73-83.

Stenhouse, L. *An Introduction to Curriculum Research and Development.* London: Heinemann, 1975.

Stenhouse, L. "Case Study and Case Records: Towards a Contemporary History of Education." *British Educational Research Journal* 4 (1978): 21–39.

Stubbs, M., and Delamont, S., eds. *Explorations in Classroom Observation.* Chichester: Wiley, 1976.

Sutton, C. R., ed. *Communicating in the Classroom.* London: Hodder and Stoughton, 1981.

Taba, H. *Teaching Strategies and Cognitive Functioning in Elementary School Children.* U.S.O.E. Cooperative Research Project No. 2404. San Francisco: San Francisco State College, 1966.

Travaglini, M. "In the Wake of Sputnik." *American Education* II (1975): 26-28.

Travers, R. M. W. *Second Handbook of Research on Teaching.* Chicago: Rand McNally, 1973.

Turiel, E. "Stage Transition in Moral Development." In *Second Handbook of Research on Teaching,* edited by R. M. W. Travers. Chicago: Rand McNally, 1973.

Tyler, R. W. *Basic Principles of Curriculum and Instruction.* Chicago: University of Chicago Press, 1949.

Wade, B. "Assessing Pupils' Contribution in Appreciating a Poem." *Journal of Education for Teaching* 7 (1981): 40–49.

Wastnedge, R. "Whatever Happened to Nuffield Junior Science?" In *Problems of Curriculum Innovation I.* Course E283, Unit 13. Bletchley: Open University Press, 1972.

Willis, G., *Qualitative Evaluation: Concepts and Cases in Curriculum Criticism.* Berkeley: McCutchan, 1978.

Winne, P. H., and Marx, R. W. "Reconceptualizing Research on Teaching." *Journal of Educational Psychology* 69 (1977): 668–78.

Wragg, E. C., and Wood, E. K. "First Encounters with Classes." Paper presented at the Annual Meeting of the British Educational Research Association, Cardiff, 1980.

Yinger, R. J. "Routines in Teacher Planning." *Theory into Practice* 18 (1979): 163-69.